What others are saying about

GANDHI AND JESUS
The Saving Power of Nonviolence
BY TERRENCE J. RYNNE

Desmond Mpilo Tutu, Nobel Peace Prize Recipient and Archbishop Emeritus of Cape Town, South Africa:

"At a time when all too many leaders persist in countering violence with increased violence, Terrence Rynne's *Gandhi and Jesus* is a sharp reminder of the strength and critical need for embracing the way of nonviolence. Through his exploration of Gandhi's *satyagraha* (pursuit of truth) and Jesus' teachings in the Sermon on the Mount, Rynne draws the reader to reflect on the potent force of active nonviolence in creating a culture of peace—within each person and throughout the human community. The author illustrates that just as Jesus and Gandhi made nonviolent love the basis of their lives, we who comprise the human family can share this vision of the world. We can choose to enhance the life and dignity of each person and shape a world that equitably supports all creation. It is my hope that the readers of this important book will be inspired to embrace nonviolence as a way of life so that, rather than engaging in an arms race, we will race toward achieving poverty alleviation, political integrity and stability, environmental enhancement and the observation of human rights so as to nurture the bodies, minds, and spirits of our brothers and sisters around the world."

Arun Gandhi, President of the M. K. Gandhi Institute for Nonviolence, University of Rochester, Rochester, New York, and the grandson of Mahatma Gandhi:

"An outstanding study of two great people and their message which is so misunderstood and maligned in modern times. This fascinating book must be read by all those who wish to save this world from disaster."

Stanley Hauerwas, Professor of Theology at Duke University and, according to *Time* magazine, America's number-one theologian:

"Terry Rynne not only provides an extraordinarily sophisticated account of Gandhi's satyagraha, but he does so in a way that defeats easy criticism of Gandhi's continuing relevance. Rynne quite masterfully draws on the work of C. F. Andrews, John Howard Yoder, Bernard Haring and Walter Wink to tell how Christians should have a stake in Gandhi. If that were not enough, he then helps us see how this Christian narrating of Gandhi can help us recover accounts of salvation that avoid some of the worst caricatures associated with satisfaction theories. I highly recommend this book."

Colman McCarthy, *Washington Post* **columnist and full-time teacher of peace:**

"As few have done before, and as none have done so clearly and wisely, Terrence Rynne unites the nonviolent teachings of Gandhi and Jesus. If ever a book like this is needed—in times so darkened by violence—it is now."

James Douglass, author of *The Nonviolent Cross* **and organizer of the anti–White Train and anti–Trident missile campaigns:**

"Terrence Rynne's *Gandhi and Jesus* gives Christians an excellent way of seeing our faith in relation to Jesus' greatest disciple, who was not a Christian but a Hindu. Through the practice of Gandhi, Terrence Rynne has liberated the nonviolence of Jesus from the violence of Christian history and soteriology. Rynne's book, especially the final chapter, 'Rethinking Christian Salvation in the Light of Gandhi's Satyagraha,' should be required reading in seminaries. As Rynne shows, the saving way of Jesus is, above all, the way of nonviolence, and Gandhi is our point of entry."

John Shea, author of *Spiritual Wisdom of the Gospels for Christian Preachers and Teachers* **and a popular spiritual writer:**

"Terrence Rynne brings Gandhi and Jesus into creative dialogue and, as a result, we come to better understand and appreciate the healing power of non-violence. At once theoretical and practical, scholarly and personal, *Gandhi and Jesus* speaks to some of the most important issues of our time"

GANDHI AND JESUS

The Saving Power of Nonviolence

GANDHI AND JESUS
The Saving Power of Nonviolence

TERRENCE J. RYNNE

ORBIS BOOKS

Maryknoll, New York 10545

Founded in 1970, Orbis Books endeavors to publish works that enlighten the mind, nourish the spirit, and challenge the conscience. The publishing arm of the Maryknoll Fathers and Brothers, Orbis seeks to explore the global dimensions of the Christian faith and mission, to invite dialogue with diverse cultures and religious traditions, and to serve the cause of reconciliation and peace. The books published reflect the views of their authors and do not represent the official position of the Maryknoll Society. To learn more about Maryknoll and Orbis Books, please visit our website at www.maryknoll.org.

Library of Congress Cataloging-in-Publication Data

Rynne, Terrence J., 1942–
  Gandhi and Jesus : the saving power of nonviolence / Terrence J. Rynne.
    p. cm.
  Based on the author's dissertation (Ph.D.—Marquette University).
  Includes bibliographical references.
  ISBN-13: 978-1-57075-766-2
  1. Nonviolence—Religious aspects. 2. Christianity and other religions—Hinduism. 3. Gandhi, Mahatma, 1869–1948. I. Title.
  BT736.6.R85 2008
  205'.697—dc22
                                    2007033085

Contents

Acknowledgments

Irst, I would like to thank James Douglass, whom I have never met, but whose book, *The Nonviolent Cross*, many years ago now, planted a seed in my spirit that has continued to grow. Through his book I began to see the power and potential of Jesus' nonviolence. Douglass recounted the very human behind-the-scenes lobbying by Dorothy Day, himself and others at the Second Vatican Council. As a result, the fathers of the council adopted a strong condemnation of the use of nuclear weapons, or any act of violence aimed at the destruction of population centers, as a crime against God and humanity. Moreover, they came very close to an outright rejection of the *possession* of nuclear weapons, not just their use. I realized that such a document, such a stance, is the result of committed, knowledgeable, credible people trying to be faithful to the truth and communicating that truth with others. I gained the hope that, as a result of a similar dynamic, the Catholic Church and the whole Christian church might one day say an unequivocal no to all modern war and embrace again the teachings of the nonviolent Jesus.

That seed prompted the research that went into this book. After twenty-five years of working in health care marketing, I was able to pursue that research. I thank Frs. Philip Rossi and John Laurance and Professor Christine Firer Hinze of Marquette University's theology department for welcoming me back into academia. Frs. Thomas Hughson, Philip Rossi, and Bryan Massingale and Professor Irfan Omar served as supportive, rigorous members of my Ph.D. advisory board. I am especially grateful to Professor Michael Duffey who served as my dissertation advisor. Professor Duffey has for years been Marquette's faithful, credible witness to nonviolence. The loving, dogged, intelligently questing spirit of a true *satyagrahi* lives on in him.

I also want to thank Colman McCarthy, the columnist for the *Washington Post* who, while still writing regularly, has dedicated himself full time to teaching peace wherever and whenever he can—in high schools, universities, and prisons. He is dedicated to sparking a peace education movement across our country. His work makes total sense to me. I cannot think of a better way to spend one's life and use one's talents.

As Gandhi said, nonviolence is the real truth and fabric of daily human living—violence its interruption. A belief in nonviolence does not come just out of theory, it has to be observed in action to be convincing. This is why I am grateful to my family members and friends for their daily witness. That witness began with the tender, mutual regard my mother and father had for one another, and the mostly peace-filled growing up years with my brother and sister. The continuing transparency of my seminary classmates to one another as they have struggled to lead lives of fidelity and service to others has been an ongoing source of inspiration. For over twenty-five years, our monthly Mass Group has shared intimately life's joys and sorrows as we try to live our faith. I see Gandhi's truth every day in the way our children parent their children. A great joy of my life is to see our fifteen grandchildren take such great delight in one another and the way the older ones gently care for the younger. In turn they have no greater joy than to be with and mix it up with one another. I am grateful to them all.

I especially want to thank my wife, Sally, who has been the best possible life partner. She is a leader and visionary. Years ago she founded the country's first women's health center associated with a hospital. Subsequently, she was asked to consult with hospitals around the country on issues of women's health and founded a national association of women's health professionals. She built a wonderful, thriving business, Health Newsletters Direct, based on the premise that women are the key health care decision makers. She too embodies nonviolence—in the way she has parented, in the way she has cherished her employees, in her passion to empower women and see a more just world.

Finally, I want to thank the leadership of Marquette University, Fr. Robert Wild, the president, and Dr. Madeline Wake, the provost, in particular. When Sally and I sold our respective companies, we started the Sally and Terry Rynne Foundation dedicated to peace and the empowerment of women. My vision was to see a center for peacemaking at a university near our home dedicated to encouraging research into peacemaking, training young people in nonviolent action, and developing a spirituality to sustain long-term commitments to the making of peace. Marquette has proven to be the ideal site for such a center due to the university's history, the number of faculty already deeply involved in researching the various facets of a more peaceful world, and a student body unusually committed to service learning. Sally and I made our first bequest to help launch the Marquette University Center for Peacemaking. The Center was fortunate to recruit Simon Harak, S.J., to be its first director. Fr. Harak is an award-winning scholar and teacher as well as a seasoned activist. The spirit of Gandhi, Jesus, Dorothy Day, Martin Luther King, Bishop Desmond Tutu, Maired Corrigan, Abraham Heschel, Jeannette Rankin, and Abdul Ghaffar Khan, Gandhi's powerful

Muslim friend and follower, lives on at the Marquette University Center for Peacemaking. Marquette promises to be a model for other universities in how to introduce young people in their formative years to the alternative vision and practice of peacemaking. Please learn more about the Center by visiting its website at www.marquette.edu/peacemaking or contacting me at my e-mail address: trynne@comcast.net

Introduction

Studying Gandhi's writings and reflecting on his life's work have changed the way I understand Jesus. When I read the New Testament I am thrilled and emboldened by the filled with compassion, brave, nonviolent Jesus I find there. Gandhi not only had a similar appreciation of Jesus but in his own life convincingly showed us that there is a way to live in this world actively working for the poor, taking on power structures and enduring violence without succumbing to violence oneself, his way of "satyagraha," which means "firmly holding to the truth" in the midst of conflict while reaching out with nonviolent, suffering love. When I read the Sermon on the Mount I hear Jesus proclaiming the same truth, the same "way": neither fight nor flight, but a third way of assertive, creative, nonviolent love even for our "enemies." When I see a crucifix I can only do what Gandhi did in the famous scene caught on film when he happened upon a simple crucifix while visiting the Vatican—bow and be grateful to Jesus for showing us the way and the power of suffering love.

I know I am not alone in finding inspiration from Gandhi to find in Jesus what the world, caught as it is in an iron spiral of violence, desperately needs. Andre Trocme, for example, the leader of the church in Chambon, France, that nonviolently resisted the Nazis and protected the lives of thousands of hunted Jewish people, wrote:

> The coming of Mahatma Gandhi, whose life and teaching surprisingly resemble those of Jesus, revived the whole issue of nonviolence just when majority theology thought it had already answered the question negatively... Gandhi showed that the Sermon on the Mount can be politically effective.[1]

Reading contemporary scripture scholarship has only confirmed for me this understanding of Jesus' life and teaching. There is great convergence of testimony from scripture scholars, as we shall see later in this book, that Jesus embodied and taught a way of nonviolent love of enemies and, in a time of violent Roman occupation of his country, gathered followers to live out that way. As one eminent scripture scholar, Norbert Lohfink, put it: "Jesus was nonviolent to the core."[2]

It is a mystery to me that more Christians have not embraced the nonviolent Jesus. It is a mystery to me that the Christian churches, in particular the Catholic Church, are not, at this point in history, clearly proclaiming, with a strong and united voice, the way of nonviolent discipleship. Given the clear witness of Gandhi and the astonishing achievements of organized nonviolent action in the sixty years since his death, the liberation of country after country, from Poland, East Germany, and the Ukraine to South Africa, the Philippines, and Czechoslovakia, and given the powerful witness of Gandhian adherents such as Martin Luther King, Lech Walesa, Vaclav Havel, and Nelson Mandela—why is it not more obvious to Christians that the Sermon on the Mount is the way forward? Given the united testimony of contemporary scripture scholarship, why do we still hang back from following the way of the nonviolent Jesus?

I believe there are three major reasons: first, we are enmeshed in a culture that believes in the myth of redemptive violence; second, we are deeply imbued with a spirit of retributive justice and as a result find it hard to hear the biblical message of restorative justice; third, some of our fundamental Christian tenets, of our "systematic theology," were conceptualized with a mindset that accepted violence as a given for humans.

The myth of redemptive violence in which our culture is enmeshed is the belief that, when one is really up against it, only might can bring deliverance. When push comes to shove, most people believe, the only logical thing is to push back. One has every right to defend one's self, one's property, one's family, one's nation. End of story. The way to maintain power is to carry a big stick and not be afraid to use it when you have to. Otherwise you just invite attack. This is undoubtedly the conventional wisdom and the way of the world. The only problem is—it is not the gospel.

The political and ethical stance of many of us Christians is more often shaped by the concept of retributive justice than by than the biblical teaching of restorative justice. "To do justice" in the retributive justice scheme means to appropriately punish those who have done wrong to society. The symbol of this kind of justice is the ancient symbol of the female figure holding the scales. Justice is not done until the scales are once again in balance. Because of this ingrained value we in our culture are fascinated with the issues of determining guilt, tracking down criminals, and administering justice—understood as appropriate punishment. This carries into popular entertainment. Witness the high ratings for television shows such as *CSI* and *Law and Order*. We just can't get enough stories about finding and punishing the guilty. *CSI* and *Law and Order* multiply themselves into *CSI Miami* and *CSI New York* and *Law and Order: Special Victims Unit* and *Law and Order: Criminal Intent.*

In cultures that emphasize a retributive understanding of justice, determining who is guilty and exacting appropriate punishment are important functions of society. Those who find and punish the guilty—the police, the private investigators, the evidence technicians, the prosecutors, the judges—are legitimately held up as important protectors of society's well-being. This retributive mindset spreads into everyday life. As Joel B. Green and Mark D. Baker note:

> The assignation of blame has reached the status of a vocation for some in the media, and the two-fold process of determining fault and meting out punishment occupies families, schools, businesses and more...Who started this fight? Who called the first name? Whose idea was this?[3]

This is a far cry from the biblical teaching on restorative justice. Throughout the Bible, especially in Paul, justice is what God is *doing* for his people, justice is God delivering them from their sin. God pursues, woos, threatens, raises up prophets, works mighty deeds, reaches into people's hearts to save them from themselves. Justice is active. The point of the pursuit of justice is not punishment but change of heart and *reconciliation* between people and between people and their God. The biblical symbol of justice is the *river*, not the woman with the scales. The deep belief in retribution, the assumption that justice means retribution, keeps people from hearing the clear teaching of Jesus on loving one's enemies. Forgiveness, for a retributive mindset, is not the act of a *magna anima*, a magnanimous person, but permissiveness or being "soft on crime." In the words of Christopher D. Marshall:

> If...justice is understood in essentially retributive terms, then acts of mercy or forgiveness will be seen as, at best, a forgoing of the legitimate claims of justice, or at worst, a distinct injustice. But if justice is understood in more relational and restorative terms— making things right and repairing relationships—then justice is actually consummated in forgiveness and reconciliation.[4]

The church in the West, influenced through the centuries by the Latin fathers such as Tertullian, a lawyer, and Cyprian, adopted the narrower legal view of justice. In so doing the church watered down its faith to what can be adjudicated as "reasonable" by the world at large. The saying attributed to John Paul II, "If you want peace, work for justice," can be totally misunderstood if interpreted to mean retributive justice and not restorative justice. The largesse and mercy that Jesus demonstrated may be less spontaneously understood by the world, but it is in fact the wisdom that the world needs. Nonviolence is in the end more reasonable than the world's belief in violence. No longer is the church the "contrast society" it was in the first three centuries—embracing the gospel of nonviolence. The church instead attempts to influence society by engaging it in debates relying on reason and "natural law" concepts alone, leaving aside the revolutionary belief in nonviolence. Imagine the impact on secular society if the entire body of Christians rejected the exclusive identification of justice with retribution, turned to a concept of restorative justice, and embraced, modeled, and lived the way of nonviolence.

Finally, some of the basics of our Christian theology have been articulated out of a violent worldview. For example, our ecclesiology, or concept of the church, reflects an understanding of how to exert power that more closely resembles the hierarchical, top-down structure of the Roman Empire than it does the nonviolent, servant-of-the-servants teaching of the gospels. No item in Christian theology is more rooted in a violent worldview than the most commonly held articulation of "what it means to be saved"—the satisfaction theory of salvation, the theory that God the Father demanded the sacrifice of his Son to make satisfaction for humankind's sin. If our very own tenets of Christian theology, the way we communicate our faith to one another, are rooted in violence, it is that much harder to hear the teaching on nonviolence.

The purposes of this book are therefore threefold: first, to share my understanding and appreciation for Gandhi's way of satyagraha; second, in the light of Gandhi's satyagraha, present the thinking of four Christian theologians who have embraced and make credible a nonviolent Jesus; third, reformulate "what it means to be saved" by making, not violent sacrifice, but nonviolent power, the root metaphor. If our systematic theology, the way we explain the truths of our faith to one another, is soaked in violence, then our ethics or moral theology will surely be soaked in and unreflectively supportive of violence—as has been the case for centuries. Our ethics or moral theology may shift to the degree that our fundamental systematic theology shifts. This is, therefore, a work of *systematic* theology, an attempt to express one of the basic truths of our faith, salvation, in a way that opens us to hearing the call to nonviolent discipleship.

CHAPTER ONE

Mohandas Gandhi: A Hindu and More

Mohandas Gandhi was a Hindu who throughout all of his life associated with, learned from, and showed deep respect for people who embraced the diverse religions of India, including Islam, Jainism, Christianity, Judaism, and Zoroastrianism. Moreover, through his education in England and his association with the British who occupied his country, he came into contact with many currents of Western thought and practice. He had an experimental cast of mind: weighing, testing, trying ideas in practice, and judging them simply in terms of whether they improved the life of humanity. Consequently, he developed for himself a constantly evolving but passionately held set of beliefs and principles that guided his behavior as he took on structures of domination and oppression. It was his own personal synthesis rooted in what he found to be universal. Nonetheless, his belief system and mindset were predominantly Hindu. As he put it:

> I must tell you in all humility that Hinduism, as I know it, entirely satisfies my soul, fills my whole being, and I find solace in the Bhagavadgita and Upanishads that I miss even in the Sermon on the Mount.[1]

To enter the mindset of another religion is no simple task. Hinduism is in some ways particularly challenging because it is not a creedal religion. Many would say it is more a culture, a lifestyle, than a religion. The tenets of the religion seamlessly weave themselves into everyday living. For example, the attitude toward the unity of all living beings plays out in many simple daily ways. In the words of Ravindra Kumar:

> [A] farmer of any country will not be seen allowing monkeys, birds and other wild animals to eat and uproot his blossoming crop. Probably, you won't find anywhere except in India, people giving food to ants and other birds with great affection. It is in India

alone where parents never inspire their children to drop eggs of birds out of their nests... practically you can well understand the uniqueness of Indian non-violence.[2]

Understanding another religion requires, as Gandhi described it, a "passing over," a letting oneself see the world through the other person's religious eyes. As C. F. Andrews explains:

> There are few things perhaps more difficult to accomplish than to put oneself in sympathetic touch with a religion which is not one's own by birth-inheritance... There is strangeness about every mood and tone of worship, as well as in the words of the sacred texts of Scripture and the revealed doctrines held to be orthodox.
>
> An easy way of realizing this is to consider the instance of a Hindu... being told about the Holy Communion Service, with its consecrated elements of bread and wine representing the Body and Blood of Christ.[3]

Fortunately, Gandhi meets us halfway, having already "passed over" to understand not only Christianity but also the broader zeitgeist of Western civilization. To enter into Gandhian thought and praxis is to enter into a body of work that is already a synthesis of Hindu and Western thought.

GANDHI'S BELIEFS

Mohandas Gandhi grew up as a Hindu, but it was not until his early adult years that he was able to fully and richly appropriate it. He seriously considered other paths, in particular Christianity, before realizing that he had all that he wanted or needed in Hinduism.

Gandhi's Childhood Years

Gandhi's mother's example of faith and devotion, in particular, stayed vividly in his memory. She was a member of the Vaishnava sect, which was heavily influenced by both Buddhism and Jainism and thus placed a major emphasis on warmth of heart and compassion for all living things. According to his autobiography:

> She was deeply religious. She would not think of taking her meals without her daily prayers. Going to Haveli—the Vaishnava temple —was one of her daily duties... She would take the hardest vows

and keep them without flinching. To keep two or three consecutive fasts was nothing to her.[4]

Gandhi's father, a prime minister in Porbandar, one of the small princely states of Kathiawad, kept a very open household in terms of religion. Gandhi remembered men of many religious traditions—Jain, Muslim, and Parsi—being welcomed into their home. All were respected as seekers after truth, all in their own ways. The Jain tradition was particularly strong in the area, and its emphasis on ahimsa (doing no harm) and the many-sidedness of truth became very important to Gandhi later in life. The only religion that he learned to think poorly of during his youth was Christianity because of the missionaries, who stood on the street corner near his school deriding the beliefs and the gods of Hinduism. In his experience, converts to Christianity immediately took up meat eating and the drinking of liquor, so he came to associate Christianity with "beef and brandy."

The trappings and glitter of the temple held little appeal for Gandhi. What did capture his heart and stir his ideals were certain plays and songs. He read a tale about the folk hero Shravana and admired the hero's devotion to his parents. He saw a live performance of a play about King Harischandra, an Indian Job who refused to lie even through subjection to many afflictions. As Geoffrey Ashe notes:

> It captured him. He went to it several times, reenacted scenes himself, identified with Harischandra, and wished he could go through the same trials... The ideal of Absolute Truth, and Absolute Duty corresponding to it, came to him with the charm, the excitement, the mad logic of a fairy tale.[5]

During this period, the final lines of a poem by the Gujurati poet Shamal Bhatt ran through his head constantly:

> For a bowl of water give a goodly meal;
> For a kindly greeting bow thou down with zeal;
> For a simple penny pay thou back with gold;
> If thy life be rescued, life do not withhold.
> Thus the words and actions of the wise regard;
> Every little service tenfold they reward.
> But the truly noble know all men as one,
> And return with gladness good for evil done.[6]

The message of "return good for evil" is clearly stated and embraced by Gandhi years before he read the Sermon on the Mount or Tolstoy. Even though religion did not have much appeal to him in these growing up years, the stories and poems conveying the values of Hinduism surely did.

Gandhi's Years in England

Gandhi arrived in England in 1888 at age nineteen to study law. Leaving India was determined by his caste to be grounds for excommunication. His family allowed him to go only after his mother had secured an oath from him to refrain from wine, women, and meat. He kept the vow but, in his first months in England, went very hungry. His search for a decent vegetarian meal led him into the company of the Vegetarian Society, where he met an interesting array of mavericks who launched him, through their beliefs and the readings they gave him, on a spiritual quest. Reading Henry Salt's *A Plea for Vegetarianism*, for example, gave him a fresh understanding of and appreciation for his country's tradition of vegetarianism.

During his second year in England he met two Theosophists, bachelor brothers, who were reading Sir Edwin Arnold's translation of the *Bhagavad Gita*, and they invited him to read it with them. Certain verses in the second chapter struck him strongly:

> If one ponders on objects of the sense, there springs
> Attraction; from attraction grows desire,
> Desire flames to fierce passion, passion breeds
> Recklessness; then the memory—all betrayed—
> Lets noble purpose go, and saps the mind,
> Till purpose, mind, and man are all Undone. (2:62–63)

Gandhi wrote:

> The book struck me as one of priceless worth. The impression has ever since been growing on me with the result that I regard it today as the book par excellence for the knowledge of Truth.[7]

Another book by Sir Edwin Arnold, *The Light of Asia*, and a personal meeting with Madame Blavatsky and Mrs. Besant of the Theosophists, who highly valued the *Gita* and the learning of the East, prompted in him an interest to read books on Hinduism. At the same time, a vegetarian friend urged him to read the Bible. He plowed through the books of the Old Testament even though the chapters after Genesis put him to sleep. When he read the New Testament, however, it was a totally different story:

[T]he New Testament produced a different impression, especially the Sermon on the Mount which went straight to my heart. I compared it with the *Gita*. The verses, "But I say unto you, that ye resist not evil: but whosoever shall smite thee on the right cheek, turn to him the other also. And if any man take away thy coat let him have thy cloak too," delighted me beyond measure and put me in mind of Shamal Bhatt's "For a bowl of water give a goodly meal," etc. My young mind tried to unify the teaching of the *Gita*, *The Light of Asia* and the Sermon on the Mount. That renunciation was the highest form of religion appealed to me greatly.[8]

At this point in his life Gandhi had to postpone reading any more religious books to study diligently for his examinations, but he told himself that he would come back to the study of all the major religions as soon as he could. That time would not come until he found himself in South Africa.

The South African Years

Gandhi passed his examinations and returned to India in 1891 after two and a half eventful years. He could not find steady, lucrative employment, however, so when he received an invitation in 1893 from a Muslim trader in Natal, South Africa, who was in need of the services of an Indian lawyer trained in England, he jumped at the opportunity.

In South Africa he made friends with many Christians, especially evangelicals and Quakers. They invited him to services, entertained him in their homes, bombarded him with books, and engaged him in argumentation. He found the life and message of Jesus very attractive but he resisted the Christians' way of describing salvation, unable to understand how a person could be saved all in one go by calling on someone else for salvation. As a Hindu, Gandhi believed that individuals need to struggle to find their own unique way, doing good and dying well, to liberate themselves from the karma of past lives and to eventually enter into oneness with the divine. Given his sense that all human beings are called to be one with divinity, Gandhi did not understand how Jesus could be the only son of God. Neither could he recognize the Sermon on the Mount in the history and practice of the Christian Church. He did not feel conversant enough with his own Hindu traditions to be able to engage his friends comfortably in disputations. Therefore, in 1894 he called for help from a friend he had met in 1891 in Bombay right after returning from England.

That friend was a poet-jeweler named Raychand, a Jain, only slightly older than Gandhi. A superb businessman, Raychand, upon closing business for the day, would always turn to his spiritual diary and his religious books. He was intensely focused on seeing God face to face. Gandhi wrote of him:

> During the two years I remained in close contact with him I felt in him every moment the spirit of vairagya (renunciation)...There was a strange power in his eyes; they were extremely bright and free from any sign of impatience or anxiety...These qualities can exist only in a man of self-control.[9]

Gandhi asked Raychand a variety of questions ranging from the nature of the soul and God to the meaning of salvation and the nature of the scriptures. In all there are twenty-seven questions, twenty questions about Hinduism and the rest about Christianity. Raychand's answer to the first question concerning the nature of the spirit is three times as long as any other. It begins:

> Q. What is the Soul?...A. As there are physical objects like a pot, a piece of cloth, etc. so there is an entity called the atman whose essence is knowledge. The former are impermanent. They cannot exist through all time in the same form. The atman is an imperishable entity which exists eternally in the same form.[10]

In addition to this long letter, Raychand sent Gandhi three ancient Hindu texts that belonged to the Hindu system of Advaita Vedanta, a system codified in the ninth century by the famous philosopher Shankara but originating in the ancient Upanishads of the pre-Christian era.

The works that Raychand sent fully engaged Gandhi's attention. He paid special attention to the practical issues concerning how one can achieve *moksha* (liberation) in this life, the moral and intellectual training required for climbing the seven stages of yogic exercises leading to the goal. Page after page of the Hindu texts emphasize personal exertion and reason—much different from the Vaishnava tradition that places the cause of liberation in the initiative of a loving God and his avatar Krishna. In the Hindu system of Advaita Vedanta, nonattachment and asceticism are the keys to *moksha*.

Gandhi found the letter and the readings very helpful. His belief in Hinduism received a solid intellectual foundation, and he began to make Hinduism his own on a more reflective level. What he found particularly important in Raychand's teaching was his stress on action.

> Of particular importance was [Raychand's] insistence on accord between belief and action; it was the way a man lived, not the

recital of a verse or the form of a prayer, which made him a good Hindu, a good Muslim, or a good Christian.[11]

In 1905, when Gandhi was asked to give four lectures on Hinduism for the Johannesburg Lodge of the Theosophical Society, his grasp of what Hinduism and religion meant to him had solidified. In his first lecture he recapitulated the fundamentals:

> This is what they believe: God exists. He is without beginning, immaculate and without any attribute or form...His original form is *Brahman*...it is bliss incarnate, and by it all this is sustained. The soul exists, and is distinct from the body. Between its original form and the Brahman, there is no distinction. But it takes on, from time to time, a body as a result of *karma* or the power of *maya*, and goes on being born again and again...in accordance with the good or bad deeds performed by it. To be free from the cycle of birth and death and be merged in Brahman is *moksha* or liberation. The way to achieve this *moksha* is to do pure and good deeds; to have compassion for all living things as well.[12]

In 1913 Gandhi wrote four letters to Jamnadas, the son of a cousin, in response to Jamnadas's questions about religion. His answers are consistent with his 1905 lectures.

During this period, despite this growing confidence in his tradition and group of Hinduism, Gandhi continued to be pulled by the attractiveness of the example of Jesus and a desire to follow his own lights wherever they might lead. In 1901 he made one more determined effort to see if Christianity was the path he should follow. In a 1925 presentation to Christian missionaries he described this step, which involved going to see Kali Charan Banerjee, a very respected Indian Christian:

> I told Mr. Banerjee, "I have come to you as a seeker—"...Well, I am not going to engage you in giving a description of the little discussion that we had between us. It was very good, very noble. I came away, not sorry, not dejected, not disappointed, but I felt sad that even Mr. Banerjee could not convince me. This was my final deliberate striving to realize Christianity as it was presented to me.[13]

Gandhi's gradual appropriation of Hinduism on a theoretical level during the years he spent in South Africa coincided with experiences and actions that were no less important—in fact probably more important than what he read or heard—for the development of his thought and praxis.

The chronology of those experiences and actions is, therefore, appropriate. In 1893, shortly after arriving in South Africa, he was evicted from his first-class railway cabin because of the color of his skin and, after protesting, was bodily thrown off the train. He spent the night sitting on the station platform, deciding whether he would go back to India or stay and fight. He later said it was the most important moment of his life when he decided to fight. As B. R. Nanda wrote, "Iron entered his soul."[14]

In 1894, Gandhi organized the Natal Indian Congress to pull together all the various parties, Muslim and Hindu, to carry on an organized fight, nonviolently, against the government, risking jail in a spirit of civil disobedience. This fight was to go on for the next twenty years.

In 1899, when the Boer War broke out, Gandhi organized an ambulance corps of Indians to minister to the sick and wounded. The corps eventually numbered 1,100 and saw action at the front. His experience of the frontline soldier's rugged ability to withstand pain and suffering and the witness of Boer women who endured prison with bravery and without complaint inspired his insights into the power of brave suffering.

In 1906, the Zulu Rebellion broke out. Gandhi again organized an ambulance corps. They ministered to those on both sides of the conflict. While he was away from his family—a wife and four sons—he realized that if he was going to continue to give his life in total service to the community, he would have to change his lifestyle. He took the vow of *bramacharya* (celibacy) at age thirty-seven and lived it for the rest of his life. Although he was a financially successful lawyer, he realized that he needed to move toward a life of simplicity and poverty.

In 1906, in response to further oppressive laws from the government, Gandhi led a major passive resistance campaign and began to struggle to articulate what it was that participants in the campaign were doing—it certainly was more than "passive resistance." He sponsored a contest in his newspaper to suggest a name; the term "satyagraha" evolved from this time.

In 1910, Gandhi's friend Hermann Kallenbach donated 1,100 acres where the *satyagrahis* could live on free of charge. Gandhi's role of living with, teaching, and forming, in an ashram setting, a community of *satyagrahis*, who took seven vows including those of poverty, nonviolence, and chastity, began in earnest.

In 1913, he led a mass campaign of civil disobedience that eventually led to the repeal of the unjust laws. Gandhi returned at last to India. General Smuts, his opponent through many of these years, is quoted as saying, "At last the saint has left our shores—I sincerely hope forever."[15]

Gandhi's struggle to claim his Hindu identity occurred in the historical context of Indians being systematically made to feel inferior by the occupying power. Indian culture and religion had been consistently held up to ridicule. According to B. R. Nanda:

In 1872 a high British administrator and scholar, Sir Alfred Lyall, stated in the Fortnightly Review that the "old gods of Hinduism will die in these elements of intellectual light and air as a net full of fish, lifted up out of water." That same year, Robert Knight, one of the most eminent and liberal-minded British journalists in India, said: "Our own conviction is profound that India will never possess Home Rule until she has cast away the false systems of religion...that have been the cause of her degradation and become Christian."[16]

Gandhi's appropriation of Hinduism as his living religion was a vital part of his claiming *swaraj* (self-governance, self-determination) for himself. By 1921 he had come a long way from the timid young man who had arrived in South Africa with the sole ambition of bringing wealth and prestige to his family by imitating the lifestyle of the English. He had embraced his religion so fully that by the time he returned to India at age forty-five he already had a reputation for holiness. He had become an ashram dweller, a political leader whose total focus was on the welfare of the lowliest Indians. His own lifestyle had come to be as simple as theirs.

By 1921, Gandhi was confidently writing about what he had come to believe. Two wide-ranging essays appeared in that year, one in Gujurati in *Navajivan* under the title "Who Is a *Sanatani* Hindu" (in our terms, an orthodox Hindu) and the other in English in *Young India* under the title "Hinduism." The views in these essays are consistent with has already been quoted. His fundamental beliefs are in atman (the innermost essence of each individual), *moksha*, and karma. Gandhi wrote:

> A Hindu is one who...believes that *moksha* is the supreme end of human striving...The central principle of Hinduism is that of *moksha*. I am ever striving for it.[17]

In a letter to Leo Tolstoy, Gandhi went out of his way to ask his famous correspondent not to criticize the belief in reincarnation:

> Re-incarnation or transmigration is a cherished belief with millions in India, indeed, in China also. With many, one might almost say, it is a matter of experience, no longer a matter of academic acceptance. It explains reasonably the many mysteries of life.[18]

He also believed in "dharma," the law built into the universe that makes all cohere. Dharma encompasses the concepts of duty, morality, virtue, and justice. It is the closest Hindu equivalent to our concept of religion. The law that sustains all is built into the universe and it is up to each human to discover for himself or herself what that dharma is. It needs to be rediscovered in every age.

From Gandhi's belief in this concept of the regular order built into the universe followed his belief in *varna*—the view that each individual's occupation fits into an order that extends before and around and after that individual's lifetime—and the legitimacy of the idea of caste. His writings on these ideas evolved over time. He eventually rejected the caste system as it had evolved in India—including the laws and customs governing inter-dining and intermarriage, which have made caste so embedded in the daily life and culture of the people of India. Moreover, from the beginning, he completely rejected untouchability as an abomination and corruption of authentic Hinduism. Nonetheless, he clung to some notion of *varna*.

Erik Erikson has a wise observation on the West's attitude toward these ideas:

> We in the West are proudly overcoming all ideas of predestina-
> tion. But we would still insist that child training can do no more
> than underscore what is given...And we certainly sense...how
> we continue to project ideas of doom and predetermination either
> on hereditary or constitutional givens, on early experience and
> irreversible trauma, or on cultural and economic deprivation—
> that is, on a past, as dim as it is fateful.[19]

Gandhi considered cow protection the special, positive hallmark of Hinduism; this view flowed from the fundamental belief in the unity of all life. As Gandhi wrote:

> Cow-protection is the dearest possession of the Indian heart. It is
> the one concrete belief common to all Hindus...Cow-worship
> means to me to worship innocence. Cow-protection means the
> protection of the weak and helpless.[20]

It evolved out of India's own history and geography. Gandhi explained by noting that

> [m]an through the cow is enjoined to realize his identity with all
> that lives...The cow was in India the best companion. She was
> the giver of plenty. Not only did she give milk, but she also made
> agriculture possible. The cow is a poem of pity...She is the moth-
> er to millions of Indian mankind.[21]

Gandhi believed in the sacred scriptures of Hinduism and considered their content but not their letter as the word of God. Nonetheless, he insisted that their interpretation always be subject to the test of reason and resisted the role of the *shastris*, the scholars of the ancient texts, as the sole, legitimate interpreters of the truth of the scriptures. Consequently, throughout his public life in India, he was accused by the "experts" of not being a *sanatani* Hindu—especially when he opposed untouchability or befriended and ate with Muslims.

In conclusion, over his lifetime Gandhi came to claim his Hinduism. He studied it. He shared it. He prayed over it. He came to embody it for millions of Indians who lived in the countryside. He used the stories and the images and the language that the common people understood. As a result, his appropriation of his Hinduism came to have a great political impact.

THE POLITICAL IMPACT OF GANDHI'S HINDUISM

Gandhi's Understanding of Politics and Religion

Some students of Gandhi see him as a religious leader, as the Mahatma, which means the "Great Soul"; others see him as a political leader who freed India from the yoke of the British. The "Mahatma" appellation was a burden for Gandhi. He always claimed to be an ordinary man and believed that all people could do what he had done. For Gandhi, religion and politics had everything to do with one another. Religion encompassed what humans believed about themselves and their ultimate destiny. Religion was an empty husk if it was not put into practice. Gandhi's particular religion, Hinduism, teaches the fundamental unity of human beings and the necessity, therefore, for Gandhi, of working together to relieve human suffering. Working to relieve human suffering necessarily means involvement in politics, the arena in which humans make decisions about their future together.

Most of Gandhi's contemporaries did not share his conception of politics. When he returned to India from South Africa, Britain was in the midst of the Great War. His colleagues thought it was time to implement constitutional schemes to take advantage of Britain's vulnerability. Gandhi, on the other hand, according to Judith Brown,

> [spoke of] creating a new society from the roots upwards, and not only spoke but acted with whatever material came to hand—in the ashram, among farmers, and with factory hands. The terms for growing indigo, land revenue assessment, or the wages of one small group of factory workers, were as significant to him as imperial policy and Congress schemes, indeed even more so, because the solution of such problems was evidence that Indians were making anew their nation, and not relying on concessions from

their rulers which would only amount to a spurious home rule, not real swaraj.[22]

Gandhi understood that power rises. He understood that no leader could maintain power without the consent of the governed. That is why he worked from the grassroots upward. He understood that if the people, especially the millions upon millions who lived in India's small villages, did not throw off their fear, their ignorance, and their sense of hopelessness, the country might end up with a narrow kind of political independence and still not have real freedom. In 1920 Gandhi said:

> It is as amazing as it is humiliating that less than one hundred thousand white men should be able to rule three hundred and fifteen million Indians. They do so somewhat undoubtedly by force but more by securing our cooperation in a thousand ways...The British cannot rule us by mere force. They want India's billions and they want India's manpower for their imperialistic greed. If we refuse to supply them with men and money, we achieve our goal, namely, *swaraj*.[23]

His notion of freedom began with the individual. In that, the notion was quintessentially Hindu. It had to be rooted in the Vedantic concept of self-liberation: not just absence of restraint and self-aggrandizement but cooperation for a secure and just community. As Madan Sinha wrote: "The self in Hindu thought is a synonym for the universal."[24]

The stress on the individual as the focus of society led Gandhi to put forward a search for freedom that begins with self-knowledge and self-freedom and that liberates people from the desire to dominate or be dominated. It led him to see that social reforms were necessary for India's freedom. Each individual had to take responsibility for overcoming the three major social problems in India: the Hindu-Muslim conflict, untouchability, and economic inequality.

Finally, his religious faith made him insist that the struggle for freedom from the grassroots up could be accomplished only nonviolently. There could be no divorce between the ends desired—a peaceful, just society—and the means utilized. Gandhi wrote:

> I do not believe in short-violent-cuts to success. Those Bolshevik friends who are bestowing their attention on me should realize that...I am an uncompromising opponent of violent methods even to serve the noblest of causes.[25]

He saw the choice between violence and nonviolence to be a stark either-or for India.

There are two alternatives before us. The one is that of violence, the other of non-violence...As they are incompatible with each other, the fruit, the *swaraj* that would be secured by following the one would necessarily be different from that which would be secured by following the other...We reap as we sow.[26]

The religion that Gandhi thought needed to be mixed with politics was not a state religion. He totally opposed any notion of a state religion and he thereby contributed to India becoming a secular state. In 1920, he wrote:

Let me explain what I mean by religion. It is not the Hindu religion, which I certainly prize above all other religions, but the religion which transcends Hinduism, which changes one's very nature, which binds one indissolubly to the truth and which ever purifies. It is the permanent element in human nature which leaves the soul restless until it has found itself.[27]

Louis Fischer noted the irony that Mohammed Ali Jinnah, who was not religious, established Pakistan as a state based on religion, while Gandhi, who was completely religious, worked to establish a secular state.[28] The way Gandhi lived out this concept of religion had immense impact on the political scene.

How the Masses Were Galvanized

Upon his return from South Africa, Gandhi had already developed a reputation among the leaders of the Indian National Congress. Often through the previous years Gandhi had appealed to the Congress and the viceroy for assistance in the struggle against the South African government. Gandhi realized, with the political astuteness frequently attributed to one of his *bania* (grocer) caste, the importance of public opinion. He labored mightily to make known the oppression of the Indians in South Africa out to the general public in India and England as well. He continually placed articles in the leading papers in England and India to publicize the situation and succeeded in generating widespread sympathy for the cause. In addition, he returned to India periodically to spread the word personally through speeches in various locations throughout the country and thus was beginning to be known by the general public.

Gopal Krishna Gokhale, one of the leaders of the Indian National Congress, visited Gandhi in South Africa and succeeded in getting an initial agreement from General Jan Smuts that was to end the oppression of Indians and therefore the need for the Indian Civil Resistance movement. When Gokhale returned to India, however, Smuts went back on his word, necessitating one last major campaign by Gandhi and his fellow *satyagrahis*. Recognizing in Gandhi one of the outstanding leaders of the coming generation, Gokhale took him under his wing when he returned from South Africa. He advised Gandhi to say nothing publicly until he had spent a year or more in India; he advised Gandhi to go on a tour of the subcontinent to become familiar with the situation in India. Gandhi did—the first of his many wanderings across India—paying special attention to the innumerable small villages across the country.

The common people took notice of Gandhi for three main reasons: his lifestyle, which embodied basic Hindu ideals; his use of the common words and symbols of the Hindu religion; and the fact that his politics insisted on action, not just endless talk.

Gandhi's dress, his travel by foot up to twenty miles a day, his personality, and his lifestyle of simplicity and self-sacrifice began to attract attention. In an article entitled "Why India Follows Gandhi," H. N. Brailsford refers to the "ancient Hindu tactic," saying that in India the saint who can control himself is considered capable of commanding the universe.[29]

Gandhi's asceticism was rigorous and constant. His fasting, vegetarianism, celibacy, and vigorous life of prayer and silence folded into his search for truth and provision of service. His religion was not a sometime thing but informed every moment of his life. The common people saw in him the embodiment of what their religion held sacred.

The first verse of the *Isopanishad* that Gandhi loved to quote continues, "Renounce the world and receive it back again as the gift of God," which accurately expresses the belief of the Hindu belief that the search for God begins with the renunciation of the world. As Vincent Sheehan wrote:

> No man could hope to get a hearing in religious matters in India, unless he has first renounced the world.[30]

The spirit of *darshan*, that one can receive a blessing from that which is holy, runs deep in the Hindu consciousness, whether it involves seeing the Ganges or the Himalayas or being in the presence of a holy person. Over time, thousands would flock from the countryside to catch a glimpse of Gandhi, if it was rumored that he would be in the area or passing through on a train. Just being in his presence, it was believed, gave them *darshan*. At his burial, four million people, one of the largest crowds at one place in history, if not the largest, gathered to see his ashes placed into the Ganges. As Sheehan noted:

> It is nothing less than the recognition of a community of spirit in which the poorest and humblest of Hindus ... can recognize in a Gandhi or a Nehru that which his own karma has not permitted

him to achieve, but which in some other life he may achieve...
The Mahatma or the Great Soul is one which has arisen above the
mass but is still of it... a visible sign of the perfectibility in nature,
thus rejoicing the hearts of the poor earthbound toilers.[31]

The second appeal that Gandhi had to the masses was the use he made
of common Hindu symbols and ideals and the stories used to convey them.
Every villager knew the story of Prahlad, for example, a young boy who suffered his father's wrath because of his clinging to the truth, *satya*. They
heard Gandhi talk about this same ideal of truth as central to his search.
They recognized it as central to the Vedanta (the system of Hindu philosophy based on the Vedas). "Ahimsa" appears in the Hindu scriptures as early
as the *Chandogya Upanishad*, and the *Mahabharata* makes ahimsa the greatest religious duty; that too is known in every village in India. *Tapasya*, or the
value of self-suffering and renunciation of self, is another fundamental value
that the people witnessed in Gandhi. He altered the significance and content of all these traditional words, but he drew on the well of the people's
traditions. He recognized that the masses in India would be awakened to
reform only through religion. He went to the traditional words to uncover
the ideas that would work for modern India.

When the leaders of Congress proposed, for example, for purposes of
greater clarity, substituting the word "independence" for *swaraj*, Gandhi
responded:

I defy any one to give for independence a common Indian word
intelligible to the masses... an indigenous word understood by the
three hundred millions. And we have such a word in *swaraj*... It is
infinitely greater than and includes independence... It is a word
which, if it has not penetrated the remotest corner of India, has at
least got the largest currency of any similar word. It is a sacrilege
to displace that word by a foreign importation of doubtful value.[32]

The final reason for Gandhi's appeal to the masses was his insistence on
action. This was especially important to the young. Nehru, for example,
first started following Gandhi because he represented something new, a distinct departure from the politics of the past, which had consisted of repre-
sentations and appeals and disputations. Gandhi stood for action, not talk.

Gandhi's first nonviolent campaigns in India, the Champaran and
Ahmedabad campaigns, were successes, using the principles of nonviolent
action or satyagraha. They captured the attention and imagination of
many in India. They were the springboards for Gandhi's elevation to the
political leadership of the National Congress. Between 1919 and 1922
Gandhi succeeded in forging a mass movement unprecedented in India.

He transformed the Indian National Congress into a political organization with a mass following. It had previously consisted of upper-class, educated elites, but Gandhi sought to change that. He wrote:

> I do not rely merely on the lawyerly class, or highly educated men to carry out all the stages of non-cooperation. My hope is more with the masses... Let not the leaders distrust them.[33]

Gandhi inspired the masses through his faith in them. He believed in achieving great things and maintaining heroic ideals. He had read Carlyle's *Heroes and Hero-worship* early in his life and was impressed by what Carlyle wrote about Muhammad and other heroes who drew to themselves bands of like-minded heroes. To quote Raghavan Iyer:

> In reaffirming the heroic ideal Gandhi was vindicating the oldest tradition in India embodied in the two great epics that are still... told in the countryside. The *Ramayana* and the *Mahabharata* ... the epics exalted a conception of manhood in which personal worth held pride of place... the pursuit of honor through action. The hero, in Indian legend, uses the potentialities that lie dormant in all... and wins the warm approbation of his fellows because he spares no effort and shirks no risk... to make the most of his powers in the service of a supreme ideal.[34]

With Gandhi, as with the tradition, fearlessness is the first quality of the hero. Hero worship is ruled out; heroism is ruled in—because all are to be heroes. Gandhi's faith in the masses was felt by them. As Naryan Desai pointed out:

> It was Gandhi's faith that created faith-worthiness among the people. The masses do not see how successful you are, nor how vocal you are. They see with their sixth sense how truthful you are.[35]

Gandhi's leadership has been described as a "hyphen connecting the middle classes and the people which transferred energy from each to the other."[36]

Gandhi's appropriation of his Hinduism was later used against him by the advocates for a separate Muslim state. He did use a Hindu term, *Hind Swaraj*, to describe the future state of India's freedom. He advocated a Hindu hymn for the national anthem. On some scores he could have been more sensitive to the feelings of those of other faiths, especially the Muslims, as he focused so intently on giving hope to the Hindu masses.

On the other hand, all his life he read and reverenced the scriptures of the other major faiths of India. He read the Koran, the scriptures of Zoroastrianism, and the Bible. Prayers from all these religions were used in his daily prayer services in successive ashrams. On no one did he rely more for counsel than the imam who followed him from South Africa and lived in the ashram. Gandhi was totally dedicated to building harmonious relations between Muslims and Hindus from the South African period onward. He made support of Khilafat an important plank of his politics.[37] He shared meals with Muslims and Christians and spoke against the prohibitions on inter-dining—much to the horror of the Hindu *shastris* and pandits (looked-up-to leaders). As a result he was constantly accused by these Hindu "experts" of not being *sanatani*.

The Hindu common people recognized him as one of them and acclaimed him a "Mahatma." The more learned found him to be more of a puzzle. As early as 1909, his very good friend, Reverend J. J. Doke, who befriended him and took him in when he was under attack by the whites in South Africa, and whose family Gandhi cherished, wrote:

> A few days ago I was told that "he is a Buddhist." Not long since, a Christian newspaper described him as a "Christian Mohammedan," an extraordinary mixture indeed…I question whether any system of religion can absolutely hold him. [38]

Gandhi was indeed open to all glimmers of truth wherever he could find them. There is no doubt that he considered himself a Hindu. As he said, Hinduism was as close to him as his mother, as his wife. Nonetheless, he constantly folded new insights into his understanding of the basic truths of his Hinduism.

GANDHI'S TRANSFORMATION OF TRADITIONAL HINDU CONCEPTS

Important Western Influences

Jesus

First of all, how can Jesus be classified as a Western influence on Gandhi?

Christianity was mediated to Gandhi and India through institutions that carried the values of Western civilization. The English Raj itself proudly and consciously proclaimed its Christian roots and values. The Christian missionaries who went to India from the United States proudly set up many of their Western values, such as thrift, cleanliness, and hard work, as virtues that India should emulate.

In many of the hundred volumes that comprise the collected works of Gandhi, there are dozens and dozens of transcripts of talks that he was constantly asked to give to Christian gatherings, especially Christian missionary gatherings. The missionaries objected to Gandhi's negative stance toward religious conversion and asked him again and again how they could best serve India. Gandhi always answered them straight on that they should first stop denigrating the culture that they had entered and begin to appreciate it instead. He then counseled them to live their faith instead of preaching it.

In a talk to Christian missionaries in Calcutta at a YMCA meeting in 1925, for example, he said:

> Bishop Heber wrote two lines which have always left a sting with me: "Where every prospect pleases and only Man is vile." I wish he had not written them. My own experience in my travels throughout India has been to the contrary...and I am *not* able to say that here in this fair land, watered by the great Ganges, the Brahmaputra, and the Jumna, man is vile. He is *not* vile. He is as much a seeker after truth as you and I are, possibly more so...I miss receptiveness, humility, willingness on your part to identify with the masses of India.[39]

Gandhi was convinced that Christianity would be more appreciated in India if Christians would do less preaching and more living of their faith in a way that was consistent with what Jesus modeled in the New Testament. He used the New Testament itself to make that point to the missionaries:

> It is not he who says, "Lord, Lord," that is a Christian, but "he who does the will of the Lord" that is a true Christian.[40]

He put it philosophically by reflecting on how far language falls from a full representation of truth and how much more powerful is the example of someone's life for communicating what he or she believes.

> Your whole life is more eloquent than your lips. Language is always an obstacle to the full expression of thought...language is a limitation of the truth which can only be represented by life.[41]

But his favorite way to make this point to Christians was through an analogy:

A rose does not need to preach. It simply spreads its fragrance. The fragrance is its own sermon ... if it could engage a number of preachers it would not be able to sell more roses than the fragrance itself could do. The fragrance of religious and spiritual life is much finer than that of the rose ... "Fool don't you see that I got it from my maker."[42]

Gandhi experienced Christianity through Western mediation: words, actions, and writings. But when he read the New Testament he felt there was a huge gap between the message he found there and the behavior of Christians in the West. In fact, he struggled with its Westernization because the country where Christianity originated, Palestine, is part of Asia. As he explained:

But today I rebel at orthodox Christianity, as I am convinced that it has distorted the message of Jesus. He was an Asiatic ... when it had the backing of a Roman Emperor it became an imperialist faith as it remains to this day. Of course there are noble but rare exceptions like Andrews.[43] ... Jesus caught a breath of wind from Asia and gave it to the world. It has been diluted in the West. You incorporated it into a system alien to it. That's why I call myself not Christian, because I do not hold with the system that you have set up based on might.[44]

On the other hand, even if he criticized the Westernized version, he was mightily influenced by Christianity and in particular the Sermon on the Mount, the concept of the Kingdom of God, the events in Jesus' life, and the symbol of the cross.

We have already seen how the Sermon on the Mount went straight to his heart when he first read it, even though related sentiments are found in Indian sources. The teaching "do no harm" is to be found in the Jain tradition. The Buddha taught, "Hatreds are not quenched by hatred. Nay rather hatreds are quenched by love." It also appears in the Gujurati hymns that Gandhi heard in his youth. Nevertheless, the truth of nonviolence jumped out at him in a fresh new way when he read the New Testament.

Such passages as "Resist not him that is evil; but whosoever smiteth thee on thy right cheek, turn to him the other also" ... I was simply overjoyed.[45]

[A]s my contact with real Christians increased, I could see that the Sermon on the Mount was the whole Christianity for him who wanted to live a Christian life...It seems to me that Christianity has yet to be lived.[46]

It disturbed him greatly when he heard Christians put aside the teaching of the Sermon on the Mount as impractical or dreamy idealism or to be practiced only by those called to be monks or the clergy—the typical ways Catholics and Protestants make the Sermon on the Mount irrelevant to daily life or realpolitik.

> For many of them contend that the Sermon on the Mount does not apply to mundane things, and that it was only meant for the twelve disciples. Well I do not believe this. I think the Sermon on the Mount has no meaning if it is not of vital use in everyday life to everyone.[47]

Gandhi spent the whole of his life demonstrating that the Sermon on the Mount could be eminently practical politics. The unthinking acceptance of violence and wars as inevitable by Christians, even church leaders, greatly disturbed him. He felt it made a mockery of the New Testament, Jesus, and the clear teaching of the Sermon on the Mount. He wrote:

> Christianity is no Christianity in which a vast number of Christians believe in governments based on brute force and are denying Christ every day of their lives.[48]

He saw the message of nonviolence and, as he came to call it, satyagraha, as desperately important for the future of humankind. He understood Jesus' message in the Sermon on the Mount to be the sacred truth that the world yearned for, the "wisdom hidden for all ages," and yet it was taken so cavalierly by professed Christians.

> [I]t has yet to make a greater contribution. After all, what are 2000 years in the life of a religion? Just now, Christianity comes to a yearning mankind in a tainted form. Fancy, bishops supporting slaughter in the name of Christianity.[49]

Nonetheless, he continued to hope that Christianity would some day be authentically lived and that the West would come to hear the message of the Sermon on the Mount afresh—if, through "experiments with truth" it could be demonstrated as a workable way to confront and overcome evil and violence. In this regard he wrote:

> [T]he frightful outrage that is just now going on in Europe, perhaps shows that the message of Jesus of Nazareth, the Son of

Peace, has been little understood in Europe and the light upon it may have to be thrown from the East.[50]

Second, he found Jesus' teaching on the "the Kingdom" helpful and important. It signified for Gandhi that the work of religion was a work for and of this world, not for the next. As he explained:

There is one thing which occurs to me, which came to me early in my studies of the Bible. It seized me immediately when I read the passage: "Make this world the Kingdom of God and his righteousness and everything will be added to you."[51]

The concept of the Kingdom, moreover, placed clear emphasis not on thinking, not on contemplating, not on worshiping and praying, but on acting. Gandhi saw Christianity as a religion that prized action and behavior; its mottoes were "Do the work of my Father" and "Do this in memory of me." In 1927 he noted:

My experience tells me that the Kingdom of God is within us, and that we can realize it not by saying, "Lord, Lord" but by doing His will and his work. If therefore, we wait for the Kingdom to come as something coming from outside, we shall be sadly mistaken.[52]

Gandhi did not believe that the Kingdom of God could be built on earth without the grace of God transforming human beings. But he believed that that transformation enabled humans to build the Kingdom even in the teeth of violent resistance. Only the grace of God could give humans the strength. But the strength was given precisely for Kingdom building. Service of others and nonviolent resistance to evil, not self-congratulations or merely individual *moksha—that* was building the Kingdom. Speaking of the nonviolent person, he wrote:

He or she must have a living faith in nonviolence. This is impossible without a living faith in God. A nonviolent man can do nothing save by the power and grace of God. Without it he won't have the courage to die without anger, without fear and without retaliation. Such courage comes from the belief that God sits in the hearts of all and that there should be no fear in the presence of God.[53]

Building that Kingdom had very practical implications for Gandhi. He saw the teaching of the Kingdom to have both personal and social implications. He was deeply moved when he read that the Kingdom belonged to the humble and the poor, that the persecuted and the meek are its citizens. In the words of K. L. Seshagiri Rao:

On the social side, the Kingdom of God meant to Gandhi the ideal society in which justice is done...and institutions are geared to encourage the best in men and women. He believed that those institutions which permitted injustice, inequity and exploitation of man by men were evil and that they needed to be changed.[54]

The idea of the Kingdom of God placed India's freedom movement in a much bigger context of human liberation. As S. K. George, an Indian Christian, has pointed out:

The Christian ideal of the Kingdom of God is the culmination and fulfillment of [the Christian's] hope of God's sovereignty on earth...But Gandhi's hope also included the extension of that Kingdom over the whole earth, till the little leaven of it had leavened the whole lump...He has had the courage to work out the implications of it in modern life, to specify the politics and the economics of the Kingdom of God.[55]

Gandhi's goal of founding a nonviolent society was much closer to the Christian idea of the Kingdom than the Hindu idea of *moksha*.

Third, Gandhi found the events of Jesus' life illuminating. When Gandhi set off on his momentous walk to the sea in 1930 launching the Salt Satyagraha, he likened it to Jesus setting his face to Jerusalem. The events of Jesus' life were a constant source of strength and insight to him, and he invoked them often. On the temptations of Jesus in the desert, he observed that

[w]hen he (a man) conquers the first temptation (of hunger), he gains mastery over his senses. That endows him with strength. That strength itself is the second temptation...When a man thus gains mastery over strength, he becomes a master of *siddhu* (miracle working powers). These *siddhis* are his third temptation.[56]

Gandhi understood Jesus as a spiritual aspirant entering into his life of ministry. The sequence of baptism, fasting, and temptations was understandable to Gandhi in terms of progressive self-purification for the sake of human service. Commenting on the baptism by John the Baptist, he wrote that Jesus

was a servant of the people or a spiritual aspirant. The first lesson He took through baptism at the hands of John, was that of humility and self-purification. He thought of aligning himself with the millions by taking baptism and a bath in the Jordan.[57]

Finally, for Gandhi the cross revealed the fate with which a person living a life of aggressive nonviolence would be faced in an atmosphere of violence. The cross said to Gandhi that Jesus was a person who, in his love for the poor, oppressed, and outcast, stood against evil with his whole being to the end, despite the threat of violence. Jesus died on the cross because of the way he had lived.

> The cross, undoubtedly, makes a universal appeal the moment you give it a universal meaning in place of the narrow one that is often heard at ordinary meetings. But then, you have to have the eyes of the soul with which to contemplate it.[58]

Gandhi's understanding of the cross illuminated aspects of Jesus' message and life that the West had overlooked or buried through the centuries. As Stanley Jones put it:

> Never in human history has so much light been shed on the Cross as has been shed through this one man and that man not even called a Christian. Had not our Christianity been so vitiated and overlain by our identification with unchristian attitudes and policies in public and private life, we would have seen at once the kinship between Gandhi's method and the Cross . . . A Hindu summed it up for me with these words: "We should exchange sacred books. The Gita gives philosophic reasons for war, while the New Testament teaches peace, and yet we are more peace-minded and you are more war-minded."[59]

Gandhi understood the cross as a clarion call to discipleship. Anyone who claims to be a Christian had better embrace the idea that they will be in for a life of suffering—if they begin to oppose the forces of oppression.

> You may certainly experience peace in the midst of strife, but this happens only when . . . you crucify yourself . . . Living Christ means a living Cross, without it life is a living death.[60]

S. K. George was inspired to look at the cross in a new way through the teaching and praxis of Gandhi. George wrote:

> Satyagraha is deliberate choice . . . aggressive love attacking evil in its strongholds . . . The Cross of Christ is the supreme, perfect historic example of such assault and victory over evil. But alas, Christianity has made of it a creed, a doctrine, belief in which is to

secure a heaven of comfort and security! It was necessary... to set it up again as a working principle of life.[61]

In a very famous scene, captured on film, Gandhi had stopped at the Vatican on his way back from the 1931 Roundtable Conference held in Britain when he happened to see a rough crucifix. His reaction was immediate and emotional:

> Chance threw Rome in my way. And I was able to see something of that great and ancient city and Mussolini, the unquestioned dictator of Italy. And what would not I have given to bow my head before the living image at the Vatican of Christ crucified. It was not without a wrench that I could tear myself away from that scene of living tragedy. I saw there at once that nations, like individuals, could only be made through the agony of the Cross and in no other way. Joy comes not out of infliction of pain on others, but out of pain voluntarily borne by oneself.[62]

Gandhi understood the cross not as passive resistance but as an assertive act of love. In 1946 he wrote to Madame Privat:

> Europe mistook the bold and brave resistance, full of wisdom, by Jesus Christ for passive resistance, as it was of the weak. As I read the New Testament I detected no weakness and no passivity about Jesus as depicted in the four gospels.[63]

The impact of the Sermon on the Mount, Jesus' life, and the cross of Jesus meant much to Gandhi and influenced his thought and work from early on in his life. It all became even clearer and more powerful for him when he read the works of Leo Tolstoy.

Leo Tolstoy

In a speech Gandhi gave in 1928 on the occasion of the centenary of Tolstoy's birth he stated:

> I would say that three men have had a very great influence on my life. Among them I give the first place to the poet Raychand, the second to Tolstoy, and the third to Ruskin.[64]

Gandhi read Tolstoy during his first years in South Africa. He read other works of Tolstoy while in jail in 1909. The three ideas of Tolstoy that influenced Gandhi greatly were: that the Sermon on the Mount taught an assertive version of nonviolence, the importance of service, and the idea of "bread labor."

Tolstoy's book *The Kingdom of God Is within You* forcefully reclaims the idea that nonviolence was central to the teaching of Jesus. In rejecting that truth through the centuries in favor of nationalism, war, and imperialism, Christianity lost its way.

Tolstoy had been an officer in the Crimean War and came to understand that the further up the social ladder one lived, the further one was from understanding the heroic life of the peasant. In the patient suffering of the common soldier from the peasant class he saw heroism, truth, and authentic love. It inspired him to throw over the trappings of society and the church.

In the *Kingdom of God Is within You*, Tolstoy wrote:

Among the many points in which this doctrine falls short of the doctrine of Christ I pointed out as the principal one the absence of any commandment of non-resistance to evil by force. The perversion of Christ's teaching by the teaching of the Church is more clearly apparent in this than in any other point of difference.[65]

In his letter to Madame Privat quoted above, Gandhi wrote:

[T]he meaning [of the New Testament] became clearer when I read Tolstoy's *Harmony of the Gospels* and his other kindred writings. Has not the West paid too heavily in regarding Jesus as a Passive Resister?[66]

Gandhi was in the middle of his early campaign of resistance when he first read Tolstoy. In 1906, he and his colleagues had taken an oath to resist even to death. At that time the campaign was not couched in or understood by Gandhi to have any religious dimension. Gandhi's reading of Thoreau had started to influence his attitude toward what they were doing in terms of conscience and a religious duty. By the time he read more of Tolstoy in 1909, he was beginning to formulate the campaign of resistance in more religious terms. After reading Tolstoy, he put aside his doubts concerning ahimsa and became a firm believer. As Raghavan Iyer noted:

His early hesitances about nonviolence were overcome by reading Tolstoy's *The Kingdom of God Is within You*...He thought Tolstoy's remarkable development of the doctrine of nonviolence put to shame the narrow and lopsided interpretations put upon it by its votaries in India despite the great discoveries in the field of *ahimsa* made by ancient Indian sages.[67]

Tolstoy emphasized that nonviolence, based on the fact that every human life is sacred, is an outgrowth of the fundamental law of love that is within the heart of each individual. Nonviolence is active and powerful in the same way love is active and powerful. In 1909, on his way back from England aboard ship, Gandhi wrote *Hind Swaraj*, a withering critique, in a Tolstoyan key, of Western civilization and a presentation of the idea of active nonviolence as an alternative path of action for Indian youth who were ready to embrace violent revolution against the British. He sent a copy of the tract to Tolstoy and a correspondence between them began.

It was at this time that the idea of "soul force" emerged in Gandhi's mind. He was trying to get away from an interpretation of their movement which made it a "way of the weak." In a speech in June 1909 on "The Ethics of Passive Resistance," he said:

> Passive Resistance, was a misnomer...The idea was more com-
> pletely and better expressed by the term "soul force." As such it is
> as old as the human race. Active resistance was better expressed by
> the term "body force." Jesus Christ, Daniel and Socrates repre-
> sented the purest form of passive resistance or soul force
> ...Tolstoy was the best and brightest exponent of the
> doctrine...In India, the doctrine was understood and commonly
> practiced long before it came into vogue in Europe.[68]

Tolstoy wrote back to Gandhi in 1910, the last letter he wrote in his life, of how important for the future of humankind was the work that Gandhi was doing in far-off Transvaal—applying satyagraha for the first time to masses of men.

As Margaret Chatterjee expressed it, Gandhi had been looking for a manly conception of love, which he did not always find in the literature of Gujurat, his home state.[69] He found it in Tolstoy.

The second idea that Gandhi received from Tolstoy was the idea of service. Tolstoy's concluding paragraph of *The Kingdom of God Is within You* reads, "The only meaning of man's life consists in serving the world by cooperating in the establishment of the Kingdom of God."[70] That theme of service pervades the book, and in another work of Tolstoy read by Gandhi, *The Gospel in Brief*, it is again the theme:

> My teaching is, that life is given to man not that others may serve
> him, but that he should give his whole life to service of others.[71]

From 1910 on Gandhi began to speak of *seva* (service) to others as the way to *moksha*. Not meditation, not *bhakti* (the devotional surrender to God), but service. J. T. F. Jordens points out that

[w]hen Gandhi declared that service was the activity that leads to the realisation of *moksha,* he made a statement nowhere to be found in the Hindu tradition.[72]

The third idea of Tolstoy that heavily influenced Gandhi was that each man should do the amount of bodily labor each day equivalent to his earning his daily bread through the sweat of his brow—what Tolstoy called "bread labor." Gandhi found the same idea in the works of John Ruskin.

When books struck him as important and true, he acted upon them. He straightaway made plans to begin his ashram, where each resident was expected to contribute to the welfare of all through daily manual labor.

Gandhi was clearly, according to his own testimony, influenced by the ideas and practices of a number of Western thinkers. He was such an independent thinker, however, and so rooted in his own culture, that the ideas from the West did not fall on absolutely virgin soil. Instead, ideas seemed to give him confirmation of directions in which he had already been moving or clarity on ideas that he had already been pondering. Some would say, for example, that he received the idea of civil disobedience from Thoreau, whereas, in actuality, he was already well into the first nonviolent campaign before he had even read Thoreau for the first time—in jail, in fact.

In any case, through the influence of these thinkers, Gandhi forged something new . His central idea of satyagraha, for example, was a rich synthesis with many contributing streams of thought and action. In the words of William Robert Miller:

> Like so many other great ideas in history, satyagraha was born of the interplay of diverse traditions. Few Westerners realize the theological richness of the term, which is generally translated as "soul force," but *sat* means not only soul in the western sense; it can also be translated as "ultimate reality." And this was just what Gandhi had in mind, for his was a Hinduism strongly modified by a deep encounter with Christian perfectionism, particularly that of Leo Tolstoy.[73]

As Raghavan Iyer concluded:

> Certainly no other influential Indian intellectual was as steeped as Gandhi was in the religious and philosophical texts of the classical Indian tradition as well as in the writings of daring Western moralists of the nineteenth century like Tolstoy, Thoreau, Ruskin, Emerson and Carlyle. It is hardly surprising that no other Indian politician or religious man became as original in his thinking as

Gandhi. His ready response to unorthodox...moralists of the nineteenth century in the West helped Gandhi to bring a pre-1914 standpoint—individualistic, heretical, heroic, humane—to the civic life of the twentieth century.[74]

Hindu Concepts Infused by Gandhi with New Meaning

Before exploring how Gandhi gave new political meaning to traditional concepts, it is important to review one other important interpretive lens that Gandhi used. It was, according to him, the most important influence of all on his life and praxis—the *Bhagavad Gita*, a popular religious poem within the epic *Mahabharata*. The way he interpreted the *Gita* had all to do with the way he conceptualized *moksha*, and understood ahimsa and *tapasya*.

We have already seen that he was introduced to the *Gita* back in his London student days. During his early years in South Africa he set out to learn it by heart as he brushed his teeth; every morning for fifteen minutes he stared at verses pinned to the wall. Recitations from the *Gita* were an integral part of the prayer services in successive ashrams for the rest of his life. He even published his own translation and extensively commented on the *Gita*'s meaning. It was the most important document for the leading of his daily and political life. As he wrote:

> What, however, I have done is to put a new but natural and logi- cal interpretation upon the whole teaching of the *Gita* and the spirit of Hinduism. Hinduism...has no one scripture like the Quran or the Bible. Its scriptures are also evolving and suffering addition. The *Gita* itself is an instance in point. It has given new meaning to *karma*, *sannasya*, *yajna*, etc. It has breathed new life into Hinduism.[75]

From the very beginning, Gandhi rejected the fundamentalist inter- pretation that the *Gita* was a work justifying violence. He interpreted the *Gita* not as a historical work but as an allegory. It describes not what one should do on the battlefield but how one must act to resolve the battle going on inside oneself.

> The *Gita* is not a historical work, it is a great religious book, sum- marizing the teaching of all religions. The poet has seized the occasion of the war between the Pandavas and the Kauravas...for drawing attention to the war going on in our bodies between the forces of Good and the forces of Evil.[76]

Gandhi turned most interpretations on their heads because he found in the *Gita* not justification for violence but a strong message of nonviolence. He explains:

> The text from the *Bhagavad Gita* shows to me how the principle of conquering hate by love, untruth by truth, can and must be applied. If it be true that God metes out the same measure to us that we mete out to others, it follows that if we would escape condign punishment, we may not return anger for anger but gentleness even against anger. And this is the law not for the unworldly but for the worldly.[77]

According to Gandhi, the main message of the *Gita* is found in the last nineteen verses of the second chapter. Arjuna asks Lord Krishna to describe the person who has achieved perfect control over himself and therefore is fully prepared to carry out the performance of his duty. The response is: the one who works without being attached to the results of his or her endeavors; the one who achieves perfect detachment.

> There can be no doubt that non-attachment is the central core of the Gita. I am certain that there is no other inspiration behind the composition of the Gita. And I know from my own experience that observance of truth or even ahimsa is impossible without non-attachment.[78]

Gandhi's interpretation of the *Gita*, along with the other influences that we have already reviewed, led him to recast some of the fundamental concepts of Hinduism: how to attain *moksha*; the meaning of ahimsa; the meaning of *tapasya*.

The final freeing of the individual soul from karmic defilement for oneness with the Spirit, or *moksha*, is not denied by Gandhi but enhanced. For him, all the works of purification are not just for final release but also for making the individual a more robust server of others. The goal is not just individual attainment but the liberation of all. In the words of Margaret Chatterjee:

> The Mahayana "all or none" principle chimed with his own conviction that if all living creatures are bound together in one great chain of existence the liberation of each is tied up with the liberation of all.[79]

It is in collective action with others that one generates and experiences the gradual spirit of liberation. Gandhi finds in the *Gita* the message of service and action for the sake of others. The struggle for freedom in one country will accrue to the struggles for freedom in countries everywhere.

Through collective action in the spirit of service and nonviolence, the circle of liberation and affection would keep expanding. Through the influence of the Vaishnava poet-saints, Gandhi saw the religious life as a horizontal expansion of fellow feeling, "an ocean of friendliness." The pursuit of perfection is an endless process but as one pursues it one would have the experience of expansiveness and "sweetness." Gandhi's second favorite Christian hymn was Cardinal Newman's "Lead Kindly Light," and its line "one step enough for me"—which expressed for Gandhi the philosophy of taking care, a step at a time, to make sure the means are pure; if they are, the results will be as well. If humans concentrate on a life of service, following the way of truth and duty where it leads them, that is sufficient for finding the way to *moksha*. Gandhi wrote:

> Life to me would lose all its interest if I felt I could not attain perfect love on earth. After all, what matters is that our capacity for loving ever expands.[80]

Gandhi therefore altered the older concept of *moksha* that stressed pursuing individual salvation through contemplation and austerities to the practical vision of serving others to change the conditions in which humans live. For Gandhi, immersion in the world, not escape from it, was the way to *moksha*.

Gandhi was confronting straight on the two errors that held the masses of India in bondage. According to K. L. Seshagiri Rao:

> First, the dangerous passivity brought about by the misunderstanding of the law of *karma*, "that everyone has to suffer the consequences of his deeds and there is no need to change things" ...The other error he saw was that meditation was considered higher than work which made it possible for the able-bodied to eat without work. Both these errors had reduced the masses of India to poverty and helplessness.[81]

Second, Gandhi changed the meaning of ahimsa. The teaching of ahimsa, whose etymological root is not "not-killing," but "physical noninjury,"[82] goes back as far as the *Chandogya Upanishad* in the seventh century BC. The aphorism from the Mahabharata, *"ahimsa paramo dharmah"* (ahimsa is the greatest duty), is known throughout India. As S. B. Mookherji points out:

> The impact of the idea on India's mass mind is reflected in a popular Sanskrit saying: "What merit is there in the goodness of a

man who returns good for good? A good man, verily, is he who returns good for evil."[83]

The Jains made ahimsa central to their religion and took it to the extremes of avoiding killing any living thing, even insects. They wear masks to avoid inhaling any living thing that might be flying in the air. As a people they ended up gravitating to business-related occupations and away from agriculture. In the acts of plowing and harvesting the destruction of life is unavoidable.

Gandhi accepted the tradition of ahimsa as a corollary of the central teaching of the Upanishads that the subjective and the objective, atman and Brahman, are identical. One should see the atman in all creatures. The true self of our neighbor is one with our own true self. To inflict harm on another is to inflict harm on ourselves. Gandhi, however, broadened the concept in a number of ways.

He made the practice of ahimsa a common duty for all, not just the saints. In addition, he made it a positive and dynamic method of political action to challenge evils that had been allowed to fester—from the domination by the British to the acceptance within Hinduism of untouchability. It was a method, in fact, that could be used in every arena of life. Gandhi wrote in 1940:

I have been practicing with scientific precision non-violence and its possibilities for an unbroken period of over fifty years. I have applied it in every walk of life, domestic, institutional, economic and political...Its spread is my life mission.[84]

Gandhi made ahimsa into a positive force—equivalent to St. Paul's notion of charity but to be distinguished from the mere feeling of love in that it involved an active fight against evil. In that fight, conducted nonviolently, the expectation was that the opponent would be converted. Gandhi was content with the negative words, ahimsa and nonviolence, because, as Raghavan Iyer points out,

[t]he negative word had its advantages for Gandhi. He wanted the acceptance of *ahimsa* to imply a deliberate stance against ill-will, a method of action based on self-restraint.[85]

For Gandhi, ahimsa was power but power in a new key, power that changed the situation, the opponent, and the practitioner all at once. The traditional Hindu virtue of ahimsa, which had always been seen as virtue to be cultivated for the sake of individual purification, was transformed by Gandhi into the principle of social uplift for all.

Third, Gandhi changed the popular understanding of suffering in the same way as he changed *moksha* and ahimsa. The pursuit of *moksha* was a pursuit of liberation for all, not just for the individual. The power of non-violence or ahimsa was not just in its ability to free an individual from the coil of *himsa* (harm or violence) and the law of karma but also in its power to change the conditions in which people lived that brought them suffering. So, enduring suffering was not just for the individual pursuing *moksha*, it was also the means by which humans could help one another overcome human suffering. In the words of Margaret Chatterjee:

> Indian metaphysical and religious thinking sees not so much evil, as suffering as the chief problem... The cycle of births and deaths strikes man in a fearsome way if he sees it as the prospect of further chains of suffering... Suffering then, in the Indian mind, has always posed itself, to the philosophers and sages, as something to be got rid of, that is as a *practical* problem.[86]

The working out of how this could be done put Indian systems of thought in a potential bind. Action to remove suffering could produce additional karma that could add to one's bondage. It was Gandhi's innovative idea that suffering itself could be the way to deal with suffering. Focusing on the sufferings of others, he saw that the injustices that afflicted the poor derived first from the "structures of domination"—what we would call the structural sources of social evil—as well as from the evil in individual human hearts. But his diagnosis went deeper.

Behind the suffering of the poor and behind the structures of evil he identified the real enemy—violence. First, violence makes the cycles of bondage tighter and tighter. One violent action leads to another and on and on. A way is needed to break the cycles. For Gandhi, that way could only be the way of self-suffering, whereby opponents are greeted with a willingness to suffer in an attempt to break through to their hearts and end the cycle. Second, violence concentrates power in the hands of a few. A way is needed to oppose and convert those who are in charge of unjust systems, a way that does not replace one oppression for another. Gandhi showed that the way is the way of nonviolent resistance and voluntary self-suffering. Third, violence leads to degradation. A way is needed that opposes violence such that practitioners find themselves lifted up to return love even as they suffer. As Margaret Chatterjee explains:

> A method is needed for every man, a moral equivalent of warfare which will release the constructive energies that all men possess and which will enable man to build up a good life for all. Gandhi believed this method to be the method of non-violence, the volun-

tary assumption of suffering by an individual and by a group as a self-purificatory act, an example to others, and as a way of converting the heart of the oppressor. [87]

The difference between the suffering of the poor and the self-suffering of a *satyagrahi* is a basic one. The suffering of the poor is not chosen. Gandhi agrees with Karl Marx that social injustice needs to be aggressively challenged but differs from Marx in seeing this as something that needs to be done nonviolently—lest we add to the total burden of suffering. Reflecting on how this came to him when in South Africa, Gandhi wrote:

> ...things of fundamental importance...are not secured by reason alone but have to be purchased with their suffering. Suffering is the law of the human being; But suffering is infinitely more powerful than the law of the jungle for converting the opponent and opening his ears...to the voice of reason...The appeal of reason is more to the head but the penetration of the heart comes from suffering...Suffering is the badge of the human race, not the sword.[88]

Gandhi gave the traditional values of *moksha*, ahimsa, and *tapasya* fresh relevance for politics and society. These spiritual values in turn gave his political vocabulary an otherworldly aura. He was both a true, resourceful believer and a shrewd politician. Understanding Gandhi's Hinduism and the Western influences on his thought prepares us to study the idea that is Gandhi's special contribution to the world—satyagraha.

CHAPTER TWO

Gandhian Satyagraha

I n 1906 Gandhi was already deeply involved in the struggle of the Indian residents of South Africa to overturn the laws that discriminated against them. He and many others had taken a vow that they would not submit to the unjust laws. The term "passive resistance" was current. Gandhi knew that historically the English people, when a minority did not approve of some offensive piece of legislation, frequently used a form of passive resistance as an alternative to armed rebellion. In *Satyagraha in South Africa* he cites the following example:

> When the British Parliament passed the Education Act some years ago the Non-Conformists offered passive resistance under the leadership of Doctor Clifford.[1]

He noted that the term was also used to describe the resistance of women in England who were fighting for the vote. In addition, it was used to describe the heroic resistance of the Boer women in the English concentration camps during the Boer War.

The approach was well known in Indian history as well. To sit in *dhurna* or mourning, remaining motionless without food and exposed to the weather, was employed by creditors at the door of debtors who refused to pay their debts. The method was at times used by whole communities to force rulers to accede to just demands. *Hartals* were strikes or work stoppages, another form of passive resistance. *Deshatyaga*, quitting a kingdom in protest, was used when all else failed to change a ruler's oppressive measures. As Raghavan Iyer comments:

> [D]*hurna, hartal and deshatyaga* were silent expressions of protest against recognized injustice, intended to arouse the oppressor's sense of shame rather than to evoke his sense of guilt.[2]

Given both English and Indian history, it was natural that the Indian residents of South Africa began referring to their actions as "passive resistance." Gradually, however, Gandhi began to see that the term "passive resistance" did not adequately express what they were doing.

Satyagraha Is More Than Passive Resistance

At one particular meeting with some supportive leading Europeans, it became apparent to Gandhi that another term, and preferably not an English term, was needed to describe the movement. An Englishman, Mr. Hosken, a magnate of Johannesburg, who was quite sympathetic to the Indians' cause, introduced Gandhi to the group in the following way:

> The Transvaal Indians have had recourse to passive resistance when all other means of securing redress proved to be of no avail. They do not enjoy the franchise. Numerically, they are only a few. They are weak and have no arms. Therefore they have taken to passive resistance which is a weapon of the weak.[3]

On the spot Gandhi changed what he had intended to say and spent his time explaining the difference between what they were attempting and passive resistance. Even this early in his career he knew that there were at least three important reasons to look for a better term.

First, Gandhi understood that what they were attempting was in no way the recourse of weaklings. It certainly was not just passive. They were taking the fight to the government in a very assertive way. It took tremendous courage and audacity to risk going to jail for one's convictions. He hated the fact that his people might see themselves as weak. He knew that if they persevered in their vows to resist the unjust laws they would feel themselves becoming stronger and stronger. They would understand their strength, and he wanted them to revel in it. He explained:

> The power of suggestion is such that a man at last becomes what he believes himself to be. If we continue to believe ourselves and let others believe that we are weak and therefore offer passive resistance, our resistance will never make us strong, and at the earliest opportunity we will give up passive resistance as a weapon of the weak.[4]

Second, Gandhi was concerned that the general populace, having associated passive resistance with the suffragists, who did not refrain from using physical force such as burning buildings and assaulting men, would see their movement as a potential physical threat to life and limb and property. This was an unfortunate misunderstanding because the

Indian populace was firmly committed to nonviolence. Gandhi went on to say:

> The result of our using the phrase "passive resistance" in South Africa was not that people admired us by ascribing to us the bravery and the self-sacrifice of the suffragists, but that we were mistaken to be a danger to person and property which the suffragists were.[5]

Third, the term "passive resistance" did not at all convey the component of their activities that entailed doing good for evil. Gandhi knew that he and his comrades were intent on showing love and support to those who were persecuting them and would not turn to violence or brute force, no matter what. They were refraining from using force not because they were incapable of it but because they were instead exerting soul force, an even more powerful weapon. He concluded:

> Again there is no scope for love in passive resistance...passive resistance is often looked upon as a preparation for the use of force...in passive resistance there is always present an idea of harassing the other party...we postulate the conquest of the adversary by suffering in one's own person.[6]

Gandhi therefore felt the need for a term, preferably in one of the Indian languages, that would more adequately convey the vivid reality and the spirit of what they were doing together. He knew that what they were doing was not at all passive. They were actively pitting their lives against injustice. It was a strategy for the strong. They were filled with love and compassion for their adversaries—not the anger and hate expressed in many "passive resistance" campaigns. They were returning good for the evil done to them and were aiming to convert and not humble their adversaries. They were not employing brute force but were using soul force. Gandhi sensed that what they were doing was in many ways a new principle of action. The term "passive resistance" did not adequately convey this new principle. As mentioned in the previous chapter, he therefore decided to sponsor a contest through his magazine, *Indian Opinion*, and offer a prize to the best essay describing their struggle.

> As the struggle advanced, the phrase "passive resistance" gave rise to confusion and it appeared shameful to permit this great struggle to be known only by an English name. Again that foreign phrase could hardly pass as current coin among the community. A small prize was therefore announced in *Indian Opinion* to be awarded to the reader who invented the best designation for our struggle.[7]

Of the few respondents to the challenge, easily the best essay was submitted by Gandhi's nephew Maganlal, who suggested the term *sadagraha*, which was translated "firmness in a good cause." Gandhi liked the term but it did not fully convey the whole of what he wanted it to connote, so he adjusted it to "satyagraha," or "firmness in the truth."

> I therefore corrected it to *satyagraha*. Truth (*satya*) implies love, and firmness (*agraha*) engenders and therefore serves as a synonym for force. I thus began to call the Indian movement *satyagraha*, that is to say, the Force which is born of Truth and Love or non-violence, and gave up the use of the phrase "passive resistance"...so that even in English writing we often avoided it and used instead the word *satyagraha* itself or some other equivalent English phrase.[8]

To understand the meaning of satyagraha, it is therefore important to clearly distinguish it, in the ways that Gandhi did, from the ideas of passive resistance, civil disobedience and pacifism. Commentators, especially Christian commentators such as Reinhold Niebuhr, have continued to confuse satyagraha with passive resistance. As it developed in South Africa, satyagraha was bold, assertive, and risk-taking.[9]

Satyagraha Is More Than Civil Disobedience

For Gandhi, civil disobedience was one of the methods to be used in a satyagraha campaign. Various forms of non-cooperation, such as strikes, boycotts, and work stoppages, were among the other methods that could be used in a satyagraha campaign.

Civil disobedience, for Gandhi, was the direct disobeying of particular laws with the willingness to accept the punishment that came with the contravention of the laws. When a government itself became lawless and unjust, Gandhi understood that civil disobedience became not only the recourse of the populace but a duty. He wrote:

> When...a Government...becomes lawless in an organized manner, civil disobedience becomes a sacred duty and is the only remedy open specially to those who had no hand in the making of the Government or its laws. Another remedy there certainly is, and that is armed revolt. Civil disobedience is a complete, effective and bloodless substitute.[10]

For civil disobedience to be "civil," it required that the resistance be carried out nonviolently.

Those only can take up civil disobedience, who believe in willing obedience even to irksome laws imposed by the state so long as they do not hurt their conscience or religion, and are prepared equally willingly to suffer the penalty of civil disobedience. Disobedience to be civil has to be absolutely non-violent, the underlying principle being the winning over of the opponent by suffering, i.e., love.[11]

Satyagraha is the whole of which civil disobedience is a part. The whole includes the methods of resistance but it also includes the commitment to nonviolence, the belief in the power of truth and self-suffering, and the desire to win over the opponent and transform the situation.

When violence erupted during the mass civil disobedience campaign of 1921–22—violence initiated by Indians—Gandhi called off the campaign and termed it a "Himalayan miscalculation" to think that the whole country was prepared to act with such disciplined nonviolence. For years he waited and planned until he thought the country was ready to try again. The threat of an outbreak of violence kept him from leading another mass campaign. He noted:

I can never give up the *idea* of civil disobedience, no matter what the danger there is of violence, but I shall certainly give up the idea of *starting* mass civil disobedience so long as there is a certain danger of violence. Individual civil disobedience stands on a different footing.[12]

By 1930, however, his attitude had started to shift. He was ready to resume the public, mass campaign even if there was some risk of the outbreak of violence. He could not control the whole country. But he had begun to see that the campaign might not cause the violence but only be the occasion for revealing the violence that was already present in the body politic. Bringing it out into the open might not be such a bad thing. He wrote:

That civil disobedience may resolve itself into violent disobedience is, I am sorry to have to confess, not an unlikely event. But I know that it will not be the cause of it. Violence is there already corroding the whole body politic. Civil disobedience will be but a purifying process and may bring to the surface what is burrowing under and into the whole body.[13]

Even so, in the Salt March campaign of 1930, Gandhi took extra care to launch the campaign in a way that would limit the opportunities for violence to break out. Only confirmed, well trained *satyagrahis*, who had spent years in his ashram, were selected to join him in his dramatic march to the seashore.

UNDERSTANDING GANDHIAN SATYAGRAHA

The Terms That Constitute the Word "Satyagraha"

Satya (truth)

The word *satya* has five meanings.

1. Satya is sat, and sat is reality itself, "what is," the real
As a Hindu, Gandhi understood *satya* to be synonymous with *sat*, "what is," the real. In instructing new arrivals to the ashram he began his training lessons in the following way:

> I deal with Truth first of all, as the Satyagraha Ashram owes its very existence to the pursuit and attempted practice of Truth. The word *Satya* (Truth) is derived from *Sat*, which means "being." Nothing is or exists in reality except Truth. That is why *Sat* or Truth is perhaps the most important name of God. In fact it is more correct to say that Truth is God, than it is to say that God is Truth.[14]

As Westerners, we talk about what is true as what conforms to reality. We typically are referring to statements or beliefs in the mind that accurately reflect reality. If they are consonant with reality, they are true. In the words of John Hick:

> Gandhi taught that truth is God. This very naturally puzzles the philosophically educated Westerner who is likely to think of the truth as the sum of all true propositions...the heart of *satya*, Truth is *sat*, reality, the real, the true, the ultimate. Indeed Gandhi treated *Satya* and *sat* as synonymous...the Gods are all manifestations of the one ultimate reality called Brahman.[15]

The *sat* in satyagraha is therefore, first, the ontologically real. *Sat* is not just a cognitive affair but the goal of all human endeavors. We are made for the truth. We pine and long for the truth. This sense, conveyed in the Psalms as well as in Hindu devotional literature, that humans are rooted in the ontologically real, came very easily to Gandhi. We catch some pale sense of this in certain expressions in English.

As Margaret Chatterjee points out:

> It also comes out in his occasional use of the word "truly" as an epithet for a person, or a mode of action which shines with the clear light of *sat*, which exists paradigmatically... "Really and truly" in ordinary language have lost their ontological overtones. One has to go back through many centuries of British history to find the phrase "good men and true" used naturally.[16]

To be in touch with the truth is to be in touch with what *is*, the fundamentally real. For Hindus that foundational reality is all-pervading and all-powerful. It is that through which all creation was sustained.

2. Satya is the source of the moral law running through the universe
All-pervading and powerful, *satya* is the force holding the universe together. Truth is therefore the source of dharma, the moral law running through the universe. In Gandhi's words:

> There is an indefinable mysterious power that pervades everything. I feel it, though I do not see it. It is this unseen power that makes itself felt and yet defies all proof, because it is so unlike all that I perceive through my senses. It transcends the senses.
>
> I do dimly perceive that whilst everything around me is ever changing, ever dying, there is underlying all that change a living power that is changeless, that holds all together.[17]

Truth for Gandhi, therefore, is both transcendent and immanent. It is ever beyond us but also beckoning us to find it within this universe and in this life. The way to the transcendent is through the immanent. As R. R. Diwakar explains:

> [Gandhi's] quest was for the both the transcendent and the immanent in equal measure. It was this belief and experience that saved him from an escape into metaphysics and made him the torchbearer for actively spiritualizing the whole of life... seeing God face to face was his passion and it meant for him the constant consciousness of an eternal presence... to serve man was to serve God.[18]

To be in touch with the truth or, to use one of Gandhi's favorite expressions, to be "attuned" to the truth, means therefore that you have the power of the universe working for you. That is why he made the search for truth, clinging to the truth, the central concern of a *satyagrahi*.

According to Stanley Jones,

> [Gandhi] believed that if you always did the true thing, you would
> have the backing of the moral universe. He felt himself the agent
> of cosmic forces working through him. He knew that the success
> would turn to ashes if the means did not coincide with truth.[19]

The *satyagrahi* could have immense strength—beyond what others
might think possible—not because of the individual human's strength but
because of the strength that flowed into him or her by being in touch with
the truth of the situation.

3. *Truth (God) is one and so is humanity;*
   Brahman (God) and atman (the Self) are one
This fundamental idea of Hinduism, that the soul of each individual
human is a spark of the divine and that with the elimination of *maya* (illusion), each soul, eventually freed from the limitations of the body, will
merge with the divine, undergirded Gandhi's belief in satyagraha. The
truth, in time, would eventually prevail over untruth. It had to. Truth alone
is real. Gandhi wrote:

> I believe in absolute oneness of God and therefore also of humanity
> ...I believe in the essential unity of man and for that matter all
> that lives.[20]

The soul is co-eternal with Brahman and will merge with Brahman in
final *moksha*. On an ultimate level, all human beings are one. Gandhi took
this belief into the fire of the controversy over untouchability and made it
the touchstone of the fight. How could there be levels of human beings
and how could some be considered untouchable, if Hindus believed that all
human beings are really one at the source? How, moreover, can one human
being be violent with another? To do violence to another is to do violence
to oneself. Referring to untouchability, Gandhi said:

> In my opinion there is no such thing as inherited or acquired
> superiority. I believe in the rock-bottom doctrine of Advaita...
> it excludes totally any idea of superiority...I believe implicitly that
> all men are born equal. Untouchability has to be rooted out
> completely.[21]

(This Hindu belief differs from the Christian contention that each
human being is a creature of God, that humans are not one with but distinct from God. Operationally, however, there really should not be much

difference between the belief systems. Christians would say that all human beings are a part of one family, that all are equal in the eyes of God, that to do violence to another is to hurt the whole. We may not say that each is identical with, or a spark of God, but we do say that in a fundamental way we are one.)

It follows from the insight that humanity is one that violence is the law of the brute and nonviolence the law of the human species. An increasing awareness and realization of one's innate divinity brings with it a deeper and deeper commitment to nonviolence towards others. Through the power of choice, even though humans are bestial in origin, humans can either increase the brutalization of nature or increasingly realize divinity. As Raghavan Iyer points out, the Indian doctrine of monism has a number of other practical consequences:

> [I]f one man gains spiritually, the whole world gains with him . . . what one man is capable of achieving is possible for all to attain . . . it is quite proper to attack a system, but to attack and resist its author is tantamount to resisting and attacking oneself.[22]

This view of truth is the reason why anyone who wanted to live in one of Gandhi's ashrams as a devoted *satyagrahi* was asked to take a vow of truthfulness—in thought, speech, and, most important, in action. In the words of Rex Ambler:

> [P]erhaps the most important feature of Gandhi's Truth, that is, in some sense it already exists and is only waiting to be realized in actual experience. It exists in people, in everybody, and not only as the ground of their common identity . . . but also as the source of their own realization of it . . . the Indian masses tended to despair of their own capabilities and were all too ready to submit to the authority of fate, or karma or British rule or even the Mahatma himself. He saw the universal availability of Truth as a source of personal liberation and independence, which would in turn provide the basis of genuine liberation and independence for India. "The Truth would out."[23]

4. Truth is established not through thought, but through action

We in the West are accustomed to thinking that truth is in the mind and that truth is an epistemological challenge. Consequently, it is difficult at first to understand Gandhi's contention that truth is found through action.

It might be helpful to understand what Gandhi meant if we come at it from a slightly different direction. Reflect for a moment on what Karl

Marx meant when he said, in the famous and last of his "Theses on Feuerbach," "The philosophers have only interpreted the world differently; the point is to change it."[24]

For Marx and for Gandhi, religion and philosophy all too often simply pondered on the world and, as a result, let it be. Just as Marx critiqued religion for being an opiate of the people, freezing people in place and encouraging them to be content with their lot, so also Gandhi was critical when religion served the existing order and failed people. Gandhi had a passionate commitment to change the way things were in order to rid the "dumb masses" of their unnecessary suffering. He was just as impatient as Marx to see the world as it was fundamentally changed. Unlike Marx, however, he did not think it would change through the iron, necessary laws of historical materialism. Gandhi believed the world would be changed only if human beings freely set themselves to the task of overcoming evil and the violence that sustained it in place.

For Gandhi, therefore, truth was a matter of living and acting in a way that relieved humanity of its burdens. One finds the truth only in service of people. The truth is not yet in place if people are suffering unnecessarily. The task is not to think about the world but to change it, for, as Gandhi wrote:

> The realization of the Self, or Self-Knowledge is not possible until one has achieved unity with all living beings—has become one with God. To accomplish such a unity implies deliberate sharing of the suffering of others and the eradication of such suffering ...No one has ever attained *moksha* by means of learning whereas many a soul did and does attain its salvation through service ...Self-realisation I hold to be impossible without service of and identification with the poorest.[25]

This contention, that truth is found by establishing it in action, is not completely foreign to the Christian tradition. For example, Nicholas Lobkowicz emphasizes that a similar idea was held by Duns Scotus, the Franciscan theologian, who held that God is the doable knowable, the *cognoscibile operabile*, the object of knowledge which may be reached by a doing that is true praxis. This tenet of Scotus, Lobkowicz contends,

> paves the way for the notion that man's ultimate achievement is practice not theory and that it is in atheoretical practice in which God is encountered or missed, the meaning of the universe fulfilled or failed ...Eventually practice will become the sole source of meaning and salvation.[26]

Gandhi entitled his autobiography *The Story of My Experiments with Truth*. For him, truth could be found only through the experimental method: hypothesize, act, hold the variables constant, test, revise, act some more. The great adventure for Gandhi was in pitting one's self against injustice and violence and transforming them by reaching the soul of the person(s) responsible, thereby revealing the real unity that underlies all appearances. The truth emerges from direct action.

Rex Ambler has written about Gandhi:

> The great illusion, the social *maya*, as we may call it, is that human beings are fundamentally different from one another, and that some are inherently superior to others and are thereby entitled to dominate them... His life's work was largely devoted to the exposure of that illusion and the realization of the Truth of human oneness. That is why his personal search for Truth so often assumed the form of social insistence on Truth, that is a social struggle to achieve at least a minimum of this unity.[27]

Truth in the narrow epistemological sense is only part of the wider meaning of *satya*. Truth is latent until it is embodied in action. For Gandhi, truth is to be discovered and created, found and enacted. Truth comes to the fore through a process of corrective experimentation.

5. Truth is absolute and relative

In 1931, Gandhi began to change his basic teaching from "God is Truth" to "Truth is God." He hypothesized that all humans could agree on the importance and centrality of truth. Even atheists and agnostics could unite with religious people on this absolute.

According to Hindu teaching, however, no human being can realize absolute truth while imprisoned in the mortal body. The best we can do is to pursue truth according to our lights. We can grasp only relative truths. Each person has a fragmentary grasp of the truth, and in order to grasp and realize a fuller truth one has to recognize the partiality of one's own perception and be open to the truth that comes from others.

The fragmentary nature of truth is why one should not impose one's truth on another. This view of truth excludes therefore the use of violence. In conflict situations a method is needed to bring out the latent truth hidden in the partial. This is where truth and nonviolence come together in the method of satyagraha. As Rex Ambler points out:

> Satyagraha is a form of action appropriate to the dual character of Truth as one in essence but diverse in practice... in order to win a greater understanding or realization of Truth, a person or group

must recognize the partiality of their own perception of truth even in the process of insisting on it...the opponent must be listened to and expected to yield his or her truth too...That is why all confrontations in the name of Truth have to be nonviolent, for violence would immediately close the door to dialogue and mutual regard.[28]

We will explore more fully the mutual relationship between truth and nonviolence in the section below on ahimsa. We will see how satyagraha affirms the relativity of truth while not falling into relativism.

This sense of the relativity of truth also led Gandhi to teach the necessity of making the means continuous with the ends sought. If one could see the truth only partially at any one moment, then one had to focus on the purity of the means. Only good means lead to good ends. Bad means lead to bad ends. Violence never issues in nonviolence. Violence never brings peace. He never tired of repeating: "One reaps only what one sows."

The duality of truth as ultimate and relative also led him to reject "isms" and orthodoxies that were not linked to orthopraxis. His appreciation of the "manysidedness," or *anekantavada* as the Jains expressed it, of truth made him open to the truths of all the religions he encountered. In Buddha and Christ he found an active spirituality. He admired the Muslim faith for its fervor, Puritanism, practical reformism, and belief in the one human family. All religions for him were branches of the one tree of truth. According to Elton Hall,

First of all he accepted the classical distinction between Absolute Truth and relative truth, *paramarthasatya* and *samvritisatya*. By definition, Absolute Truth cannot be wholly captured by any formulation or instanciation, just as relative truth can never be absolutized. Absolute Truth is real precisely because it cannot be stated. In Johannine Christian terms it is prior to the Word.[29]

In conclusion, an understanding of all that Gandhi held about truth illuminates even more clearly why there was a need for a brand new term to describe what he and his colleagues were about. They were not just protesting. Gandhi understood that unless they embraced truth and nonviolence as a creed they would quickly give up. Only a deep theological vision would give them the ballast they needed to persevere. Gandhi wrote:

[The *satyagrahi*] must have a living faith in nonviolence. This is impossible without a living faith in God. A non-violent man can do nothing save by the power and grace of God. Without it he won't have the courage to die without anger, without fear and without retaliation. Such courage comes from the belief that God sits in the hearts of all and that there should be no fear in the presence of God.[30]

A belief in God as truth would put people in touch with the power that held the universe together. It was an unfailing source of strength that would allow them to endure prison bravely and even with good humor. This vision, that in fact, all humans are one with one another, would prompt action to remove the *maya* of separateness. It would ignite in the *satyagrahi* the commitment to fight and transform the causes of unnecessary human suffering. It would point out a way to stand up to violence without succumbing to the temptation to use violence in return. The practice of satyagraha flows from this theological vision. The vision is inseparable from the practice. The practice is made effective, creative, and enduring through the vision.

So far we have seen that satyagraha includes methods of resisting injustice, methods such as passive resistance, non-cooperation, and civil disobedience. We have also explored the theological vision and understanding of God as truth, which is part and parcel of satyagraha. In the next three sections, on *agraha*, ahimsa, and *tapasya*, we will see that satyagraha is, in addition, a distinctive way of living.

Agraha (firmly hold)

Conflict is part of the human condition. Gandhi did not think conflict could ever be removed from the human condition. His vision of the future was not that of a world where people would never be at odds, a scene of perpetually low and mild voices and concord ever reigning. His understanding of human beings assumed that, because people would have varying perceptions of relative truths, there would always be differences of opinion and even sharp divisions between people.

Moreover, his realization that the world was not the way it should be, that there was much to be done to change society and stand up to oppression, necessitated confrontation and conflict. He knew that *satyagrahis* would have to be fighters. The issue was not how to avoid conflict but how to fight fairly and effectively. As Mark Juergensmeyer points out:

> It is action to be done in the context of conflict, which is why satyagraha is often described as a method of fighting...not so much a method of resolving fights as one of waging them...he often seemed to encourage engagement, especially when silence would imply consent to an ongoing form of injustice...Like Hobbes and Marx, he saw this persistent state of conflict as the greatest challenge facing socially responsible individuals and institutions.[31]

Gandhi did not think conflict was removable from the human scene. He did think, however that violence could be minimized, and that humans could achieve a predominantly nonviolent society. He understood the need for the state to have a policing power for the maintenance of order. Such policing power was not to be equated however, with warmaking power, which he hoped could be eradicated. He wrote:

> A government cannot succeed in becoming entirely nonviolent because it represents all the people. I do not conceive of such a golden age. But I do believe in the possibility of a predominantly non-violent society.[32]

Gandhi was not a patsy. He was a fighter. He constantly seemed to find the center of action. He taught that not resisting injustice and claiming to be nonviolent was actually cowardice.

> In contrast, non-violence of my conception is true battle against evil; it is active confrontation and not a device of tit for tat.[33]

Satyagraha is in fact a philosophy of conflict. By pursuing, through direct action, a fuller truth than that possessed by either party in a conflict, one tries to resolve conflicts, not through compromise, but through a higher synthesis.

Joan Bondurant entitled her excellent book *Conquest of Violence: The Gandhian Philosophy of Conflict*. She distinguishes the Gandhian dialectic for resolving conflict from Marx's dialectic in the following way:

> With Marx the dynamic quality of the dialectic is only partially retained, for the content of the process is supplied through the dogma of the class struggle...It is here that Gandhi departs. The method loses its dynamic when it becomes entangled in historicism...What results from the dialectic process is a synthesis not a compromise...When persuasion has been effected, what was once the opponent's position is now the position of both antagonist and protagonist.[34]

As we shall see, the norms for resolving conflicts and achieving a higher synthesis between parties in conflict will be ahimsa and *tapasya*. Gandhi's "experiments in truth" were fundamentally an attempt to find a way for human beings to fight well and morally. According to Juergensmeyer,

> What makes Gandhi different from...many other thinkers is his insistence that conflict itself can be moral...He felt that the

process of fighting, as well as its goals, can be virtuous . . . Truthful fighting . . . requires the fighters to suppress their own narrow positions in favor of . . . a principle to which all parties in a dispute would presumably assent and through which all would gain.[35]

Satyagraha is a way of exerting power. Given Gandhi's view that the world was bound to be riven with conflict, it is not surprising that what he liked about the term "satyagraha" was that it claimed a place for the assertive use of power. He understood the *agraha* component, translated as holding fast or holding steadfastly, to be the part of the word that conveyed the notion of coercion, force, and power. He wrote:

Truth (satya) implies love, and firmness (agraha) engenders and therefore serves as a synonym for force.[36]

It may help here, to avoid confusion later, to pause and define and distinguish some terms that are often used indiscriminately: "power," "coercion," and "force." Joan Bondurant's definitions are helpful:

Force. The exercise of physical or intangible power or influence to effect change.

Violence. The willful application of force in such a way that is intentionally injurious to the person or group against which it is applied.

Injury. Includes psychological and physical harm.

Non-violence. The exercise of power or influence to effect change without injury to the opponent.

Coercion. The use of physical or intangible force to compel action contrary to the will or reasoned judgment of the individual or group subjected to such force.[37]

Gandhi did not refrain from using force, the intangible kind. Nor did he refrain from coercion when it was required—but it was always done non-violently. Far from being people who do not engage the world, *satyagrahis* engage it full bore. Gandhi wanted *satyagrahis* to be as courageous and as powerful as soldiers—and as well trained and prepared to face violence.

Putting the two words, *satya* and *agraha*, together makes "satyagraha." It is fortunate that there is such a word. It communicates better than the pale, purely negative expressions that typically substitute for it, such as "passive resistance" or "nonviolence," the fullness of what Gandhi had in mind.

In the words of R. R. Diwakar:

It is our good fortune that Gandhi gave us a new word for this new way of life... truth, that which is according to what is or exists; and the *agraha*—insistence or adherence. Both together now indicate a new way of life. The word nonviolence or love is not included in the compound word. It is understood that the insistence on truth is to be nonviolent...There are several compound words in Sanskrit with *satya* as a component. For instance *satya-sandha*, wedded to the truth...But I have not so far come across in the whole of Sanskrit literature the words *satyagraha* or satyagrahi. It was reserved for Gandhi to coin the word as well as to evolve its full connotation during his eventful life.[38]

Terms Associated with Satyagraha

Ahimsa (refusal to do harm; nonviolence)

As was noted in chapter 1, ahimsa was a cardinal virtue of Hinduism through the centuries. Gandhi, under the influence especially of Tolstoy and the Sermon on the Mount, made it the centerpiece of his thought and praxis and a *sine qua non* of the pursuit of human liberation. Even though it is not literally included in the word "satyagraha," it is essential to the practice of satyagraha. In this section we will explore five facets of the meaning of ahimsa.

1. Gandhi's critique of the myth of violence
To understand ahimsa as Gandhi understood it, one must first have an understanding of how thoroughly he rejected *himsa*, or violence. He rejected violence on the basis of his religion, his personal experience, and his reading of history.

First, on the basis of his understanding of humanity and his religion Gandhi rejected violence. He was proud of India's religious tradition and understood that it prepared the country to embrace the alternative creed of nonviolence. He explained:

The most distinctive and the largest contribution of Hinduism to India's culture is the doctrine of ahimsa. It has given a definite bias to the history of the country for the last three thousand years and over and it has not ceased to be a living force in the lives of India's millions even today...that an armed revolution has almost become an impossibility in India, not because, as some would have it, we as a race are physically weak, for it does not require much physical strength so much as a devilish will to press a trigger to shoot a person, but because the tradition of ahimsa has struck deep roots among the people.[39]

Gandhi's awareness of the futility of violence grew out of his understanding of the nature of the spirit and its relationship to the body. He thought that turning to violence was the surest way to kill the human spirit, for, as he noted,

[t]he man with a sword, whom does he protect and whom does he kill? Physical strength stands no comparison before spiritual strength. Non-violence reveals the strength of spirit, while the sword that of the body. With the use of the sword, spirit degenerates into matter. By resorting to non-violence, the soul recovers its spiritual nature.[40]

Second, he rejected violence on the basis of his own observations. He could not understand why the human race clung to its belief in violence and enthroned it as an abiding law when it so clearly led to endless cycles of entrapment.

What is happening today is disregard of the law of nonviolence and enthronement of violence as if it were an eternal law. The democracies, therefore, that we see at work in England, America and France are only so called, because they are no less based on violence than Nazi Germany, Fascist Italy or even Soviet Russia.[41]

He witnessed the ongoing carnage that resulted from the practice of retaliation. He witnessed it in the Hindu-Muslim conflicts. He witnessed it between countries. He witnessed it between individuals. He said:

My experience daily growing stronger and richer tells me that there is no peace for individuals or for nations without practicing truth and non-violence to the uttermost extent possible for man. The policy of retaliation has never succeeded. We must not be confounded by isolated illustrations of retaliation, including fraud and force, having attained temporary and seeming success.[42]

Third, Gandhi's rejection of violence stemmed from a broad and deep reading of history. As Gandhi read history he could see the destructive power of violence for his own country when it turned to violence. He read the history of Europe in the same way, and he hated seeing that same history playing itself out again in the Second World War. Reflecting, for example, on India's history, using as an example the Sepoy Mutiny of the previous century, when the Muslim fighters within the British Army had mutinied over being compelled, against their religious values, to use cartridges greased with pig fat. He contrasted the results of that violence with what nonviolence was accomplishing in India since the first of the mass actions of non-cooperation in 1920.

> Read history with my eyes. Take the history of the Mutiny. It was a war of independence fought with violent weapons... You will see that though the greased cartridges may have been an immediate cause, it was just a spark in a magazine that was ready. But look at the result. The U.P., the storm center of 1857, has for generations since remained under a paralysis as perhaps no other province... Take now this 12 years experiment. It is a short time in the history of the nation. The experiment and its mighty results would have been impossible without the great force of non-violence.[43]

He read the history of India's relationship with England clearly. He recognized that the Empire had been built through violence and that England would not give up India without a great fight; but he understood that fighting nonviolently stood a much greater chance of success than the humankind-old way of vengeance, violence, and the sword. He did not see England as a soft, beneficent power. He knew the kind of violence that England would unleash if given cause. He wrote:

> But this Empire says that for its own imperial glory it will stoop to any atrocity... Do you think the killing of a few will frighten the Empire into giving us swaraj? That Empire which is established on the corpses of thousands of Englishmen, which has shed rivers of British, Sikh and Pathan blood, is that Empire going to be frightened by the murder of a handful of people? Most certainly not.[44]

Gandhi understood the history of Europe in a similar fashion. The so-called great figures of the past such as Napoleon, when all was said and done, understood the futility and soul-destroying impact of violence. Quoting from an old issue of *My Magazine*, Gandhi noted:

> Napoleon knew that it was folly to rely on force. "There are only two powers in the world," he said, not after he had been defeated and exiled, but while he appeared to be at the height of his success.

"Those powers are the spirit and the sword. In the long run *the sword will always be conquered by the spirit.*"

But why, we may ask, did Napoleon, if he saw so plainly the uselessness of war, continue to make war? Why did he use the sword until it was wrenched from his hand at Waterloo? Partly because Napoleon, like the rest of us, could not always practise what he preached, but we're not always as wise as he. When he pleaded for peace they would not believe he was sincere. To the Emperor of Austria after a fierce battle he addressed this personal appeal:

"Amid grief and surrounded by 15,000 corpses, I implore your majesty, I feel bound to give you an urgent warning. You are far from the scene, your heart cannot be so deeply moved as mine is on the spot..."[45]

In 1938, Gandhi predicted that Hitler, Stalin, and Mussolini would all demonstrate one more time the emptiness of violence. They would appear to be effective through violence and then they would collapse and pass from the scene, leaving more hatred and devastation in their wake. He contrasted what he saw coming with the way of nonviolence.

Hitler and Mussolini on the one hand and Stalin on the other are able to show the immediate effectiveness of violence. But it will be as transitory as that of Jhenghis's slaughter. But the effects of Buddha's non-violent action persist and are likely to grow with age.[46]

Gandhi understood that the seeds of the Second World War were planted during the First World War. The Allies' treatment of Germany in the Versailles Treaty and their division of the spoils prepared the scene for more violence. In fact, he saw Hitler refining violence into an ever more deadly poison. In 1939, Gandhi wrote:

[T]he toll of the late war has shown that both the combatants were guilty of falsehoods, exaggerations and inhumanities. The Versailles Treaty was a treaty of revenge against Germany by the victors...What wonder if Messrs Hitler and company have reduced to a science the unscientific violence their predecessors had developed for exploiting the so-called backward races for their own material gain?[47]

As the war gathered momentum, Gandhi lamented the growing brutalization of humanity. Britain used the same methods as Hitler. Violence for violence. The orthodoxy of violence was embraced by the whole world as the one and only truth. In 1940 he wrote:

> But in seeking to avenge the wrong by the wrong method of violence brought to very near perfection, Hitler has brutalized not only Germans but a large part of humanity. The end of it we have not yet reached. For Britain, so long as she holds to the orthodox method, has to copy the Nazi methods if she is to put up a successful defence. Thus the logical outcome of the violent method seems to be increasingly to brutalize man.[48]

By 1946, all that Gandhi had predicted had come to pass. Those whom violence had raised up, violence had cast down. His reading of history and his understanding of violence had once again been proven true. He could only wonder when humanity would give up the myth. When would it see that the apparent power of violence was empty and destructive? He thought that with the atom bomb humankind would finally understand the futility of all violence and be ready to embrace the alternative power—nonviolence. He wrote in 1946:

> Look at Italy. Garibaldi was a great man. He brought deliverance to Italy. And Mussolini did make her look great. But where is she today? Look at Japan, look at Germany. The very violence which brought them to the pinnacle of power has razed them to the ground. And has not the atom bomb proved the futility of all violence?[49]

At a fundamental level, what motivated and energized Gandhi was his reaction to the lot of the "poor, dumb millions." In the spirit of Vaishnava Hinduism influenced by Buddhism, the real human being was defined as the one whose heart melted in pity at the suffering of other human beings.

Gandhi understood that behind so much senseless suffering was not just violence but also belief in the saving power of violence. At the same time that he confronted senseless human suffering and therefore encountered violent reactions, Gandhi realized that he needed to do what he could to free humans from the belief in violence. As Margaret Chatterjee points out:

> In a manner which is strikingly contemporary, Gandhi pinpointed violence as the chief malady of our times. If anyone asks Gandhi what is wrong with violence he has his answers ready. One violent action leads to another; for example, violent speech provokes angry retorts from the other side. Secondly, violence concentrates

power in the hands of a few. He is thinking here of the violence typified in colonialism and the economic systems which deprive the poor by concentrating wealth in feudal and capitalist structures. Thirdly, violence leads to suffering and degradation ... Warfare is the externalization of violence in the human heart. Violence *is* evil. This is why the words "*"ahimsa paramo dharma"* (the prime duty is nonviolence) possess for Gandhi near mantric power.[50]

History and experience showed Gandhi that *himsa*, violence, was a dead end. That awareness was one of the reasons he embraced ahimsa, nonviolence, as the alternative and antidote to violence. In addition, Gandhi knew that, unlike violence, ahimsa worked—and the results lasted over the short and long haul.

2. Ahimsa as an active force

Despite the negative prefixes in the words "ahimsa" and "nonviolence," Gandhi understood ahimsa to be the most active force in the world. Ahimsa went beyond refusal to do harm; it entailed doing good to those who did one harm. Gandhi accepted the value of the term "nonviolence" because it staked out a position squarely opposed to violence, but he regretted that it did not convey all that the *satyagrahi* brought to the fray.

For Gandhi, ahimsa was the quality or attribute within a *satyagrahi* that made him or her act, in situations of hate and conflict, in a positive, non-judging, creatively forbearing and loving way. It was the animating principle of the non-cooperation movement. When violence arose during the first mass demonstration in 1920–21, the animating principle was canceled out. Ahimsa was the energizing power that gave the movement its punch and impact. For Gandhi, when expressed in direct action, it was the most active of forces. He explained:

> [W]ithout a direct active expression of it, non-violence is meaning-less. It is the greatest and the activest force in the world. One cannot be passively non-violent. In fact "non-violence" is a term I had to coin in order to bring out the root meaning of *ahimsa*. In spite of the negative particle "non," it is no negative force...It is a force more positive than electricity and more powerful even than ether.[51]

Gandhi knew enough of the New Testament to relate ahimsa to what the West has come to understand as love in the "high" sense of the term. He also knew the negative, syrupy connotations that could be attached to the term "love." He translated and explained ahimsa in many ways and in many situations. He labored to express the dynamism and profundity of the term for a Western audience. In a speech to Christian missionaries, for example, he said:

Ahimsa means "love" in the Pauline sense, and yet something more than the "love" defined by St. Paul, although I know St. Paul's beautiful definition is good enough for all practical purposes. Ahimsa includes the whole creation, and not only human. Besides, love in the English language has other connotations too, and so I was compelled to use the negative word.[52]

At a later time, speaking to Christians who had asked him if nonviolence or ahimsa was a positive quality, he further clarified why he did not simply use the word "love." It did not adequately express for him the "if under attack, respond with positive feeling" quality that he found to be so important in the fight against violence. "Love" typically is used in a setting where there is no conflict, where one is attracted to another, or when one is beneficently reaching out to another out of one's fullness. The term ahimsa, on the other hand, underlines that the setting for the *satyagrahi's* work is one of conflict, not neutrality or noblesse oblige. He wrote:

If I had used the word "love," which non-violence is in essence, you would not have asked this question. But perhaps "love" does not express my meaning fully. The nearest word is "charity." We love our friends and equals. But the reaction that a ruthless dictator sets up in us is either that of awe or pity according respectively as we react to him violently or non-violently. Non-violence knows no fear. If I am truly non-violent, I would pity the dictator and say to myself, "He does not know what a human being should be. One day he will know better when he is confronted by a people who do not stand in awe of him, who will neither submit nor cringe to him, nor bear any grudge against him for whatever he may do."[53]

This connotation of ahimsa, as the positive, surprising response to hate, is why Gandhi found the Sermon on the Mount so compelling and so accurately communicating what he was trying to get across. Later in his life, a questioner commented on how often he referred to the Sermon on the Mount and asked him to comment on the text, "If any man will take away thy coat, let him have thy cloak also." Gandhi responded:

To take what is required may be profitable; to have more given to you is highly likely to be a burden... When you give more to a

robber than he needs, you spring a surprise on him, you give him
a shock although agreeable...Historical instances are on record
to show that such non-violent conduct has produced a wholesome
effect on evil-doers. These acts cannot be done mechanically; they
must come out of conviction and love or pity for the other
man...Suffice it to say that Jesus put in a picturesque and telling
manner the great doctrine of non-violent non-cooperation.[54]

Gandhi did not interpret the Sermon on the Mount as so many
Christians have through the centuries—as a quixotic, unrealistic set of max-
ims. He understood the language for what it was, a pointed, graphic example of how people could creatively deal with violence—not giving in to it,
surprising it with resourceful action that transforms the situation. The
example invited listeners to envision similar situations of oppression in
which they might be involved and to behave in a similar fashion, turning the
tables on the oppressor in a nonviolent manner. Gandhi understood the
Sermon on the Mount to be the most realistic and practical of teachings.

3. Ahimsa as a force pitted against violence

On the other hand, Gandhi often used the word "love" to convey another facet of ahimsa: that it was a way to assume and exert power. Most people recognize that love is powerful—that it influences, energizes, and
changes people. Love can transform situations. It can cause people to act
in ways that transcend self-interest. It can connect people who are at odds,
and it can do all this without using violence, to which it is the clear
antithesis. Gandhi wrote that he was fascinated by the law of love and that
it was the philosopher's stone for him that could provide a remedy for
humanity's ills.

Ahimsa was therefore for Gandhi the power that meets, stands up to,
and quenches violence. It is the only power that can do so. It is the only
way out of the perpetual cycle of retaliation and hate. As he explained:

Non-violence in the form of love is the activest force in the world.
As the Gujurati poet Shamal says, "There is no merit in returning
good for good; most men do this. Merit lies in returning good for
evil..." The seers of old saw that the only way of dealing with the
situation was to neutralize hatred with love.[55]

A *satyagrahi*'s milieu is conflict. A *satyagrahi*'s project is removing the
causes of oppression and suffering. Such a project usually invites violence.
Ahimsa is the inner quality that is the buckler and shield of the *satyagrahi*.
If ahimsa is strong enough within a person, it enables one to prevail even

over the frightening specter of violence. Writing, for example, of the power of the sword of the British government, Gandhi describes the sterilizing, quenching power of ahimsa.

> Bravery of the sword they know. And they have made themselves proof against its use by us. Many of them will welcome violence on our part. They are unconquerable in the art of meeting and suppressing violence. We propose, therefore, to sterilize the power of inflicting violence by our non-violence. Violence dies when it ceases to evoke response from its object.[56]

4. Ahimsa as the normal law of human nature

For Gandhi, ahimsa was an inner quality of the soul, but he also understood it to be a metaphysical reality. Just as truth is the underlying law of the universe, so also Gandhi understood ahimsa to be the underlying law of human nature. If the truth is that all human beings are one, then the normal, natural way of relating to one another is ahimsa.

If ahimsa is the normal law of human nature, then violence is bestial. For Gandhi, the striking fact was that, despite the continuing cascade of violence, the world survived. He believed it survived because, in actuality, ahimsa was stronger than *himsa*. People throughout the world were on a daily basis listening to, supporting, forbearing, and cherishing one another. The force of ahimsa was the true human dynamic. Gandhi recognized that history was written as a record of wars. He maintained that wars were, in fact, the interruptions of the real course of events, the real fabric of history: people giving birth, raising children, building cultures. He saw ahimsa as the force that holds the world together and keeps it from flying apart.

The true badge of humans is their ahimsa to one another. It is what separates them from other animals, which act according to their instincts alone. Gandhi ascribed physical domination to the world of the animals and soul-force to humans, saying:

> One animal subdues another simply by its physical might. Its world is ruled by that law, but not so the human world. The law which is most in harmony with human nature is that of winning over others by the power of love—by soul force.[57]

Gandhi knew that the message of nonviolence went against the conventional wisdom and natural instincts of the animal in humans to return like for like and tit for tat. He attempted to reframe the question by redefining what was "natural." He did so by pointing out what everyone also knew—that ahimsa was all-pervasive. It was as common as a parent showing patience with a fractious child, as "normal" as a teacher anticipating the restlessness of a classroom and changing the subject or the pace of the day, as normal as a friend reconciling with a friend. He extended this kind of normal behavior to the uncommon situation of confronting violence and described nonviolence as "natural," even as he granted that the more virulent the violence the greater the ahimsa required to meet it. He wrote:

> The safest course is to lay down laws on the strength of our usual experience, and our usual experience is that in most cases non-violence is the real antidote to violence, and it is safe to infer from it that the highest violence can be met by the highest non-violence.[58]

5. Ahimsa as the way of the strong and the brave

Gandhi, throughout his thirty-year public life in India, attempted to keep India from turning to violent revolution. He knew that India could not defeat the strongest military power on earth, one that had all the guns and tanks and planes in the world. He knew that that way would be an unending tale of blood and hate, a way that would leave no way out. He also knew, however, the appeal of violence, especially to the young. To many in India, resisting the British with violence was the only manly thing to do. Some of his political critics opposed him precisely because they believed that his non-cooperation movement was negative and his nonviolence emasculating.

He understood those sentiments and recognized the appeal of war. When he managed an ambulance service for England in the First World War, he came to admire the courage and tenacity of the "Tommies" on the battlefield. He understood the calls to courage, sacrifice, and greatness that people responded to in war. He knew that calls to nonviolence could have the same appeal. All through his life he insisted that nonviolence took even more bravery than violence and war.

> One need not assume that heroism is to be acquired only by fighting a war. One can do so even while keeping out of it. War is one powerful means, among many others. But if it is a powerful means, it is also an evil one. We can cultivate manliness in a blameless way.[59]

For the *satyagrahi* who is called to resist oppression and who therefore has to face violence, there is no room for cowardly behavior. Gandhi often said:

> My creed of non-violence is an extremely active force. It has no room for cowardice or even weakness. There is hope for a violent man to some day be non-violent, but there is none for a

coward...The heroism of ahimsa cannot be developed from cowardice. Bravery is essential to himsa and ahimsa. In fact it is even more essential in the latter for ahimsa is nothing if it is not the acme of bravery.[60]

Gandhi took great pride in all those who followed in the way of satyagraha. His contention that ahimsa took great courage was borne out in very visible ways as *satyagrahis*, both men and women, both young and old, again and again withstood lathi (long, steel-shod, bamboo rod) charges and police brutality, and did so nonviolently. He took particular pride in the behavior of the thousands of Khudai Khidmatgars, Muslims in the Northwest Territories, Pathans who followed Abdul Ghaffar Khan in the way of nonviolence. Khan had found the message of nonviolence in the Koran before he had even met Gandhi. In a speech to a group of their leaders in 1938, Gandhi said:

I know it is difficult; it is no joke for a Pathan to take an affront lying down. I have known Pathans from my South African days ...They were a rough and ready lot. Past masters in the art of wielding a lathi...they held life cheap, and would have killed a human being for no more thought than they would a sheep or hen. That such men should have, at the bidding of one man, laid down their arms and accepted non-violence as the superior weapon sounds almost like a fairy tale.[61]

Abdul Ghaffar Khan became one of Gandhi's closest friends and followers. About him Gandhi said:

It was Khan Saheeb who told me that he never felt as strong and brave as when he, out of his own free will, renounced the lathi and the rifle.[62]

For Gandhi, the Khudai Khidmatgars demonstrated real power, the power of ahimsa, not the power of violence.

A *Khudai Khidmatgar* will command the cooperation of all sections of the community, not the sort of obedience that a Mussolini or Hitler can command through his unlimited power of coercion, but the willing and spontaneous obedience which is yielded to love alone.[63]

The highest encomium Gandhi could give to those possessing ahimsa was that they were behaving as Kshatriya. Only members of the Kshatriya caste, one of the four main traditional castes of Hinduism, were called to be warriors. The calling of the *satyagrahi* was not a puny challenge. It meant preparing oneself to lose all, to die for others. A *satyagrahi* had to be ready to lose all, even life. It therefore required great inner preparation. If a soldier trained to learn to kill, one who adopted nonviolence had to learn the art of dying and the spirit of sacrifice. Gandhi wrote:

> [O]ne has to develop the spirit of sacrifice to such a high degree that one would not hesitate to sacrifice one's family, property and even one's life.[64]

For Gandhi, only the brave could practice satyagraha. In the words of Erik Erikson:

> Ahimsa, he realized, had not been invented by meek or defenseless people, even as in Western civilization Puritanism was the way of life not of repressed people, but of essentially lusty ones: ahimsa was preached to man when he was in full vigor of life and able to look his adversaries straight in the face.[65]

Tapasya (self-suffering)

Gandhi never tired of repeating that ahimsa was the only way to truth (i.e., the underlying oneness of atman and Brahman). Only actions that were purely nonviolent established truth between people. Only nonviolent action aiming to overcome oppression and the violence behind oppression could change the world to be more in accord with the underlying truth that ran through the universe. Nonviolence, ahimsa, was the means and truth the end.

The question arose—how could the *satyagrahi*, in a situation of conflict, know that he or she was in the truth? Gandhi's answer was that the *satyagrahi* had to cling to the truth as he or she saw it and press home its claims, but if the opponent disagreed and responded with force, then the *satyagrahi* was the one who accepted the subsequent suffering in the name of finding a broader zone of truth, a higher synthesis, that could bring both parties together. This was the principle of *tapasya* or self-suffering. He wrote:

> Truth will not be suppressed by violence . . . Difficulty however lies in knowing where truth lies. It is easy enough to accuse one's opponent of representing untruth. But this inherent inability to demonstrate the absolute truthfulness of one's position makes tolerance an absolute necessity for the progress of ordered life. Without the freedom to everyone to express his opinion unfet-

tered by interference from those who hold the contrary, ordered life becomes an impossibility.[66]

Gandhi insisted that *satyagrahi* should remain free of anger or hate against their opponents. The resistance was against the injustice, not against those committing the injustice.

> Man and his deed are two distinct things. Whereas a good deed should call forth approbation, the doer of the deed, whether good or wicked, always deserves respect or pity as the case may be. "Hate the sin and not the sinner" is a precept which, though easy enough to understand, is rarely practiced and that is why the poison of hatred spreads in the world.
>
> This ahimsa is the basis for the search for truth... It is quite proper to resist and attack a system, but to resist and attack its author is tantamount to resisting and attacking oneself. For we are all tarred with the same brush, and are children of the one and the same Creator.[67]

The resistance was, for example, against the oppressive regime the British imposed on India, not against the British people. As Gandhi explained:

> Your quarrel is not with the British people, but with the Imperialistic spirit of exploitation of the weak races of the earth.[68]

Gandhi knew, from experience, the practical value of this principle. After having fought a pitched battle with the government of South Africa over the course of twelve years, when he and his colleagues had finally convinced the government to discontinue its oppressive laws, they were at peace with one another. No bitterness or hatred remained, because of the way the fight had been waged—with respect and nonviolence.

> In South Africa whatever the Indians had won as a result of satyagraha did not leave any ill-feeling behind it. For eight long years General Smuts fought uncompromisingly against the claims of the Indian community. But in the end he recognized the justice of the claims and became my lifelong friend.[69]

The *tapasya* component of satyagraha means that when push comes to shove in a dispute, rather than retaliate with force, the *satyagrahi* takes it, endures the suffering—not out of passivity, but knowing first, that retaliation never goes anywhere, and second, that the opponent's heart can be reached by the witness of voluntary suffering endured for the truth. Gandhi noted that,

> [f]ar from seeking revenge, a votary of non-violence would pray to God that he might bring about a change of heart of his opponent, and if that does not happen he would be prepared to bear any injury that his opponent might inflict upon him, not in a spirit of cowardice or helplessness, but bravely with a smile on his face. I believe implicitly in the ancient saying that "non-violence real and complete will melt the stoniest hearts."[70]

The aim of satyagraha is to reach the heart of the opponent so that together they can reach a higher synthesis of truth and a resolution of the conflict. Gandhi wrote:

> Let my friend understand the implications of non-violence. It is a process of conversion... But there is no such thing as compulsion in the scheme of non-violence. Reliance has to be placed upon the ability to reach the intellect and the heart—the latter rather than the former... Its secret lies in bearing anything that may be inflicted on us... We want to win, not by striking terror in the ruler but by awakening their sense of justice.[71]

The *satyagrahi* wears the opponent down. Gandhi never forgot how successful the mass satyagraha movement using these principles had been in South Africa. He had faith that they would work everywhere, but he also had experience of their having worked many times. He enjoyed quoting General Smuts in this regard.

> "I on my part had inflicted severe hardships on Gandhi's men but they had borne them silently. How long could I inflict such severities on such people?"[72]

Self-suffering is the substitute for inflicting violence on others. Gandhi certainly did not enjoy seeing his people suffer, but he knew it was a way superior to that of violence. As he explained:

> Suffering injury in one's own person, is on the contrary, of the essence of non-violence and is the chosen substitute for violence to others. It is not because I value life low that I can countenance with joy thousands voluntarily losing their lives for satyagraha, but because I know that it results in the long run in the least loss of life

and what is more, it ennobles those who lose their lives and morally enriches the world for their sacrifice.[73]

As the opponent's heart is reached there opens the possibility of finding a solution to the conflict. Partial truth can be supplied with more partial truth and harmonious alternatives can be envisioned. The conflict
waged by a *satyagrahi* is on two levels, that of truth and that of power.
According to Mark Juergensmeyer:

> Gandhian fighting always has a deeper level, a struggle for Truth,
> even in the midst of a struggle for power on behalf of a truthful
> cause. If this is the case, satyagraha should be thought of not only
> as a political strategy but as an epistemological concept. It is a
> way of knowing, by pitting opposing perceptions of it together
> …a process for discovering an emerging truth. The Sanskrit
> term for truth, satya, is based on a verb, so it is appropriate to
> think of it in fluid terms; not something one must determine
> before engaged in the fight, but something that emerges in the
> process of fighting.[74]

Gandhi believed that no one was beyond the pale and that every
human being, even the hardened of heart, could be reached through self-
suffering. He was under no illusions about people. He was true, however,
to his belief in the fundamental unity of humankind. He accepted the challenge that is put even now to such a claim for the power of self-suffering
and nonviolence, namely, "You mean, even Hitler?" Yes, he meant even
Hitler, Mussolini, Stalin, et al. He wrote:

> It is based on the assumption that it is possible to convert Fascists
> and Nazis. They belong to the same species as the so-called
> democracies, or better still, war-resisters themselves. They show
> in their family circles the same tenderness, affection, consideration
> and generosity that war-resisters are likely to show even outside
> such circles. The difference is only of degree.[75]

He admitted that the Fascists and Nazis would, given their beliefs,
ingrained habits, and practices, be much harder to reach. It would take an
effort times three:

> It is therefore a matter of rule of three to find out the exact
> amount of non-violence required to melt the harder hearts of the
> Fascists and Nazis.[76]

In sum, all four of these components work together to form satyagraha: resisting oppression assertively (*agraha*) through nonviolent, loving action (ahimsa) to find the living truth in the situation (*satya*), a truth that is discovered and authenticated through self-suffering (*tapasya*), a truth that transforms the situation and brings opponents together.

For Gandhi, one other set of actions was integral to the full practice of satyagraha, that of the constructive program.

A Constructive Program

For Gandhi, the *satyagrahi*'s call was to befriend through nonviolent action those suffering under the weight of violent oppression, but it was also, more positively, to build a nonviolent society. Along with the non-cooperation and civil disobedience movements designed to transform the relationship with the British from one of dominance to one of mutual regard and India's freedom, Gandhi pursued at the same time the building of alternative social, economic, and political structures that would enable India to live without dependence on or rancor for the British once they finally quit India. This constructive program had two components: an aggressive movement to rid India of its twin evils of untouchability and communal violence between Muslims and Hindus, and, second, a push to build alternative social, political, and economic structures to relieve the plight of the poor. The main initiatives for building these structures that would insert nonviolence into the social fabric were the *khadi* movement (reintroducing into the country the production of homespun cloth, a capability that had been lost when the British had undercut the industry; making *khadi* had been the poor village farmers' way to augment income during the non-growing season) and educational and village uplift.

Gandhi, over the years from 1919 to 1947, led only three major mass non-cooperation movements in India, one a decade—much to the chagrin of many of his followers. The first major campaign of 1920–22, as we have seen, Gandhi discontinued when it was marred by violence against the British. The second, the Salt March campaign (1930–33), galvanized the country and caught the attention and the imagination of the world. The final "Quit India" campaign (1942–44) eventually led to the transition in political power. In contrast, Gandhi spent all of the intervening years, when he wasn't in jail, on the constructive program: building the *khadi* movement, fighting untouchability and communal violence, advocating for alternative educational and conflict resolution structures, and working on experiments in village uplift.

These initiatives were just as much experiments in finding the truth through nonviolence and self-suffering as were the non-cooperation and civil disobedience campaigns. In the words of John Chattanatt:

The nonviolent, active search for truth not only permits but positively requires a great variety of positive actions aimed at preventing as well as eliminating evil.[77]

Looking back, the effectiveness of the nonviolent non-cooperation campaigns is clear. They delegitimated the rule of the British. The British response of jailings and violence eventually disenchanted even the moderate middle class who shared in the spoils of the Raj. People began to recognize how the empire had disempowered the populace, induced many to define themselves in imitation of their masters, and drained the wealth of the country. As B. R. Nanda notes:

Gandhi's critics did not appreciate the long delays between them [the campaigns]. Gandhi didn't mind because he knew the object of the campaigns was not to crush the opponent but "to set in motion forces that could lead to his ultimate conversion..." the repression of the non-violent struggles had the effect of eroding the moral authority of the British authorities and their Indian collaborators... [H]is nonviolent struggle alienated from the imperial regime moderate men and women in India.[78]

Moreover, the successive campaigns lifted the spell of fear that enveloped the Indian masses. Nehru always attributed the casting off of fear to Gandhi, saying that when Gandhi said, "Be not afraid," it changed everything. At the same time, the British people began to see more clearly the nature of their own violence. Pressured by both world opinion and the mirror held up to them by India's nonviolence, many began to see themselves as oppressors. Many more began to think that keeping India in the Empire was more trouble than it was worth. B. R. Nanda continues:

The successive campaigns... also wore out, however slowly, British rigidity into skepticism and skepticism into fatigue.[79]

On the other hand, the constructive program, the apparently apolitical work of Gandhi, brought him close to the masses. They in turn gave weight and power to the political movement that he headed. The effectiveness of the constructive program is a much more difficult thing to assess. In 1927, he published in *Young India* a brief stocktaking of progress—both of the nonviolence campaigns and of the constructive program. Of the non-cooperation movement Gandhi wrote:

The mass awakening that took place in 1920 all of a sudden was perhaps the greatest demonstration of the efficacy of nonviolence.

The Government has lost prestige never to be regained. Titles, law-courts, educational institutions no longer inspire the awe they did in 1920. Some of the best lawyers in the country have given up law forever as a profession and are happy for having accepted comparative poverty as their lot. The few national schools and colleges that remain are giving account of themselves... It is possible to multiply illustrations of this character and prove that wherever there is real national life, a bond between the classes and the masses in India, non-cooperation is the cause of it.[80]

Of the constructive program he wrote:

Take again the three constructive items of the programme. Khadi is a growing factor in national regeneration and is serving over 1,500 villages through an army of nearly two thousand workers and is giving tangible productive relief to over fifty thousand spinners and at least ten thousand weavers, printers, dyers, dhobis and other artisans. Untouchability is a waning thing just struggling for existence. Hindu-Muslim unity of 1920–21 showed its vast possibilities... Real swaraj will have to be not a donation rained on us from London, but a prize earned by hard and health-giving non-cooperation with organized forces of evil.[81]

By the end of his life, this appraisal, at least on the score of communal violence, turned much more dire. On the other hand, many followers, such as Vinoba Bhave, carried on the specific work of the constructive program after Gandhi's death. It is beyond the scope of this book to evaluate the current vitality of the movement in India. Many feel that it is not very alive—at least in the Gandhian form—although the government of India struggles to solve the very problems that concerned Gandhi. As India's most recent national election demonstrated, the poverty of the masses remains at the center of India's political agenda.

One thing that is certain is that India does not suffer from the disease of undying hatred of the British. Gandhi's spirit of satyagraha seemed to have inoculated the populace against self-hate, reprisals, and wasteful living in the past. As we shall see in a later section, it seems that those national liberation campaigns, for example in Poland and South Africa, that embraced the Gandhian spirit of satyagraha and included a constructive program emphasizing the development of alternative social and political structures ended up with a smoother transition to independence and more harmonious subsequent relations between the formerly oppressed and their oppressors than those that did not.

In summary, satyagraha is both a theological vision and a way of life, or better a way of life that flows from being caught up by a theological vision. As a way of life, satyagraha is first a life of dedicated nonviolent direct action in service of the oppressed and the poor that aims to change the relationships of power through a mutual discovery of truth—if need be through self-suffering. It also includes a commitment to prevent or remove, through constructive action, the causes of human suffering. Second, it is a way of life rooted in a theological vision. That vision sees the fundamental unity of humankind in God, sees the way of force and violence as dead ends, believes that love is the natural human condition and that with enough imaginative, tenacious soul force, conflicts can be resolved.

Those who embrace satyagraha understand that those who do not share this vision and who are not transformed by it will not think that the way of life is "realistic." Those who are embraced by the vision and who live it, find that, in the give and take of real life, it is surprisingly realistic.

A Reflection on the Mechanics of How Satyagraha Works

The realism of satyagraha stems from the fact that it is effective. Gandhi knew that what he crafted and shaped over his lifetime, this "new" way of addressing human problems and violence, which was "as old as the hills" but was new as it was applied to masses of people acting in concert, could be used by young and old, rich and poor. It could be used in all situations of conflict, from those within families, to conflicts between ethnic groups, to movements of liberation, and even, as we shall see, as an alternative to war, a way to defend a country from attack. It is appropriate to pause at this point and comment on the underlying dynamics that make satyagraha so effective when it is practiced in its pure form.

The effectiveness of satyagraha lies in its understanding of human psychology, its method of conflict resolution and in its use of cascading coercion. First, satyagraha's effectiveness lies in its understanding of human psychology. In a helpful article entitled "Satyagraha as a Mirror," Richard Gregg quotes the eminent psychiatrist Carl Rogers to the effect that people never change their habits of thinking, acting, or feeling unless something happens that changes their picture of themselves. Gregg takes that insight and applies it to the practice of satyagraha.

> The suffering of the satyagraha is as it were, a mirror held up to the violent party, in which the violent ones come gradually to see themselves as violating human unity and its implication. They see themselves as others see them.[82]

The face of the one suffering as a result of the violent party's actions is the mirror held up to the violent one. Gregg continues:

> The voluntary suffering of the satyagraha is so unusual, so dramatic, so surprising, so wonder-provoking. Wonder naturally evokes curiosity and attention...They sense the disapproval of the onlookers and wanting social approval, they begin to search for ways to save face.[83]

The face of public opinion is the second mirror held up to the opponent in a satyagraha campaign. Gandhi made masterful use of public opinion for this very reason. If everyone—the public, other nations, one's closest associates—begins to think of the opponent in a certain negative way and if that image is consistently mirrored back to the opponent, it begins to be very hard to shake. Convictions begin to waver; questions begin to enter into the self-consciousness. The stronger and the clearer the picture, the harder it is to resist. Our knowledge and our consciousness are, at root, social constructs. A negative identity sits hard. One wants to shake it off, to change it. In the words of Rita Dadhich:

> In order to raise the consciousness of the exploited through recourse to satyagraha, Gandhi relied greatly on creative public opinion against the opponent's actual deeds...a process of conflict resolution by mutual understanding and by educating public opinion through reason, discussion and self-suffering...even the tallest will not dare to practice it or openly lend support to it.[84]

A third mirror held up to the opponent is the ongoing positive regard that the *satyagrahi* has towards the opponent. That regard conveys a positive image. The opponent consistently treated with trust and love begins to experience an identity worthy of that trust and positive regard. This in turn provides the basis for changing habits, attitudes, and behaviors and opens the opponent to the search for alternative solutions to conflicts. Weyburn Groff, reflecting Gandhi's own words, wrote:

> Ahimsa involves trust in the goodness of the opponent, and love toward those who hate you, and is the means to resolve the conflict. It is the greatest force because it appeals to the heart of the opponent, not merely to the intellect.[85]

The three mirrors—the face of the suffering one, the face of public opinion, and the identity that the *satyagrahi* sees in the opponent—offer the opponent a different picture of himself or herself without which, as Carl Rogers pointed out, no one ever really changes. Gregg concludes:

> All this suggests that satyagraha operates at a deeper level than nationality, military power, book education or socioeconomic theory. It is a process working in the very elemental nature of humankind as a biological species.[86]

Second, satyagraha's power stems from the fact that it is a particularly effective form of conflict resolution. It aims neither at compromise nor at mediation. Moreover, it does not result in a forced victory of one party over another. The aspects of satyagraha that we have reviewed in this chapter make, as some thinkers point out, for superior conflict resolution. The idea of *anekantavanda*, the many-sidedness of truth, means that any one party in a dispute has to remain open to the possibility that another party will also have a grasp of partial truth. The search for a resolution to the conflict will therefore involve a search for a solution that incorporates various partial glimpses of truth into a more adequate whole.

The book *Gandhi's Way: A Handbook of Conflict Resolution*, by Mark Juergensmeyer, begins:

> The basic idea of Gandhi's approach to fighting is to redirect the focus of a fight from persons to principles... Every fight, to Gandhi, was on some level a fight between differing angles of vision illuminating the same truth.[87]

In compromise solutions, both parties lose a little. In mediated conflicts, one of the parties is usually adjudicated as more right than the other. In forced victories, due to threats of one kind or another, one party goes up, the other goes down. In the Gandhian approach, the emphasis is on imagining together alternative solutions that will recognize and satisfy both parties' visions of fairness.

The use of nonviolent action in satyagraha is what prevents the relative nature of truth from turning into relativism. Satyagraha provides a means for finding the truth—nonviolent action. It also provides a criterion for determining the truth—and that criterion is whether the course of action makes human living more possible and richer. In the words of Joan Bondurant:

> Through the operation of non-violent action the truth as judged by the fulfillment of human needs will emerge in the form of a mutually satisfactory and agreed upon solution.[88]

The third reason why satyagraha works so well—at least in mass campaigns—is the way it uses various types of nonviolent coercion, layered on in increasing levels of intensity. Bondurant analyzes a number of campaigns either led by or advised by Gandhi during his years in India and concludes that at least the ones aimed at opposing established political order typically proceeded in the following fashion.

First comes a period of negotiation in which every effort is made to come to agreement through normal channels using creative disputations and presentations that address as clearly as possible the underlying facts and the principles on which the aggrieved parties are taking their stand. Every effort is made to state the opponent's case fairly and to understand the opponent's point of view. If there is no resolution, the aggrieved parties prepare for direct action. In this second stage, those who will participate in direct action take time to reexamine their motives, decide on procedures, restate their minimum demands, and prepare themselves for possible violence to themselves.

They then move to the third step of agitation, attempting to activate public opinion on their behalf. This stage uses symbols, slogans, parades, white papers, and so forth—an array of means to attract attention and a sympathetic hearing.

Before moving on to more vigorous actions, the fourth step is to issue an ultimatum making clear what will follow, inviting agreement, and offering face-saving, alternative resolutions to the problem.

The fifth step is economic boycott or other forms of strike. The sixth step is non-cooperation. Various types of non-cooperation, such as nonpayment of taxes, boycotts of schools, and ostracism are used, depending on the situation. The seventh step is civil disobedience. The eighth step is usurping the functions of government. The final step is establishing parallel government.

All this is done with a positive regard for the opponent and a willingness to suffer—which is, of course, still another form of coercion. This application of increasing intensities of coercion is analogous to the way war is traditionally described, namely, turning up the suffering of the enemy and making them suffer so much that they eventually concede defeat. It is, on the other hand, completely different from war, in that the coercion is nonviolent. As Richard Gregg notes:

> The object of nonviolent resistance is partly analogous to war—namely to demoralize the opponent, to break his will, to destroy his confidence, enthusiasm and hope. In another respect, it is dissimilar, for nonviolent resistance demoralizes the opponent only to re-establish in him a new morale that is finer because it is based on sounder values. Nonviolent resistance does not break the opponent's will but alters it.[89]

THE IMPORT, SIGNIFICANCE, AND CONSEQUENCES OF SATYAGRAHA

In this section we will make three points to help bring out the full significance and value of Gandhi's concept of satyagraha. The first point is that satyagraha is more than pacifism. The second is that Gandhi offers what William James called for, namely, a "moral equivalent to war." The third is that the dynamic of satyagraha has been "successfully" played out again and again in multiple situations of intense conflict, not just in India during Gandhi's time, but all over the world over the last sixty years.

Satyagraha Is More Than Pacifism

People all too facilely equate satyagraha with pacifism. Just as they dismiss pacifism as unrealistic in a world of power politics, so also do they then dismiss satyagraha out of hand. Gandhi in fact engaged in spirited debate with pacifists for many years. During the 1930s many English pacifists severely condemned Gandhi.

Satyagraha is distinguished from pacifism in three ways. First, if pacifism is a refusal to participate in war, satyagraha's spirit of non-cooperation runs deeper. It requires non-cooperation with the whole system that supports a state built on militaristic assumptions and principles. As Gandhi wrote:

> To refuse to render military service when a particular individual's time comes is to do the thing after all the time for combating the evil is practically gone. The disease is deeper...He or she, therefore, who supports a State so organized is, whether directly or indirectly, participating in the sin...Refusal of military service is much more superficial than non-cooperation with a whole system which supports the State...A state that rests on military violence is a bad state.[90]

Second, satyagraha goes well beyond refusing to serve in a war to fighting against and overcoming the causes underlying war. Gandhi had no use for the passive approach of refraining from participating in war because he was so firmly committed to action. For him, the *Gita*, as well as the Sermon on the Mount, enjoined acting against evil and violence. According to Gene Sharp:

> It is a far cry from pacifism to Gandhi's idea of nonviolence. While pacifism hopes to get rid of war chiefly by refusing to fight and by carrying propaganda against war, Gandhi goes much deeper and

sees that war cannot be avoided, so long as the seeds of it remain in man's breast and grow in his social, political and economic life. Gandhiji's cure is therefore very radical and far reaching. It demands nothing less than rooting out violence from oneself and from one's environment.[91]

Gandhi rejected the distinction between just and unjust wars—even though he could side with those whose cause was just on ideological grounds—because he unequivocally rejected the violent means employed by the so-called just war. He believed passionately that nonviolent means were always superior to violent means. Consistent with that stance, he lobbied constantly for an India that would not turn into a military power and he advocated that it choose a path of nonviolent resistance even for its self-defense as a state. Satyagraha was his preferred method for resolving even conflicts between states.

In contrast to the limited antiwar posture of the pacifists, Gandhi addressed the root of the problem: the inhuman race to exploit the weaker peoples of the world. He wrote, "All activity for stopping war must prove fruitless so long as the causes of war are not understood and radically dealt with."[92] He believed that if the great powers disarmed themselves they would not only escape the ravages of war but would earn the eternal gratitude of posterity. They would have to, at the same time, as Rashmi-Sudha Puri wrote, "give up their imperialistic designs and exploitation of the weak and hapless, while revising their own way of life."[93]

Third, Gandhi had an understanding of violence that went well beyond where most pacifists stood. His understanding evolved over the years through his various experiments with truth. Some are surprised, for example, that he not only enthusiastically participated on the side of the British in the Boer War, the Zulu rebellion, and World War One, as the leader of corps of medics, but also, when back in India, actively recruited Indians to serve as soldiers in the First World War. His explanations for his behavior were straightforward and pragmatic. He believed then in the ideals of the British Empire, thought he benefited from it, and therefore thought he owed something in return. Moreover, pragmatically he thought such a service to be training for Indians in bravery and proof both to themselves and to the British that they deserved freedom. Although he was always personally opposed to carrying a gun and to violence, it was only with the coming of the Second World War that he began to unequivocally condemn the violence of war. His attitudes evolved.

Many are also surprised by the way he accepted the role of violence in many situations—in defense of the defenseless for example, or the fending off of a robber, or even in the ending of a life of unending pain.

He consistently maintained that it was better to be violent than to be a coward, while always maintaining the superiority of nonviolence. He saw violence and nonviolence as constituting a continuum, not as absolute opposites. At points of the continuum, violence and nonviolence inter-twine. G. Ramachandran wrote:

> It has become more or less a dogma, among students of Gandhian thought, to assume that violence and nonviolence are opposites which cancel each other out...Life is not a clear-cut progression from the infra-red of brute violence to the ultra-violet of ethereal nonviolence.[94]

Gandhi recognized that violence and nonviolence intertwine. Humans have to make their judgments and take their stances. Gandhi maintained both that nonviolence could always prevail but also that it sometimes did not prevail—if, for example, because of inaction, the violence had been allowed to become too strong to defeat, or if one's nonviolence was not strong or pure enough to stand up to and quench the violence. His understanding of violence and humanity's responsibility for it went far beyond simply refraining from active service in a war.

Satyagraha Offers the "Moral Equivalent of War"

Gandhi understood more than just the horror of war; he also understood the enduring appeal of war. He understood that humans found in war, when conducted on behalf of those values they held dear, such as family, homeland, or hard-won freedoms, a spirit of sacrifice and community; their individual lives became more important and even noble as they fought and risked death. We have already seen the emphasis Gandhi placed on bravery and fearlessness and how he compared *satyagrahis* to the finest of the Kshatriya or warrior caste. Gradually, as the world began to move toward the Second World War, he applied the doctrine of satyagraha to the problem of a country being invaded by an enemy and to the situation of a people subject to elimination by a dictatorship. He began to see that satyagraha was not just the way for a subject people to gain their freedom; it was also an alternative to war. He was, in effect, responding to the famous challenge laid out by William James in 1911:

> Militarism is the great preserver of our ideals of hardihood, and human life with no use for hardihood would be contemptible ...We must make new energies and hardihoods continue the

manliness to which the military mind so faithfully clings. Martial virtues must be the enduring cement; intrepidity, contempt of softness, surrender of private interest, obedience to command, must still remain the rock upon which states are built.[95]

In recent years, other writers have reflected on the enduring appeal of war and the challenge of replacing it in the human psyche with something just as invigorating, soul-stirring, and ennobling.[96] Stanley Hauerwas, for example, makes this challenge part of his critique of the Methodist and Catholic bishops' statements on war and peace.[97]

As early as 1931, when Gandhi was asked how a disarmed neutral country could allow other nations to be destroyed, he first answered that he would refuse to offer supplies to the invading army attempting to pass through his country. He then suggested that a nonviolent army confront the invading army:

> Reenacting Thermopylae . . . you would have presented a living wall of men, women and children and invited them to walk over your corpses. You may say that such a thing is beyond human experience and endurance. Then I can tell you that it was not beyond human experience last year. We showed that it is quite possible. Women stood lathi charges without showing the slightest cowardice. In Peshawar thousands stood a hail of bullets without resorting to any violence whatsoever. Imagine such men and women standing in front of an army wanting safe passage. It would be brutal enough, you would say, to walk over them, but you would still have done your duty and allowed yourself to be annihilated. An army that dares to pass over corpses would not be able to repeat that experiment. You may, if you would, refuse to believe in such courage on the part of the masses of men and women, but then you would have to admit that non-violence is made of sterner stuff. It was never conceived as a weapon of the weak, but of the stoutest hearts.[98]

By 1938, when asked about Mussolini's invasion of Abyssinia, Gandhi answered in a similar vein that Abyssinia should take up a nonviolent stance and pledge complete non-cooperation because then Mussolini would have no interest in Abyssinia:

> Thus if they had simply said: "You are welcome to reduce us to dust or ashes but you will not find one Abyssinian ready to coop-erate with you," what would Mussolini have done? He did not want a desert. He wanted submission and not defiance.[99]

Gandhi consistently affirmed the possibilities of satyagraha and its superiority to the cycle of violence, even in the extreme situations, such as Hitler's persecution of the Jews. In 1938, he wrote, "If there ever could be a justifiable war in the name of and for humanity, a war against Germany, to prevent the wanton persecution of a whole race, would be completely justified."[100] Even recognizing how horrendous and how unjust Hitler's actions were, he still advocated satyagraha as, in the long run, a superior alternative to war, and less destructive of life. He refused to accept that any individual was beyond the reach of soul force, if delivered by masses of people. The combination of non-cooperation and the willingness to bravely suffer even death, if embraced by a mass of people, he believed had unlimited potential. In 1938, he wrote:

> But, says a comforter, "Hitler knows no pity. Your spiritual effort will avail nothing before him."
>
> My answer is, "You may be right. History has no record of a nation having adopted non-violent resistance. If Hitler is not affected by my suffering; it does not matter. For I shall have lost nothing worth preserving. My honor is the only thing worth preserving. That is independent of Hitler's pity. But as a believer in non-violence, I may not limit its possibilities. Hitherto he and his likes have built upon their invariable experience that men yield to force. Unarmed men, women and children offering non-violent resistance will be a novel experience for them. Who can dare say that it is not in their nature to respond to the higher and finer forces? They have the same soul that I have."[101]

Gandhi gave the same advice to the Chinese against the Japanese, the Czechs against the Germans, and to his own countrymen under the threat of invasion from Japan. This application of satyagraha as a policy of national defense crystallized in his mind into the idea of a "peace brigade," a committed mass of people, thoroughly trained in the principles of non-violence, who would be willing to put their lives on the line in the situation of an invasion of their country. A summary of his remarks appeared in *The Hindu* on September 24, 1938:

> When asked how non-violence could check foreign aggression, Mahatma Gandhi is reported to have replied that if India had one crore of non-violent volunteers, he was confident that no nation could conquer India. If they failed in their attempt to prevent aggression, then the fault was theirs, not in the philosophy of non-violence but in their methods of practicing it. Mahatma Gandhi

was convinced that non-violence, if properly applied, could not only solve India's problems but also the world's.[102]

In summary, Gandhi offered the world a "moral equivalent to war." It certainly answered William James's stipulation that an alternative to war would be found that preserved "hardihood." Nothing could be more brave than a mass of people confronting an army outfitted with guns and tanks, a mass of people baring their breasts to bullets—as brave as any soldiers risking their lives in order to kill the "enemy." Like war, satyagraha demands public spirit, organization, endurance, self-sacrifice, and discipline for its successful operation.

More important, nonviolent civil defense holds out the opportunity of ending international conflicts, conflicts between nations, with much less destruction than traditional wars. Gene Sharp has estimated that if India had used a full-scale war with traditional guerilla approaches, as had been done in Algeria, the death toll would have been "3 to 3.5 million versus the actual death toll from the nonviolent struggle of 8,000."[103]

Finally, as Gandhi reflected on the history of wars and violence, he posed the very practical question of effectiveness. For him, war never led to peace because it used means that were antithetical to peace. War always left behind the latent seeds of hate and retribution. Killing, especially in conflicts over ideology, led to mutual demonization.

Gandhi saw in satyagraha an alternative to war that would not continue or escalate the cycle of hate and retribution but would instead quench it. A people responding to violence with nonviolence would end the cycle just as surely in conflicts between states as it did in the conflict of a people trying to throw off an oppressive rule.

Sixty Years of Experiments in Satyagraha

Gandhi understood that satyagraha, applying the principles of nonviolence and self-suffering to the struggle of masses against the forces of oppression and violence, including war, was a new discovery that was just beginning to be understood and would take continuing experiments to validate and refine. Gandhi retired from the Congress because he wanted to more fully understand and experiment with nonviolence. He wrote in 1935:

I have retired from the Congress because, among other reasons, I want to impose silence upon myself...to explore the yet hidden possibilities of non-violence...to understand the ultimate truth of things which, at present, I seem to see only dimly. And after a laborious search I have come to the conclusion that if I am to see it in any fullness I can only do so by non-violence in thought, word and deed.[104]

If Gandhi practiced this alternative way of dealing with hate and violence, he did not exhaust its possibilities or apply it in all possible settings. That was the legacy he left to those who came after him. As Naryan Desai wrote, "We need a great scientist to discover a new force of nature but do not need such geniuses to implement the truth discovered . . . we do not need Edison every time we turn on a light switch."[105]

Since Gandhi's death, many people have put into practice the principles of satyagraha in many different contexts. Recently a number of books have appeared that describe some of the many nonviolent resistance campaigns that have taken place over the last sixty years.[106]

Walter Wink says that despite these examples of the effectiveness of nonviolence, most people still cling to what he calls the "myth of redemptive violence." Then, he says, came 1989–90.

In 1989 alone, thirteen nations comprising 1.7 billion people—over thirty-two percent of humanity—experienced nonviolent revolutions. They succeeded beyond anyone's wildest expectations in every case but China. And they were completely peaceful (on the part of the protesters) in every case but Romania and parts of the southern U.S.S.R. If we add all the countries touched by major nonviolent actions in this century, the figure reaches almost 3 billion—a staggering sixty-four percent of humanity.[107]

Of all these nonviolent revolutions, perhaps the four that most clearly emulated the principles and practices of Gandhi have been the civil rights movement in the United States under the leadership of Dr. Martin Luther King, the revolution in South Africa under the leadership of Nelson Mandela and Desmond Tutu, the overthrow of Ferdinand Marcos in the Philippines, and the Solidarity revolution in Poland.

Martin Luther King, before being exposed to the life and teachings of Gandhi, had thought that the ethic of the Sermon on the Mount could be only a personal ethic, applying, at best, to relationships between individuals. He discovered that it was, instead, an ethic that could be practiced by groups of people and applied to the struggles between groups of people. King wrote:

Gandhi was probably the first person in history to lift the love ethic of Jesus above mere interaction between individuals to a powerful and effective force on a large scale. Love for Gandhi was a potent instrument for social and collective transformation. It was in this Gandhian emphasis on love and nonviolence that I discovered the method of social reform... Gandhi resisted evil with as much vigor and power as the violent resister, but he resisted with love instead of hate.[108]

In South Africa, apartheid seemed invulnerable. Violent resistance had been tried and easily crushed during the 1970s. When leaders turned to nonviolent resistance, and began to build alternative structures of their own, much as Gandhi had counseled in India, they began to move forward. People began to act as if they were free and to break the cycle of cooperation. As Peter Ackerman notes:

Stay-aways, strikes, and boycotts put pressure on white business owners and employers, and they undermined white attachment to the status quo. Rent boycotts defunded local councils, and street committees usurped their functions. Faced with this variegated challenge, the regime reacted with open force. Repression subdued the civics committees, but it also cost the regime any chance of avoiding economic punishment by the international community.[109]

Desmond Tutu commented:

I suppose that human beings looking at it would say that arms are the most dangerous things that a dictator, a tyrant needs to fear. But in fact, no—it is when people decide they want to be free. Once they have made up their minds to that, there is nothing that will stop them.[110]

In South Africa, as in India, the populace, as a result of the principles and practice of disciplined nonviolence in the Gandhian mode, has carried on its "truth and reconciliation" efforts surprisingly free of the spirit of vengeance and hatred for former oppressors.

In 1986, Cardinal Jaime Sin, the Catholic archbishop of Manila, invited three long-time students of Gandhian nonviolence—Richard Deats and Hilda and Jean Goss-Mayr—to the Philippines to train people in nonviolence. They trained thousands who in turn trained many others. When the decisive election was held, half a million poll watchers were ready for action. When Marcos called on the army to kill Defense Minister Juan Ponce Enrile and General Fidel Ramos for fomenting a revolt, one million people responded to Cardinal Sin's call to nonviolently defend them and their followers. As Michael Duffey described the scene:

The churches of Manila organized a human blockade of thousands of lay people, nuns and seminarians on the causeway down which Marcos's marines and their tanks finally came. The tanks slowed to a standstill in front of the sea of Filipinos celebrating the hour of national liberation; their drivers refused radio commands to proceed to the rebel encampment... almost all of Marcos's military forces defected. On February 25, he requested safe passage for his family out of the Philippines.[111]

In 1989, workers in Poland, after unsuccessfully trying violent resistance in the 1970s, conducted an eight-year-long nonviolent struggle against the regime. As a result, Poland became the first non-communist country in Eastern Europe since Stalin. Solidarity not only gathered fifty million workers into freely elected trade unions, it also created, in alliance with the Catholic Church and other nongovernmental organizations, à la Gandhi's constructive program, an alternative set of social, political, intellectual, and cultural institutions parallel to those dominated by the communist party. As Gene Sharp wrote, "The main thrust of the underground Solidarity movement was... the construction of an independent society, 'which consisted of removing as large a public domain as possible from the government's control.'"[112] As a result, as in South Africa, the new government, under Solidarity, was able to assume control without the turmoil that comes with a violent overthrow of a government. The institutional infrastructure had already been put in place.

In the next chapter I will present four Christian theologians who have fully embraced nonviolence, in the spirit of satyagraha, as central to Christian discipleship.

CHAPTER THREE

Selected Christian Theologians
Who Have Embraced Nonviolence

In this chapter I will review four Christian theologians who, in various ways, have been significantly influenced by Gandhi and his teaching on satyagraha. Not only was Gandhi heavily influenced by Jesus and the example of the cross, he in turn has heavily influenced Christian theologians to discover for themselves the centrality of nonviolence in the life and death of Jesus and its centrality for Christian discipleship.

The four that I have selected are C. F. Andrews, John Howard Yoder, Bernard Häring, and Walter Wink. These four are not the only Christian theologians who have embraced nonviolence or been influenced by Gandhi. I could have reviewed, for example, the thoughts of Dietrich Bonhoeffer, Bernard Lonergan, James Douglass, Martin Luther King, Rene Girard, Raymund Schwager, Stanley Hauerwas, or Thomas Merton, among others, but these four are sufficiently varied and their stances sufficiently clear and compelling to serve as representative of the others.

I have chosen the four for different reasons. C. F. Andrews was selected first because no other Christian was personally closer to Gandhi than Andrews. He witnessed and collaborated with Gandhi in the struggle for freedom, and his immersion in Gandhi's spirit of satyagraha compelled him to rethink his Christianity in terms of nonviolence. John Howard Yoder was selected because his book, *The Politics of Jesus*, has opened the eyes of many Christian thinkers to the centrality of nonviolence for Christian discipleship. Bernard Häring was selected, first, because he is widely acknowledged as the leading Catholic moral theologian of the twentieth century and, second, because his work is a clear challenge to the church as a whole to clearly proclaim the message of nonviolence. Finally, Walter Wink, the only one of the four who is still living and writing, was selected because of his work on the "third way" of Jesus, demonstrating that Jesus taught neither passivity nor violent revolution, neither flight nor fight, but a way of life very similar to what we recognize in Gandhi's satyagraha.

As I review each of these thinkers in turn, I will attempt to indicate what contribution their thinking, under Gandhi's influence, may make toward a contemporary theory of Christian salvation.

C. F. ANDREWS: A CHRISTIAN *SATYAGRAHI*

The first representative theologian I will consider is C. F. (Charles Freer) Andrews.

C. F. Andrews had the opportunity to observe and reflect upon satyagraha firsthand. He was one of Gandhi's closest friends, a partner in praxis and theory. Their letters to one another reveal many disputations over how to apply ahimsa. He was the only English Christian in the inner circle of India's fight for independence and he struggled "shoulder to shoulder with Gandhi in the struggle for India's political emancipation."[1] Horace Alexander, a friend of both Andrews and Gandhi, wrote:

C. F. Andrews was the best possible man to interpret Gandhi to the West, for he knew him more intimately than any other Westerner. As far as I know, he was the only Englishman, perhaps the only man, who in recent years called Mr. Gandhi by his first name "Mohan." To nearly all others Mr. Gandhi was "Gandiji" (which practically means Mr. Gandhi) or "Bapu," (Father or Daddy) or "Bapuji." He had become the senior, the one for whom love was mingled with respect or even reverence. For many he was the oracle. None were left to whom he was an equal.[2]

Gandhi himself described Andrews in a speech he gave to his countrymen right after the horrific Jallianwala Bagh massacre and made the witness of Andrews a reason why Indians should not harbor hatred for Englishmen. Gandhi said:

Mr. Andrews is like a brother to me. I therefore find it difficult to say anything about him. The sacred relationship between us stands in the way...Mr. Andrews has poured out his very life for India. He is no ordinary Englishman. He is a man of great learning, comes of an illustrious family, is a poet and theologian. If he had wished, he could have become a high dignitary...But he has not cared for wealth or for position and, today...he is ever on his feet in service of India. What is our duty towards such an Englishman? As long as there is even one Andrews among the British people, we must, for the sake of such a one, bear no hatred to them.[3]

C. F. Andrews was an Anglican priest who went to India in 1904 as a young missionary/college teacher, learned to love India with a passion, challenged the "mission to the heathens" mindset of the Christian churches in India, developed an original theology of enculturation, became the sole English Christian in the inner circle of the fight for independence from Britain, and brought and interpreted the message of Gandhi to the West through his three volumes, *Gandhi's Ideas* (1929), *Gandhi at Work* (1930), and *Mahatma Gandhi: His Own Story* (1931). By the time of Andrews's death in 1940 he was known throughout the world not only as Gandhi's great English friend and colleague but also, in his own right, *Deenabandhu*, "The Friend of the Poor," due to his tireless work to end indentured servitude and his unfailing responses to communities in need.

Andrews was asked in 1914 by Gokhale, the great Indian leader, to go to South Africa to assist Mohandas Gandhi in his struggle. It was the first time Andrews met Gandhi. They bonded as brothers at their first meeting. As Andrews witnessed the example of Gandhi and his followers in South Africa, he found in their behavior the clearest example of the teaching of Christ in the Sermon on the Mount that he had ever seen. He realized that in order to find Christ in the land of South Africa he had to go outside the Christian Church to the bands of Hindu passive resisters who told him of their joy in prison and who spoke kindly of their jailers.

Andrews recognized the contributions that both Marx and Gandhi had made to understanding the social nature of evil. He thought that satyagraha represented new hope for humankind in its struggle against evil and suffering. He wrote:

> It is one of the strangest phenomena of our modern age that those who have made us face this social aspect of evil have not been orthodox Christians, but men who either discarded "religion" altogether, like Karl Marx . . . or belonged by birth to another religion, like Mohandas Karamchand Gandhi, . . . a Hindu, [who] pointed us so nearly towards a truly Christian solution and . . . carried it out so far in action as to make it appear practicable.[4]

Uniquely early on—before he had even met Gandhi and was only hearing stories about Gandhi's work in South Africa—Andrews recognized the theological and human significance of Gandhi. In an article of 1907 he was reflecting on Gandhi: "In the East the idea is everything and advance is not made by material circumstances merely, but by personal devotion of multitudes towards the guru who sacrifices himself for the idea."[5]

Andrews wrote in his autobiography what he had thought about Gandhi after first spending time working with him in 1914 and observing close up the method of satyagraha:

In Mahatma Gandhi...this sovereign power of winning victories through suffering was apparent in every aspect of his hard life of pain. To be with him...gave me a high courage enkindled...by his own. His tenderness toward every slightest thing that suffered pain was only a part of his tireless search for truth, whose other name was God...His one message was that long-suffering and redeeming love are alone invincible.[6]

By 1938, toward the end of his life, looking back at all that he had observed in both South Africa and India in terms of the practice of Gandhian nonviolence, Andrews was clearer than ever that Gandhi's days in South Africa, when he invented satyagraha, were important for the history of the world. Describing for a new audience the story of satyagraha in South Africa, he concluded:

This was the last act of that great drama, whereby Mahatma Gandhi won his passive resistance struggle against overwhelming odds in South Africa. Future historians will record it as a turning point from violence to non-violence in the history of India and the world.[7]

Andrews's experiences in India, especially his witnessing and experiencing Gandhian satyagraha so intimately, compelled him to read the New Testament with what he felt were clearer eyes.

Andrews's Understanding of the New Testament

As a result of his experiences with Gandhi in South Africa, Andrews confessed that he had a whole new appreciation of Jesus' teaching in the New Testament about the oneness of humanity. He realized how deeply offended Christ was by racial and religious exclusiveness and how it called forth his severest condemnations. For the first time he understood how Jesus had deliberately shocked the Pharisees by saying that publicans and sinners would enter into the Kingdom because the Pharisees were causing such unnecessary burdens for people and such unnecessary divisions between people based on man-made religious rules, noting that

Christ himself, with all the reckless courage of youth and the power of God in his heart, had risked his life in his own village ...over this very question...The first disciples of Jesus...had followed their Master step by step, eradicating one prejudice after another from their own lives...They had to learn that God's way of thinking was exactly opposite of their own foolish racial way.[8]

This fundamental belief in the oneness of humanity is the foundation of Gandhi's satyagraha, the belief that all persons at bottom will recognize their common humanity if confronted in love and a spirit of self-suffering. Through his experiences of racial hate and prejudice in South Africa and India, Andrews understood in a new way just how fundamental this belief was for his own Christian faith. As he wrote:

> Probably on no issue was the New Testament more explicit and the teaching of Christ himself more plain, than on this. "In Him," St. Paul writes, "there is neither Greek nor Jew...barbarian, Scythian, bond or free: but Christ is all and in all."[9]

The second New Testament teaching for which Andrews developed a new appreciation was the nonviolent peacemaking taught in the Sermon on the Mount. Andrews sorted through the issues concerning the historical setting in which Jesus worked and taught. He came to understand very well the political and economic dynamics at work in Jesus' time. Therefore, even though Andrews wrote excellent and popular works on developing a thriving inner spiritual life, his interpretation of the New Testament accented its social and political thrust. He was far from a quietist. In the words of Chaturvedi and Sykes:

> The last memorandum that Andrews ever wrote was a protest against the impressions which he felt had been given by one of the Metropolitan's broadcasts, that from the Christian point of view resistance, even non-violent resistance, to injustice and oppression was wrong. "Our Lord," he wrote, "was in the direct line of the great Prophets...He challenged the State rulers in Jerusalem on the...corrupt form of their own theocratic rule. He fearlessly dealt, from first to last, with public affairs."[10]

In his interpretation of the Beatitudes section of the Sermon on the Mount, for example, Andrews consistently emphasizes the political implications of the blessing statements. For Andrews, the peacemaker has to carry all the other seven blessings in order to bring peace to others. Andrews points out that

> [t]he character which Christ has thus set forward before our eyes in the Beatitudes as truly blessed stands out uncompromisingly for purity, love and truth in a world given over to violence and brute force. From first to last, in His own life, He repudiated violence in all its forms, and would not accept from the powers of evil all the kingdoms of the world and the glory of them by lowering, however slightly, His moral standard.[11]

Andrews's understanding of Matthew 5:38–42, in particular, reflects his experience with the flesh-and-blood satyagraha campaigns and something of Gandhi's understanding of the Sermon on the Mount, which we have seen "went straight to his heart." Andrews first carefully places the sayings in their historic settings:

> To be struck on the right cheek was regarded as a challenge and an insult. According to the code of honor of those days it would require some immediate requital. In all probability it would be the beginning of a long dispute involving the family or tribe ...
>
> The cloak or upper garment was much more costly than the vest or shirt underneath. Jesus implies that if a small demand were made of us under some form of compulsion, such as a lawsuit, then instead of resisting it, a much more valuable gift might be given freely, without any lawsuit at all, with a view to win the heart of the oppressor.
>
> The compulsion to "go a mile" refers to a custom on the great high roads of the Roman Empire whereby an officer of Government was free to take forced labor from any locality in order to do his own official work.[12]

Placing the sayings in their historical contexts immediately changes the way one interprets the intent of the sayings. They are specific examples of real situations of oppression with which Jesus' audience would be quite familiar. Jesus is putting them in those settings and asking them to imagine how they would behave now that they have met him, witnessed how he behaved, and heard what he taught. How would they behave if they were trying to emulate him in such settings of oppression? The passage is an invitation to his hearers to use their imaginations. It is a particular type of language—not commandments or rules but picture language. As Andrews notes:

> He is using the "picture language" which all simple, country people like to hear in homely talk. For it can be taken away and remembered without any danger of becoming vague and indefinite. The extreme form renders it a perfect vehicle for transmission. It also sets the mind to work to discover beneath the picture the true inward meaning.[13]

Jesus' audience knows very well Leviticus 24:20, the *lex talionis*, the law of requital: "Eye for eye, tooth for tooth, burning for burning, wound for wound, stripe for stripe." According to Andrews, the words of Matthew 5:44, "Love your enemies, do good to them that hate you, and pray for them that despitefully use you and persecute you," had to have struck

Jesus' listeners as such a stark contrast to the law of requital as to be coming from an entirely different world. Andrews, with his appreciation of the
contribution of the East and with his universalist vision, then puts the
teaching about returning good for evil into the historical chain that began
centuries before with the Buddha, continued through the suffering servant
of Isaiah, and culminated with our Lord's passion and death on the cross.

> We have to go back a very long way in human history if we would
> trace back the silent growth of this idea of returning good for evil.
> In the life of Gautama the Buddha it formed the supreme discov-
> ery which he made when he sought to break the chain of suffering
> wherewith human life had hitherto appeared to be inextricably
> bound.[14]

For Andrews the message of Matthew 5:38–44 is therefore both a
method and a spirit. Taken together they describe the new way of life that
Christians are to live, an alternative approach to the two ways that humanity had accepted as the only possible approaches to the problems of violence and oppression: the way of withdrawal and the way of retaliation.
Andrews knows it is "natural" that, when someone has personally injured
us, we are inclined to retaliate and answer blow for blow. He knows that
typical human justice demands that the scales be evened and a penalty
required. It is precisely against these "natural" instincts that he places the
"turn the other cheek" message.

> And yet our Lord tells us to do just the opposite: to offer no resist-
> ance even if he continue his persecution. In highly figurative lan-
> guage Jesus tells us to go to the extreme in showering generosity
> on the persecutor. We are to go to extravagant lengths in trying to
> win his love and change his heart. "If he compel you to carry his
> burden for one mile, carry it two miles instead"—i.e., until you
> have completely won his heart.[15]

Andrews knows that Gandhi's satyagraha is in part a method, and that
Jesus' teaching is a method, a technique to be used and applied in a whole
range of real, practical settings in which the believer confronts violence,
but he is leery of the term because he is afraid that the reader will fall back
into the trap of understanding the Sermon on the Mount as a set of rules
and regulations to be slavishly copied, so he qualifies his statement:

> I have called this, inadequately, a method. It is far more than that,
> it is a spirit. The word "method" implies a copying of detail in the
> picture—what we have come to call a "technique." But that is very

far from the thought of Jesus. Indeed, the very illustrations which
He gives make the literal copying of what He tells us so rare as to
be almost impossible.[16]

Andrews then tells the story of an old missionary in Lahore who, when
he was preaching in the bazaar, actually received a blow on the right cheek
from someone who had read the verse. The missionary had waited a long
time to do exactly what his Master had counseled and turned his left cheek
to the one who had struck him and, as a result, won the heart of his perse-
cutor. The language is clearly not prescribing specific behavior in a specific setting that is so rare to be almost unique; instead, as Andrews says,

> What is needed is to watch for those golden occasions of return-
> ing good for evil in the daily life which are in accord with the spir-
> it of Christ's teaching, and then eagerly to seize them and act as
> He would wish us to act. There is probably no part of his teaching
> ...where literalism may be more harmful than beneficial.[17]

Far from being either an invitation to weakness or an unrealizable
ideal, the teaching of the Sermon on the Mount is, for Andrews as it was
for Gandhi, an invitation to heroic, imaginative action in the face of personal and social violence, oppression, and evil. For Andrews, it is the distinctive Way of the followers of Jesus.

Answers to Questions about Jesus' Teaching on Nonviolence

Andrews's book, *The Sermon on the Mount*, is the work that most fully sets
forth his basic understanding of Christian nonviolence. Specific questions
about this teaching arise in other contexts and he answers them in his writings. Some of those questions are:

First question: "Gandhi in his teaching on satyagraha clearly desires to reach
and convert the opponent. Jesus' words to the Pharisees, on the other
hand, are so scathing that he seems to completely write them off. Is Jesus'
teaching then different from Gandhi's?"

Andrews agrees that Jesus' words are scathing and his indignation
tremendous, but notes that they are followed with a torrent of pity:

> He lashed at them with tremendous moral judgment because they
> despised the poor and rejected them...But you will notice that every
> time the indignation rises there comes at the end a torrent of tears,
> pity, compassion even for the oppressors...He loves his enemies.

Have you noticed in those words over Jerusalem...how at the end he breaks down in tears and weeps over that city of pride?[18]

Second question: "Is the teaching of the Sermon on the Mount meant for a select few? Is it not a 'counsel of perfection'? Isn't it for those who leave behind the ordinary, human ties of marriage and daily living?"

Andrews agrees that the Sermon on the Mount calls for heroic action. He recalls that Christ died young, at the height of his manhood, and his summons to vigorous action is that of a young man. Therefore, according to Andrews, his message will always appeal to the young and the daring spirit in human beings. Andrews writes:

More than any other figure in human history Jesus represents, for all time, the youth of man confronting undismayed, obstacles inconceivably great and conquering them by the daring of his spirit. Other founders of religions of the world, each in their own sphere supremely noble, have lived long lives on earth and died in old age, leaving their message of truth behind them. Christ has this one surpassing quality; he represents for all time...the religion of youth...Christ appeals to...—the faith that can move mountains.[19]

The appeal to the heroic, for Andrews, receives no apology because the odds are so great and the work required to build the kingdom so momentous, but he insists that the heroism is possible only because of faith, a faith that introduces people to a supportive community through which people can be capable of great things. He repeats a legendary story that

carries this great truth at its center, how Jesus, as he returned to the Father, was asked by those angels who earnestly desire to gaze into the mystery of man's redemption, "What have you left behind to carry out the work?" He answered, "A little band of men and women who love me." "But what if they fail when the trial comes? Will all you have done be defeated?" "Yes," said Jesus, "if they fail, all I have done will be defeated." "Is there nothing more?" "No," said Jesus, "there is nothing more." "What then?" "They will not fail," said Jesus; and the angels wondered as they saw the sublime confidence of love which this betokened.[20]

People are able to live this life of nonviolence not because of leaving the ties that bind of marriage and life in this world, but because of the community of faith that supports and inspires them. In fact, Andrews argued strenuously with Gandhi against insisting that a vow of celibacy be a condition for joining his ashrams. He argued, based on Jesus' positive attitudes toward marriage and his body- and world-affirming message, against what he saw as Gandhi's flight from and denigration of the body. The community of faith, not body-denying asceticism, for Andrews, is what frees humans for heroic action. He recounted how John's community of faith drew the followers of faith away from fear of the vast, powerful Roman world, so they were ready to face death itself. "The wonder of all wonders was this," wrote Andrews, "that these young disciples actually passed through the horrors of Domitian's reign of persecution without a murmur, without flinching, and without even a cry for vengeance."[21]

Andrews insists that the heart of the message of Jesus is the requirement that his followers go well beyond what most consider "natural" and act with extravagant love. Jesus' demand is much higher than that of the world around him. The Greek word *perisson* is key for Andrews's spirituality — "what do you do in '*perisson*,' i.e. in excess, out of your fullness (which you have received through others in faith)"? Finally, in answer to the question, he points to the history of the early Church and to the lack of any double standard or two-class approach:

> One further striking historical fact is this, that none of the Apostles ever attempted to set up a double standard of this kind in the earliest days of the Church... The first preachers of the good news of the Kingdom took men and women, often of the lowliest type, freed men and slaves, just as they were, and by the power of the Holy Spirit transformed them in their own surroundings, making saints out of quite ordinary people.[22]

Third question: "Is not the Sermon on the Mount unrealistic? Surely it cannot be applied in a world of realpolitik? Was Jesus overlooking the fact of evil, violent human beings and corrupt organizations and states?"

In answer, Andrews insists that Jesus was not oblivious to the strength of evil in the world. In fact, because of the clarity of his vision, he understood the sacrifices that would need to be made to stand up to those powers:

> Our Lord Jesus Christ gave repeated warnings to His disciples concerning the immense strength of these forces of evil in the world which would have to be met and conquered. It was just because His pure eyes saw so clearly that He did not underestimate them for a moment... Experience has shown us clearly, even in our own lifetime, what incredible sacrifices have to be made when evil is so strong in the world.[23]

For Andrews, as for Gandhi, this is precisely the significance of the cross of Jesus. Evil and violence in the world are so threatening and immense that the only way for change to come about is to be found in the example of Jesus who set his face to Jerusalem to take up the cross. As John Hoyland wrote:

> Christ had brought it about by bearing the Cross, by setting His face steadfastly to go up to Jerusalem, . . . and by consciously and deliberately taking upon himself that vast experience of patiently-borne pain for the changing of the evil will in man.[24]

Andrews admitted that he more clearly understood the teaching of the Sermon on the Mount and the significance of the cross because of the personal example of Gandhi. He embraced nonviolence because of Gandhi's witness and because of his understanding of the life and teaching of Jesus. The two intertwined in a way that is impossible to sort out.

In 1924 Andrews came to Gandhi's side to protect him from visitors, and to care for Gandhi during his great fast against untouchability. He also took over the task of editing *Young India*. He wrote an editorial describing the last day of Gandhi's fast and his own reactions to it, which concludes:

> Below the summit of the ridge, in the open spaces where the modern golf links had been made, I watched the golfers come and go. The clubs were swung and the balls were hit; muscular men and women marched forward, while little boys carried their clubs behind. Physical activity was there in every limb—physical and temporal power. Instinctively my gaze turned back to the frail, wasted, tortured spirit on the terrace by my side, bearing the sins and sorrows of his people. With a rush of emotion there came to memory the passage from the Book of Lamentations—"Is it nothing to you, all ye that pass by? Behold and see, if there is any sorrow like unto my sorrow?" And in that hour of vision I knew more deeply, in my own personal life, the meaning of the cross.[25]

Andrews's Thoughts on the Future of Nonviolence

Andrews understood quite early that Gandhi's teaching, and by extension Christ's teaching, was the answer William James was looking for in his famous essay when he described one of humankind's greatest needs—finding the "moral equivalent to war." He expected people who came after him and Gandhi to continue their experiments with truth and develop the principles and practice and further.

> A thoroughly scientific treatment of the subject would be required in order to show both points of weakness and points of strength in

its present development, thus making possible on a large scale the very same principles that he [Gandhi] himself has used.[26]

Andrews recognized with some realism that in comparison to the history and study of war that had been going on intensively for centuries, the history of experiments in satyagraha had been very brief. Preparation for a moral resistance campaign deserved no less a wholehearted effort than that which went into preparation for war. He wrote:

> When we consider, even for a moment, the vast and detailed preparations that are made for a struggle of violence such as war, and how military training occupies many years of a man's lifetime and with large numbers becomes a life profession, it should be abundantly clear that the moral effect needed to supplant war cannot be made in an impromptu manner.[27]

Both Andrews and Gandhi realized that nonviolence applied to mass action was a new phenomenon and that their experiments with it were at the very early stages of its potential development. Both were hopeful that others would come along after them and surpass anything that they had accomplished. Toward the end of his life Andrews even saw signs that more and more Christians were embracing nonviolence. (This was at the end of the 1930s, when pacifism in England was increasingly popular. Much of that enthusiasm was to dissipate during World War II and with the experience of Hitler.) At the end of his book, *The Sermon on the Mount*, Andrews presents a brief history of the Christian groups who clung to the idea of nonviolence as central to Christ's message: from the Montanists, to the Cathari and Albigenses, to Francis of Assisi, the Lollards, the Quakers, and the Moravians, through Tolstoy and the Dukhobors. He then concludes:

> Now at last in the West, at the end of all this long development outside the main body of the Christian Church...large groups of Christians have banded themselves together as brothers, with the determination to carry out the principle of the Sermon on the Mount, "Love your enemies,"...while gladly expressing a willingness to suffer for their convictions as in the first day of the Church.[28]

C. F. Andrews received many great gifts during his life. The greatest ones were his friendships with some remarkable people, especially Rabindranath Tagore and Mohandas Gandhi. Through his friends he came to know and appreciate India and Islam and Hinduism from the inside. He always testified that his appreciation of this magnificent culture and these world religions made his faith in Jesus Christ stronger and his Christianity more open and world-affirming. His firsthand experience of satyagraha in action enabled him to read the New Testament with fresh eyes. There was no doubt in his mind that Gandhi's great appreciation for the Sermon on the Mount was exactly right. For him and for Gandhi, the message of non-violence was the teaching the world needed and was yearning to see put into practice.

From Gandhi's point of view, Andrews was the person who made Christianity live. He knew him and loved him well. Whenever Christian missionaries would ask him how they should bring the message of Christianity to India he would answer, "Live it. Be like Andrews."

John Howard Yoder: Disciple of the Nonresistant Jesus

John Howard Yoder (1927–1997) was a Mennonite theologian, a professor at the University of Notre Dame, and a fellow of the Joan B. Kroc Institute for International Peace Studies. Yoder has had a profound influence on contemporary Christian theology. His contribution stems from the fact that he proposed afresh two fundamental questions: Do we find in the New Testament that Jesus taught a sociopolitical ethic? And, if Jesus did propose a distinctive sociopolitical ethic, what is its content and is it normative for his followers? Those two questions were asked and answered by Yoder especially in his books *The Politics of Jesus, The Original Revolution, He Came Preaching Peace*, and *Christian Attitudes towards War, Peace, and Revolution*. What was noteworthy and powerful about Yoder's approach was that he answered the questions using the latest tools of historical/critical biblical scholarship, bridging the gap between scripture studies on the one hand and moral and systematic theology on the other.

Yoder studied under both Karl Barth and Oscar Cullmann at the University of Basel on his way to completing his doctorate in theology. He was influenced by both of them in the way that he read the scriptures, but he was especially influenced by Cullmann's careful study of the political environment of first-century Palestine. During the 1950s and 1960s he used the scholarship of many scripture scholars in addition to Cullmann as he developed his work on the politics of Jesus. Among them were C. H. Dodd, Hans Conzelmann, Rudolf Schnackenburg, John L. McKenzie, SJ, Robert Morgenthaler, Robert North, SJ, Krister Stendhal, and Hans Dieter Betz. When he issued a second edition of *The Politics of Jesus* in 1994, he added epilogues to each of the chapters as well as the testimony of then-current respected scripture scholars: C. F. Moule, Markus Borg, N. Thomas Wright, Dominic Crossan, Richard Horsley, Walter Brueggemann, A. E. Harvey, Gerard Lohfink, SJ, Adela Yarbro Collins, John P. Meier, Raymond Brown, and Walter Wink. The later scholarship for the most part confirmed and sharpened the earlier work, which described the political context of first-century Palestine and demonstrated the political implications of Jesus' actions and teaching.

In taking this approach of first and seriously attending to the scriptures to determine whether Jesus taught a political ethic and if it was presented as normative for his followers, Yoder challenged the typical ways that these fundamental questions had been addressed. In particular he directly challenged the "realism" school of Reinhold Niebuhr and the "natural law" ethics of people like Paul Ramsey. He was also indirectly challenging the way Catholic social teaching, as expressed in the papal encyclicals of the last century, had been developed and expressed.[29]

In *The Politics of Jesus* Yoder set out to determine if there is a way to relate current New Testament studies with social ethics, especially the issues of power, violence, war, and revolution. As Yoder wrote, "Theologians have long been asking how Jerusalem can relate to Athens; here the claim is that Bethlehem has something to say about Rome—and Masada."[30]

About this work Stanley Hauerwas, the well-known Duke theologian and a former colleague of Yoder's on the faculty of the University of Notre Dame, wrote that "when Christians look back on this century of theology in America, *The Politics of Jesus* will be seen as a new beginning."[31] Hauerwas has also written, "John did not provide new answers to old questions; but rather like Wittgenstein, he changed the questions."[32]

John Howard Yoder's corpus of work can be understood as one long excursus on power—how to exercise power as a disciple of Jesus in a world of violence. For Yoder, the issue of violence in all its forms—political and social domination, economic exploitation, and especially mass organized state violence, was at the center of his theological reflections. As he wrote in *The Original Revolution*:

> The issue of war is a crucial and most typical touchstone. Perhaps it is the most crucial test point for our age. The point where we are asked whether it is ultimately Jesus or some other authority whom we confess as the light of the world.[33]

That concern came primarily from two sources: his experience in Europe after the Second World War and his Mennonite tradition. At the age of twenty-one he was sent by his Ohio Mennonite community to help in the settlement and reconstruction effort in Europe; there he witnessed firsthand the devastation to the cities that had been caused by the war and the problems of resettling the fifteen million internally displaced people fleeing en masse before the advancing Russian troops. Earl Zimmerman notes:

> The stream of refugees included Mennonites from Prussia, Poland, and the Ukraine...By the end of 1949, MCC [the

Mennonite Central Committee] had helped resettle more than eleven thousand refugees. Most of them migrated to either Canada or Paraguay, two countries that agreed to receive them as a group.[34]

This experience of the horrific destruction of World War II stayed with Yoder all his life and partially explains why he had such a passion for addressing the morality of war and the challenge of violence from the standpoint of the New Testament.

The second source of his sharp awareness of violence and the threat it posed to the survival of the planet came from his Mennonite heritage. The Mennonite experience was forged in the Peasant Wars of the sixteenth century. The Mennonites held that the life and teaching of Jesus were normative for Christians. As they read the New Testament, they saw that Jesus was clearly nonresistant and taught nonresistance to his followers. They opposed therefore, within the church, coercion of belief. These teachings threatened the political and religious authorities, and for those beliefs the Mennonites were massacred or forced to migrate to other lands.

John Howard Yoder grew up in the Oak Grove Mennonite Church, just outside Smithville in northern Ohio. His great-great-grandfather, his great-grandfather, and his father together provided leadership at Oak Grove for over one hundred years. His maternal great-grandfather, Christian Good, was a conscientious objector in the Civil War. According to Mark Nation,

[a]mong the facts passed down to John Yoder about his great-grandfather Good [was this:] ... "When commanded to shoot he said 'but those are people. I don't shoot people' so that the confederate army put him in the kitchen."[35]

Yoder knew well the various ways that the ethic of Jesus, with its political implications, had been dismissed through the centuries. Yoder's work can best be understood in dialogue and disputation with those rationales of dismissal. This section will proceed therefore through the following topics: six ways of declaring Jesus' ethic irrelevant; the New Testament on the politics of Jesus; critiques of Constantinianism and Reinhold Niebuhr; and Gandhi's influence on Yoder.

Six Ways of Declaring Jesus' Ethic Irrelevant

Yoder recognized that, for the most part, mainstream ethical theory considered Jesus not to be relevant to the questions of social ethics. He outlined the six most prevalent ways that Jesus' ethic was held to be irrelevant. (In the second edition of *The Politics of Jesus* he added six more.)

The first approach, influenced by Albert Schweitzer, had been recently articulated by Reinhold Niebuhr, who had said that the ethic of Jesus was an "interim ethic." Jesus and his early followers expected the world to end. Therefore they did not pay any attention to the issues involved in building a viable, enduring society. The values taught by Jesus, such as rejection of violence and self-defense and the accumulation of wealth, are not designed for a society that has to endure. Nonresistance might be appropriate for a small group of people waiting for the world to end, but it is not relevant for a world of nation states and naked aggression. Yoder summarized Niebuhr's thinking in the following way: "At any point where social ethics must deal with problems of duration, Jesus quite clearly can be of no help . . . Thereby the survival of society, as a value in itself, takes on a weight which Jesus did not give it."[36]

The second basis of rejection is the contention that Jesus lived in a simple rural environment and was concerned only with issues of face-to-face relations. He had no intention of teaching about complex institutions, or issues such as class struggles, power cliques, or international relations.

The third basis for a claim of irrelevance is the fact that Jesus and his early followers lived in a time when they had no control over their political situation. Now, because Christianity has made great strides in history and its principles undergird all of Western culture, Christians have to face issues of responsibility that Jesus never even considered. Yoder quotes Paul Ramsey in this regard:

> Jesus deals only with the simplest moral situation . . . the case of one person in relation to another. He does not undertake to say how men, who themselves ought not to resist at all . . . when they themselves alone receive the blows, ought to act in more complex cases.[37]

The fourth contention that leads to a dismissal is the belief that Jesus cared only about spiritual and existential matters and not social or political matters. What mattered to him was only what went on inside individual human hearts and minds.

Fifth, Jesus was a radical monotheist who wanted people to turn away from things of this world so they could worship God in spirit and in truth. The discontinuity between the divine and human means that all human values are relativized. God cannot be identified with any one ethical answer.

Finally, Jesus came to save humans from sin, and that gift of salvation is a forensic act. It has nothing to do with what people do. Proper behavior is irrelevant. Only faith matters. Jesus did not care to give precise guidance to humans on how they should behave.

The New Testament on the Politics of Jesus

Following Oscar Cullmann, Yoder first lays out what the political environment was like in first-century Palestine. Jesus lived in an occupied country, under a puppet government. Violent uprisings, inspired by religious beliefs, occurred both before and after Jesus' life. Every person in this society faced some basic political choices—choices not dissimilar from those faced by anyone born a displaced person in a country under foreign occupation.

The first alternative was to accept the situation for what it was and make the best of it, the way of realism. Making this choice would mean accepting Roman rule but making sure that the important values of the Jewish culture were kept alive—worship in the temple, recognition for and teaching of the Jewish law, and guarantees from the government that people could practice their own monotheist religion. Yoder wrote:

> That was in Jesus' age the strategy of the Herodians and the Sadducees. These were not, as a superficial reading of the Gospel narrative might make one think, nasty and scheming people; they were intelligent leaders following a responsible strategy. Their concern was to do the best one could do in the situation.[38]

The second alternative open to Jesus was the desert. He could disentangle himself from the complexities of urban life and the temptations to be unfaithful by removing himself to the wilderness with the Essenes. He clearly appreciated the value of the desert as a place for prayer but rejected this alternative and set his face to the city.

The third alternative was the path of seceding from the dominant culture, not geographically but through religion. The Pharisees maintained their purity by segregating themselves ("Pharisee" means separate), by declaring certain areas of life—certain foods, certain coins, certain persons—off limits.

The final alternative was that of revolutionary violence. This was a real option for Jesus. He appeared to outsiders to be closer to this group than the others. As Yoder wrote, "He used their language, took sides with the poor as they did, condemned the same evils they did, created a disciplined community of committed followers as they did, prepared as they did to die for the divine cause."[39]

Jesus did not take the path of the righteous, violent revolutionaries. He did not set out to change society by changing leadership at the top. Moreover, he differed from the Zealots, as this group was called, in that he associated with the impure, the sinner, the publican, and even the Roman. Yoder maintained that Jesus did not choose any of the four alternatives but instead developed a new way and a new potential for being human in the social and political world.

In *The Politics of Jesus* Yoder guides us through the gospel narrative of Luke. He comments briefly on the politically charged introductory passages, such as Mary's Magnificat, with its "pulling the mighty from their thrones" and "exalting the lowly" language that reads like a Maccabean revolutionary ode; the story of the birth of Jesus, with its themes of Caesar's census, registration, and taxation; and the narrative of John's ministry and death, about which Josephus wrote that John's imprisonment was connected with Herod Antipas's fear that John might foment an insurrection. Yoder then explains the political significance of the main narrative, beginning with the temptations in the desert. The first temptation equates to "feed the crowds and you will be king." About the second temptation there is no ambiguity concerning the political nature of the reward: "all the kingdoms of the world." Even the third temptation, Jesus throwing himself from the pinnacle of the temple, can be understood as dramatically announcing the beginning of a messianic freedom fight.

The speech that launched Jesus' public ministry, quoting Isaiah 61, states the messianic expectations in explicit sociopolitical terms. Jesus applies the passage to himself and announces that God's Kingdom is now here—with him: good news to the poor, release for the captives, sight to the blind, liberty for those who are oppressed, and ending with the phrase "to proclaim the acceptable year of the Lord." Yoder refers to Andre Trocme, Sharon Ringe, and Robert North, SJ, who understand this phrase to refer to the jubilee year. In the jubilee year, the land lies fallow and the accumulated injustices of land seizure are set aright for the sake of the poor. In any case, the imminent implementation of a new regime that Jesus proclaimed is, as Yoder wrote, "a visible, socio-political restructuring of relations among the people of God achieved by divine intervention in the person of Jesus as the one Anointed and endued with the Spirit."[40]

As Jesus moved on through his public life, gathered followers, and challenged the religious and political powers of his day, opposition from those powers began to build. His public life was an "apparent threat serious enough to justify his execution."[41]

In the eyes of the religious and political powers, Jesus' commissioning of followers was perhaps the most serious political action Jesus took. He was no longer just a solitary individual preaching a message; he was now founding a movement. He was gathering a committed following. The new social order he was proclaiming began to be visible, real, and therefore threatening.

This new social order that Jesus founded is definitely in the world. It is not a monastery or a separatist enterprise. But it is sharply at odds with the existing social order. In its very inclusivity it is different. The values of this new order are the values of Jesus, namely love of one's enemy, rejection of violence as a political option, and a servant style of leadership rather than one of domination. Love even of the enemy because, according to Jesus, that is the way God is. Yoder explains:

> Christians love their enemies because God does so, and commands his followers to do so...No one created in God's image and for whom Christ died can be for me an enemy, whose life I am willing to threaten or to take, unless I am more devoted to something else—to a political theory, to a nation, to the defense of certain privileges, or to my own personal welfare—than I am to God's cause.[42]

For Jesus, the teaching on nonresistance is rooted in the way God acts towards humanity. God shows unending, non-coercive patience with humanity. He makes the rain fall on the just and the unjust. As J. Denny Weaver has written, "Since Jesus makes present the rule of God, it is clear that God's rule confronts evil nonviolently."[43]

The nature and style of leadership in this new organization differs from what is common in the world. Jesus said that he came to serve and so should his disciples. Yoder summarized in very powerful words what this political revolution, this new society, was like:

> When He called His society together Jesus gave its members a new way of life to live. He gave them a new way to deal with offenders—by forgiving them. He gave them a new way to deal with violence—by suffering. He gave them a new way to deal with money—by sharing it. He gave them a new way to deal with problems of leadership—by drawing on the gift of every member, even the most humble. He gave them a new way to deal with a corrupt society—by building a new order, not smashing the old. He gave them a new pattern of relationships between man and woman, between parent and child, between master and slave, in which he made concrete a radical new vision of what it means to be a human person. He gave them a new attitude toward the state and toward the "enemy nation." At the heart of all this novelty is what Jesus did about the fundamental human temptation: power.[44]

In this context, the cross is a clear political act. When Jesus set his face toward Jerusalem he rejected violence as the means to set the political order right. At that moment, writes Yoder, "The cross is beginning to loom not as a ritually prescribed instrument of propitiation but as the political alternative to both insurrection and quietism."[45]

The gathering storm of resistance to Jesus by the authorities was due to the fact that they perceived him to be a political threat. They were not sure if he was going to lead a violent uprising but they knew that he was riling up the crowds, that he was gathering a band of followers around him, and that he was saying and doing things that deviated from their norms. From his side, Jesus was doing all that he could to make clear his message and inviting all to see his vision of God and of society. It all built to the point where they killed him as an insurrectionary. The punishment of death on the cross was for such an offense. In Yoder's words:

> Christ is agape: self-giving, nonresistant love. At the cross this nonresistance, including the refusal to use the political means of self-defense, found its ultimate revelation in the uncomplaining and forgiving death of the innocent at the hands of the guilty. This death reveals how God deals with evil...But the cross is not defeat...this sacrifice was turned by God into a victory which vindicated to the utmost the apparent impotence of love.[46]

Having demonstrated the political nature of Jesus' life and his death, Yoder goes on to make the case that the way of life proclaimed by Jesus and practiced in the early church, the way of nonresistant love even for the enemy, is normative for Christians. He reviews the epistles, documents older than the gospels, and finds the consistent theme of discipleship, or imitation of Jesus, to be at the center of what was taught. Discipleship and imitation of Jesus are defined precisely in terms of his suffering, nonresistant love. No one expects his followers to imitate him in terms of his mendicancy (although the Franciscans will do that later in history) or in his trade or in his not being married. Imitation is not a general imitation but imitation of a very specific behavior, namely, imitation of the way Jesus confronted evil—with nonresistant love.

"Following Christ," and "taking up one's cross" are requirements for the Christian. Over the centuries those words have been translated in ways that have changed their fundamental meaning and emptied them of their political content. Enduring a crisis of inner angst or guilt, as in Christian existentialism, is not what the cross is about. It is not patiently enduring natural disasters or illness, as in pastoral care—except by extension. Jesus' suffering was not some unexplainable and undeserved evil that came upon him accidentally like a disease, a storm, or an earthquake. On the contrary, Jesus' cross was a form of suffering that Jesus could very well have avoided. As Yoder wrote:

> The cross of Calvary was not a difficult family situation, not a frustration of visions of personal fulfillment, a crushing debt, or

a nagging in-law; it was the political, legally-to-be-expected result of a mortal clash with the powers ruling society.[47]

According to Yoder:

There is . . . but one realm in which the concept of imitation holds—Discipleship of Jesus requires following his example of nonviolent, loving resistance to the powers of domination and oppression. But there it holds in every strand of the New Testament literature . . . This is at the point of the concrete social meaning of the cross in its relation to enmity and power. Servanthood replaces dominion, forgiveness absorbs hostility. Thus—and only thus—are we bound by New Testament thought to "be like Jesus."[48]

In these earlier writings, Yoder prefers the term "nonresistance," which is consistent with his Mennonite heritage. We shall see that, as his thought evolved, he began to use such terms as "nonviolent resistance."

With this summary of Yoder's presentation of the New Testament findings on the politics of Jesus, we can now explicitly address the six ways that Christian thinkers have rendered Jesus' life and teaching irrelevant for a current sociopolitical ethic. Yoder responded to the first idea of Schweitzer and Niebuhr concerning Jesus' "interim ethic" by saying that they had misunderstood the eschatology of the New Testament. Jesus taught that God's Kingdom had really come into human history. It was "already" but also "not yet"—already here but not yet fully present until the end of time. Far from being an "interim ethic," the model of Jesus' actions and teaching for his followers hold for all time right up to the end time.

To the second idea, that Jesus lived in a simple rural environment and cared only about personal relations, the picture that contemporary scholarship presents is of a Palestine that was at the crossroads of trade routes and civilization, where East and West have met in conflict all through history. Jesus could not but be in the middle of political conflict. Moreover, he moved out of village life, went to the center of the country's political and religious action, and established a community whose demands transcended personal and family relations.

In response to the third contention, that Jesus and his followers had no control over their political situation, Yoder responded that Jesus taught his disciples that they could and should control their own community and could build a model of freedom, love, and equality within the empire that could serve as a model of change and development for the rest of the world. That is precisely what the early church proceeded to accomplish. Moreover, the disciples were faithful to the teaching concerning a new way to exert power, that of suffering love—not only as individuals, but also as a social unit, the church dealing with society.

In response to the fourth contention, that Jesus cared only about spiritual matters, a reading of the New Testament reveals one who cared about people's daily physical needs. He cared deeply about the poor, the hungry, the sick, and the root causes of unnecessary human sufferings. He was a prophet in the tradition of the Hebrew prophets, who announced jubilee.

In response to the fifth contention, that radical monotheism makes human values relative, the New Testament testifies to one who linked worship of God in truth with the practical service of human beings.

Finally, Yoder disagreed with a view of salvation that is forensic and that breaks the link between discipleship and behavior. For Yoder, the death on the cross was a historical act, not a necessity imposed on Jesus. Our salvation is directly bound up with discipleship, following the way Jesus lived. His life and death on the cross are inseparable. Our salvation is not a forensic act, outside of time, unconnected to a way of life.

Yoder's Critiques of Constantinianism and of Reinhold Niebuhr

As a historical theologian, Yoder looked back on the history of Christianity and regretted the loss of Christianity's commitment to nonresistance. That loss occurred when Constantine declared Christianity the religion of the empire, when the church in turn condoned the use of violence against the empire's enemies, when Augustine asked the emperor to use the sword to get the heretics, the Donatists, back in line. Before Constantinianism, the church had followed the example of Jesus and rejected the sword.

For Yoder, once the power had been ceded to the state to punish and coerce with the sword those who were called God's enemies, Christianity lost its power to fight and minimize violence; the church became instead the legitimator of the state and could no longer be held guiltless for the subsequent history of violence. Yoder wrote:

> The confusion leads to the paganization of the church and the demonization of the state ... the church is no longer the obedient suffering line of true prophets; she has a vested interest in the present order of things and uses the cultic means at her disposal to legitimize that order. She does not preach ethics, judgment, repentance, separation from the world; she dispenses sacraments and holds society together ...
>
> Once admitted in principle, this attitude could later bless nationalism just as consistently as it had blessed imperialism ... the belief that political means can be used against God's enemies to oblige an entire society to do God's will ... The Constantinian heresy ultimately reverts to a purely pagan view of God as a tribal deity.[49]

As Yoder studied the history of Christianity, he saw that in the Middle Ages the pacifist sentiment still lived as an undercurrent in the life of the church. Thousands of unarmed pilgrim penitents on the road were a very visible presence of people renouncing violence because they were Christians. Yoder notes that

> [s]oldiers were allowed access to the sacraments by way of exception. The lives of saints continue to be told as stories of nonviolence, of suffering love, and even of conscientious objection. Martin of Tours, for whom Martin Luther was named...was a conscientious objector. He served with the Roman army in southern Gaul in peacetime, but when war came he refused to fight and became first a conscientious objector, then a bishop, and soon a saint in the later Catholic roster.[50]

With the Reformation, that order was swept away. There were no more tangible islands of peace and holiness in the middle of a world at war. The princes assumed power over the local churches. The nation-state was the organ of the Reformation. The princes financed the churches and created their governing bodies and gave them legitimacy. That arrangement was confirmed in the Peace of Westphalia and the doctrine of *cuius regio, eius religio.*

The Reformation heightened the moral autonomy of the civil order. Luther underlined that fact with the doctrine of the two kingdoms, one for the word of God and one for the state, which is definitely not under the church. The prince was no longer under any criticism of the bishop. It was up to the state to keep order and straighten out wrongs, and thereby it was given an even stronger mandate for violence. As Yoder wrote:

> Not only is the nation the organ of Reformation...The nation is the savior of the Reformation. The Reformation did after all have to be saved by war...Before that there were wars of Christians against Christians, but they were for territory or for pride or for money...Now however there are wars against other Christians for religion. This decreases still more the notion that Christian religion would ever be a restraint on war...The acceptability of war is greater since the Reformation than before.[51]

As a result of this history, today the nation-state is assumed by many to be an unassailable value. The state has the obligation to do whatever it has to do to assure its survival. It has a blank check for violence. Citizens give their first loyalties to the nation-state. Yoder wrote, "[T]he overwhelming loyalty of most persons in our age is to the nation...it is to the nation that young people give their enthusiasm. For the nation young people will risk their lives. For the nation they will, if need be, kill and destroy in war."[52]

Yoder's critique of Constantinianism is an appeal to Christians to hear once again the central message of nonresistant love and to restore Jesus and his life and witness as the norm for Christian ethics. If the message of the New Testament does not make the case for you, Yoder is saying, consider then the history of Christianity and reflect on what has happened because the church gave up its central witness of nonresistant, suffering love of even the enemy. Observe the history of violence that has ensued.

In just about every book Yoder wrote he refers negatively to Reinhold Niebuhr's thought and on a number of occasions gives a detailed critique of Niebuhr's thought. He does so for two reasons. He recognized that Niebuhr's thought, or at least the sentiments behind Niebuhr's thought, had been embraced by most American Christians. Niebuhr had been a pacifist during the 1920s and 1930s, but with Hitler's arrival on the scene he disavowed the easy optimism of those years. He became convinced that those who thought the message of nonresistance could be translated into politics were not only naïve but irresponsible. They had forgotten the message that the world was fallen and they had no real awareness of sin. He agreed that Jesus taught nonresistance, a pure type, not the coercive type practiced by people like Gandhi. Niebuhr appreciated those who embraced the New Testament ideal for their purity and their high-mindedness. They kept those who carried the heavy load of citizen responsibility (those whose heads were not in the clouds) aware that such higher ideals existed in the world. Niebuhr's "realism" made him an advisor to presidents and the U.S. State Department during the Cold War, and his social ethics in effect endorsed the military footing and practices of the United States as a necessary evil for the protection of the country.

Yoder always understood his mission to be an ecumenical one. He prized his Mennonite heritage but felt that his "sect" had a gift for the whole church. He knew there was no hearing by the larger community of Christians for the message of nonviolence, and therefore no way out of humanity's vicious cycle of violence, if people accepted as normative the assumptions that underlay Niebuhr's thought. That is the first reason that he consistently challenged those assumptions.

The second reason had to do with his care for the Mennonite tradition. Many of his colleagues accepted Niebuhr's understanding of the value of nonresistance as a pure ideal and as such a goad for other Christians. They took it as a backhanded compliment for their tradition. It confirmed their stance of pure disengagement from politics and society. They could be patriotic and pure at the same time. Yoder did not want them to feel complimented. He certainly did not agree that nonresistance meant disengagement from the world. He wanted them to see instead that it gave them a new way to exert power and be responsible.

Yoder called Niebuhr the most important American theological mind of the twentieth century and recognized that he made Christianity relevant again for many people. He appreciated the fact that Niebuhr put the issues of violence and war right at the center of his theology, as very few have done. Yoder wrote: "The restructuring of theology around the issue of violence and war was at the center of his entire enterprise. The entire theology of Niebuhr is unfolded backwards from his outgrowing of pacifism."[53]

Yoder challenges Niebuhr's concept of sin as unbiblical and he denies that those who embrace the message of nonresistance have a shallow understanding of sin and evil in the world. In fact, they recognize that Jesus went to the cross for that stance. There is no cheap grace for a Christian who follows Jesus' way. Throughout history, those who practice nonviolence in violent societies have been met with resistance and scorn. Those who embrace nonviolence, however, believe not only in the cross but also in the resurrection. Niebuhr, by exclusively stressing the human predicament, leaves no room for the message of regeneration and salvation that is the good news of the gospel. There is no room for the doctrine of the resurrection. Humans are evil by nature, not by situation. In Niebuhr's thought there is room for the grace of pardon but not for the grace of enablement.

The second criticism that Yoder presents of Niebuhr's thought is that he has no ecclesiology, no living appreciation for what a vital church community can do for the individual. Niebuhr's contention is that nonresistance might be possible for an individual but not for a group. Central to Niebuhr's thought is that as human beings gather into groups there is less and less room for altruism; they can act only in self-interest. Yoder contends that this assertion can be tested in fact. He says that an individual by himself or herself would find it just about impossible to lead a vigorous life of nonviolence. But with the help and support of a community of believers it does become possible. That is the meaning and role of the church—to support one another in a common witness of faith. That too is the gift of the Holy Spirit to the church—to be able to stay faithful and perform what would not be possible without grace. As Craig Carter describes Yoder's thinking:

> The ideal of love has been realized in history in the man Jesus and, because of the power of his resurrection flowing into the church through the ministry of the Holy Spirit, it is possible for admittedly sinful and imperfect people to bear a visible witness to the ideal of love, not in their individual piety or goodness, but insofar as they covenant themselves together into an alternative community that lives (and suffers) without resorting to violence.[54]

Yoder's third criticism is that Niebuhr fundamentally rejects the authority of the New Testament and the life and teaching of Jesus as the norm of theology. Instead Niebuhr makes "common sense" normative. His epistemology is still that of a liberal who accepts the philosophy of the age, scientific empiricism.

> He still believes that the way you get the truth is by thinking more carefully with all the data you've got. The Bible is just one symbolic source of images and input. It is not an "authority" ... [He advocates] being open minded and reasonable and letting all of the arguments speak for themselves, and then making your own decisions.[55]

Yoder's final thought on Niebuhr is not as theological and is more practical. The faith that Niebuhr placed in violence—even though he considered it a lesser evil that a "responsible" person would just have to accept as the price one has to pay for the privilege of living in a real world—has proved, as time has passed, a little too sanguine. Just what have our wars accomplished? As Yoder notes, "Canadians are not sure you needed an American revolution to be free. Civil War historians are not sure that tragedy was necessary."[56] On the other hand, when people reflect on the last twenty years and see all that assertive nonviolence has accomplished, the Niebuhrian case seems to weaken even further. Yoder points out that

> [t]he actual historical experience of people taking some cues from Jesus has raised our estimate of the effectiveness of nonviolence. If the lines (the rising chart of what nonviolence can do and the falling graph of the utility of violence) haven't crossed on the graph, at least they are close enough that the Niebuhrian case that we have to do the violence sometimes on effectiveness grounds is getting weaker and weaker. Then what we have to prove by transcendence or "revelation" is getting smaller and smaller.[57]

Yoder's critique of Niebuhr is one other way for him to capture the attention of the larger Christian Church and put before it the case for nonviolence. At the same time, he is pushing his own Mennonite community away from its stance of noninvolvement. He almost seems sheepish in making the final point against Niebuhr on effectiveness grounds rather than on the grounds of discipleship; i.e., the reason we have to follow this way is that we believe in Jesus and his way. Christians do not have to expect that the whole of society will accept it, but to be faithful, we who believe in Jesus have to follow it. Here the two critiques come together. Christendom, Constantinianism is finished. The church is a voluntary society. It is not coextensive with the society/state as it was in the days of

Christendom (and it never should have been; it should have always maintained its separateness and its distinctive teaching of nonviolence over against the state's sword). Our greatest contribution to the state is to be faithful to the way of Jesus, to be the Church. While insisting that the state be just and use the sword only justly, the church should demonstrate in its own praxis that there is a new way, that of love of enemy and nonviolence.

Gandhi's Influence on Yoder

Yoder's belief in and commitment to nonresistance came to him originally through his participation in the Mennonite tradition, not through Gandhi. Nonetheless, the influence of Gandhi is apparent throughout Yoder's writings. In the early writings, Gandhi is something of a straw man. Gradually, however, Gandhi's thought and witness begin to influence Yoder. Finally, Yoder evidences full-fledged respect for Gandhi in ways that shape and sharpen his own understanding of the way of nonviolence.

Gandhi: Too Coercive? Not Loving? Only a Technique?

Early on, Yoder and his fellow Mennonites thought Gandhi, even though he seemed heroic and had gathered attention for nonviolence as no one had before him, might not be the real thing—as they understood the tradition of nonresistance to evil. Yoder speculated, for example, that one of the sources of the too easy pacifism embraced by so many after the First World War had to do with—in addition to the secularized Puritanism of Emerson and Thoreau, and an extrapolation of the power of revival— "some awareness in the 1920s of Gandhi." Yoder noted:

> The social gospel which is optimistic about solving problems [teaches that if] we clear away provincialism, misinformation, and sectarian separatism, it will all work out for the best...Stop war by educating. You stop it by forbidding it and putting sanctions behind the prohibitions...Just as true with or without Jesus ...You don't need any deep critical analysis of economic structures that make for war or the ethnic or social egoisms that make for abiding polarizations.[58]

Yoder's early Mennonite theological mentor, Guy Hershberger, on the first page of his *War, Peace, and Nonresistance*, argued that biblical nonresistance was not the same as Gandhi's campaign in India. He thought Gandhi's campaign was really a form of warfare, since its primary purpose was to bring about the submission of the opposition through compulsion.[59] Hershberger was following Niebuhr, who dismissed Gandhi's approach as not the real thing because Jesus' nonresistance was not coercive in nature.

Yoder was able to sort out the issue of coercion quite well. He understood, as did Gandhi, the difference between violence and the use of power that changes people and situations without violating them as human beings, even when that change comes about against their initial will. Such use of power could still be considered nonviolent and not against the way of Jesus—who really was trying to see his adversaries change. For example, Yoder wrote that power,

> even if it be called "coercive," is of a personal, humane kind as long as the individual toward whom it is directed is conceived as a person and his life is protected. The pressures of education, gossip, excommunication, or ostracism are still personal and permit the one against whom they are directed to be restored to the community.[60]

Hershberger also dismissed Gandhi as not really coming from a spirit of agape. It was not until Hershberger was in contact with Martin Luther King that he changed his mind. He could not deny that King's movement, following in the footsteps of Gandhi, was suffused with real charity—even for the enemy. In Yoder's words:

> The discussion of Gandhi shouldn't be left there. Hershberger, as I said, was responding not really to Gandhi but to Gandhi's early western interpreters who were mostly not very religious people. They were saying that we have here a method that will really work to gain valid social goals without bloodshed ... Hershberger spent considerable time visiting in the South in those early days. He came back saying that it was a good thing ... He saw it as church-based, as loving, as willing to bear the cross.[61]

Yoder had two other, related misgivings about Gandhi's nonviolent campaigns. The first was that nonviolent direct actionists might not be so much interested in speaking to those in power as wielding power themselves. The other misgiving related to the issue of effectiveness. Most of his written references to Gandhi included mention of Martin Luther King. It was as if Gandhi could be more readily understood and appreciated if mediated by King's example. While admitting that the witness of Gandhi and King had changed peoples' perspectives on the issue of "effectiveness," Yoder went on to wonder if the commitment to nonviolence could survive when it is not immediately effective. He wrote:

Now that the experience of Gandhi and Martin Luther King has demonstrated that in some kinds of situations nonviolent methods can effectively bring about social change in the desired direction, it is appropriate for both these types of ethical thought, those for which effectiveness is the final consideration and those for which it is considered only instrumentally, to take account of this new information...It is effective when one can appeal to the conscience of the oppressor, as with Gandhi in India appealing to British self respect, or the American Negro appealing to the U.S. Constitution. Can it be effective against sadists and brutes? Can it maintain its conviction for months or years without any visible success?[62]

Here Yoder reveals a far too positive view of the nature of the British Empire, the same empire that had inflicted brutalities all over the world in the name of God and country, brutalities that Gandhi himself had witnessed in the vicious Boer War. Yoder's underlying thought nonetheless is clear—what happens to a belief in nonviolence when it is not "effective"? Yoder believed, and he probably came to know that Gandhi also believed, that a life of sustained commitment to nonviolence against all odds is possible only if it rests on faith in God—in whom all humans are one—and that faith is nurtured by a supportive, believing community. On the other hand, his comment about sadists and brutes is answered only over time as nonviolent direct action did indeed stunningly overthrow "sadists and brutes."

Underlying Yoder's continuing concern over the issue of practical effectiveness, it seems to me, is his acceptance of the Barthian idea that one follows the teaching of the Word of God for no other reason than it is the Word of God. Follow the teaching on nonresistance for no other reason than that it is taught by Jesus, for no other reason than discipleship. To import mere human reasons into the equation is to be disrespectful of the Word of God. To embrace nonviolence on the grounds of effectiveness is too earthly and too insecure a motive. It is only gradually that Yoder begins to see that faith and practicality do not have to be so separate. His nonresistance begins to resemble more and more the Gandhian idea of satyagraha.

Yoder's Respect for Gandhi

In his book, *Nevertheless*, Yoder outlined nineteen different versions of religious pacifism, alluding to Gandhi in many of them. At the end of the book he indicated that Gandhian satyagraha could be considered under the pacifism of programmatic political alternatives, the pacifism of nonviolent social change, the pacifism of the virtuous minority, or the pacifism of redemptive suffering. He indicated an enhanced appreciation for Gandhi when he wrote:

> The willing acceptance of suffering is a part of the Gandhian method and of the Anabaptist and Mennonite nonresistant traditions, yet for them the suffering is conceived as instrumental. It is the price of nonviolent resistance or a way to touch the heart...In the Gandhian movement this concern for winning over the adversary is very closely linked with a concern for the discipline of one's self.[63]

He then admitted, with respect, that "Gandhi's strategy fits none of our molds."[64] Yoder also wrote:

> Gandhi and King demonstrated the power of truth made effective through active noncooperation with evil. It is costly, though hardly more costly than war. To recognize the sacredness of the adversary's life and dignity, to refuse to meet him on his own terms, is at once a moral victory and the beginning of a tactical advantage— but you will only do it if you believe.[65]

Gradually, Yoder's nonresistance began to morph into a much more positive and aggressive mode. He began to actively advocate, as did Gandhi before him, nonviolent civilian defense as an alternative to war. In a book written ten years after *The Politics of Jesus*, Yoder rejected the Niebuhrian dichotomy between pure Christian love and action for justice, refusing to concede that this ethic of "obedience" sacrifices "effectiveness." It does reject some ways of deriving ethics from effectiveness calculation, but it represents a commitment to and not against "long and broad usefulness."[66]

That is a long way from his words in *The Original Revolution*: "The ethic of discipleship is not guided by the goals it seeks to reach, but by the Lord it seeks to reflect. It is no more interested in 'success' or in 'effectiveness' than He."[67]

This idea of "long and broad usefulness" begins to be expressed by him in a mode that is quite similar to Gandhi's idea that ahimsa is really the underlying law of the universe. Yoder's expression is: "Nonviolence goes with the grain of the universe." Effectiveness in the long run is not at all counter to that which goes with the grain of the universe.

Toward the end of his magnum opus on the history of Christianity and war, violence and revolution, Yoder says that being willing to die is not necessarily a sacrifice of effectiveness and he indicates that the examples of William Penn, Gandhi, and King "are examples of political involvement which can at least be interpreted as extensions of the New

Testament baseline in a situation that gives you more room."[68] Instead of rejecting the concept of effectiveness out of hand, he comes much closer to Gandhi, who at the end of his life did not consider himself to have been successful but nonetheless never lost faith in the potential for success; at the same time, under the tutelage of the *Bhagavad Gita*, he sought to focus on good means and to not be attached to the ends. Yoder expressed it in a similar fashion: "among the many ways to be effective is to not care about effectiveness."[69]

Yoder seems surprised and heartened by the attitude of James Douglass, a Catholic inspired by Gandhi. In his book, *The Nonviolent Cross*, Douglass expresses his refusal to choose between effectiveness and faithfulness. Yoder summarizes his thought:

> Douglass affirms a clear unity between the nature of God and the course of events. If the truth is revealed and someone is willing to love it, suffer with it, it will prevail, not only in some distant eternity or some other world but on the surface of the course of events... Douglass leans on Gandhi and expects effectiveness.[70]

Joel Zimbelman confirms that Yoder in his later works often employs the term "nonviolent resistance" rather than "nonresistance" to specify the fundamental imperative of the Christian community.[71] Yoder's student Glen Stassen follows the arc of Yoder's thought and suggests another term, one that comes even closer to Gandhi's full, positive term satyagraha. He suggests "transforming initiatives."[72] This understanding of Jesus' way is consistent with but different from much of the Mennonite tradition, which often despaired of a Christian's involvement in the world. Yoder's reading of the New Testament convinced him that Jesus' way of suffering love was not *Against the Nations*, the title of Stanley Hauerwas's book with which he took exception. Yoder's last published work was instead entitled: For *the Nations: Essays Public and Evangelical* (emphasis mine). He believed, with Gandhi, that the way of nonviolence led a believer into the middle of the public square with good news for the world rather than into rejection or withdrawal. A spirit similar to Gandhi's is found in the following words:

> When Paul wrote that the word of the cross is weak to those who look for signs, but God's saving power to those who believe, he was promoting not otherworldly mysticism but the kind of political reality which brought down Bull Connor in 1963, Ferdinand Marcos in 1986 and Erich Honecker in 1989... That suffering is powerful, and that weakness wins, is true not only in heaven but on earth.[73]

BERNARD HÄRING: *PERITUS* OF PEACE

Bernard Häring (1912–1998), a Redemptorist Catholic priest, was recognized during his lifetime as the leading Catholic moral theologian of the twentieth century. He was the eleventh of twelve children in a relatively successful farm family in Germany. He remembered his mother as a paragon of nonviolence and his father as a man of courage. In his memoir, *My Witness for the Church*, Häring recounted that when Hitler came to power in 1933 he distributed free radios to every family. His father said, "As long as this criminal screams on the radio, there will be no radio in my house."[74]

Shortly after joining the Redemptorist community, he was drafted by the Wehrmacht and served throughout the war as a medic chaplain. He faced a military court four different times, twice with a possible death sentence. One of those cases was due to his offering Mass for Polish peasants. He led a group of unarmed and wounded soldiers to safety out of the circle of the Battle of Stalingrad. He was rescued by Polish peasants from a Russian prisoner of war camp and served for a time as their pastor. He later wrote that from the war experience "emerged...the vocation to work for the cause of peace and the healing power of nonviolence...all should enroll themselves among the apostles for the healing power of nonviolence as the way to peace."[75]

The experience of the war made Häring a committed pacifist and more—one who was committed to waging peace. He felt embarrassed to be spending his considerable intellectual powers on questions that, in comparison to the issues of war and peace, were hardly of first rank importance, saying:

> I find it absolutely laughable and at the same time frustrating that at my age I still have to pour out so much of my energy on questions like flexibility and inflexibility concerning the forbidding of contraception and in the struggle against sexual rigorism. I am most deeply convinced that my main calling is and must be that of an untiring peace apostle for the elimination of war, for a world culture that is free from violence, for a radical love that will not allow us to become enemies, for a "transformation of armament" to a nonviolent defense.[76]

After the war Häring was selected by his superior to train in moral theology at the University of Tübingen. Häring had been expecting to be sent to Brazil after ordination. Recalling this moment, he wrote:

> I told my superior that this was my very last choice because I found the teaching of moral theology an absolute crashing bore.

He mollified me with the answer: "we are asking you to prepare yourself for this task with a doctorate from a German university precisely so that it can be different in the future."[77]

Moral theology after the Council of Trent had as its purpose the training of priests to fulfill their roles in the confessional, emphasizing the lines between right and wrong in all kinds of settings, giving priests tools to be pastorally responsive and accurate judges of guilt. The manuals of moral theology focused therefore on the minimum requirements for salvation. The Tübingen school, on the other hand, which included such luminaries as Karl Adam and Romano Guardini, taught that moral theology should focus not just on sin, law, and penance but on the call of God in grace and the response to that call by Christians. It should focus on the fullness of the life to be lived by the Christian in the world and be based on a strong biblical foundation. That vision is what Häring brought to the writing of his famous three-volume work, *The Law of Christ* (1953). About Häring's contribution Charles Curran wrote:

> A more biblically oriented approach to the whole of moral theology first appeared in the Tübingen school in Germany and is best exemplified in the manual of Bernard Häring which despite its transitional character stands as the greatest contribution to the renewal of moral theology since the sixteenth century.[78]

Häring was invited to the Second Vatican Council as a *peritus*, a learned, respected expert. As the council unfolded he was asked to give presentations on many subjects to national episcopal groups. He was especially concerned about the document *The Church in the Modern World*. His interventions helped the fathers adopt the "signs of the times" approach found in the document. He was especially proud of the contribution he made to the text on peace. Häring later wrote, "I did everything humanly possible to bring about a strong statement on the right of conscientious objectors and a recommendation of nonviolent defense."[79]

Häring's approach to moral theology departed from the Scholastic categories of the manualist tradition in favor of a biblical ethic centered on the New Testament teaching on the Kingdom of God. That teaching emphasized God's breaking into the here and now of human history with a summons to Christ's followers to construct, through faithful discipleship, the Kingdom in this world, while braving the sin of the world. When the central call of Christ is understood to be not just protecting oneself from sin but building the Kingdom of God in the midst of a sinful world, then the horizons expand to the fullness of a life in Christ. Häring therefore opened moral theology to dogmatic, spiritual, and liturgical theology—each of which contributes to the understanding of that fullness.

Beginning as he did with the biblical teaching of the Kingdom of God in history, Häring insisted on the need to focus on what God was doing through human beings in the present, the signs of the times. Häring's method was to put the teaching of scripture into dialogue with the signs of the times in order to illumine the proper direction of the Christian's path. As Kathleen Cahalan notes:

> Häring does not look to the Bible initially for norms and principles to define moral and immoral behavior. Rather, he searches Scripture for the broad themes, patterns, and images which shape the divine-human relationship. He then looks for the norms and principles in the Decalogue and Sermon on the Mount, which he considers to be guides and signposts for persons in their response to the divine call.[80]

There was no more important sign of the time for Häring than the violence epidemic—the arms race, the nuclear stalemate, the spread of nuclear weapons, ever increasing terrorism, kidnapping for ransom, the taking of hostages whose only crime is their nationality, and the ideology behind it all, namely, an all-pervasive belief in the efficacy of violence. He remembered what his professor, Romano Guardini, had said years before, that

> the decisive question of the forthcoming era would be the question of power: will humanity be able to control it enough to guarantee its rational use for justice; or will the era be one of prepotent power, of man controlled by irrational power?[81]

Häring understood the role of and the need for power for a Christian living in this world. The issue of violence is for Häring, as it was for Niebuhr and Yoder, the central issue of moral theology—because it is, given what humanity has developed in terms of lethal force, a matter of life and death for the whole world. Häring wrote:

> ...especially in view of the signs of the present time, when the alternative of non-violent conflict-solving becomes a question of "to be or not to be" for humankind... Especially in the view of the eruptive signs of the times, the fundamental option of faith in Jesus Christ requires faith in redemption from violence.[82]

Häring agreed with Rene Girard that humankind has to face up not only to the threat of ultimate violence but also to the scapegoating myths behind that threat. In the past, individuals were selected for ritual scapegoating and murder. Now it is whole peoples that are selected for sacrifice—

as at Auschwitz. With the system of mutually assured destruction (or MAD), whole nations and even the whole of humankind become scapegoats and hostages. Häring quotes Girard, who says that, according to these ideologies,

> entrance into paradise depends on a previous extinction or violent conversion of categories of people to whom fault is attributed.[83]

Häring joins with Girard in signaling that humankind is at a crossroad and that a final and irrevocable rejection of violence imposes itself as an inexorable necessity. This is the sign of the times that Häring brings to the reading of sacred scripture.

Häring's reading of scripture is therefore especially alert to what gives direction to humanity dealing with violence, domination, and oppression. He finds, following the scripture scholars Norbert Lohfink, Rudolf Schnackenburg, Rudolf Pesch, and Heinrich Spaemann, that nonviolence is at the heart of the gospel. In fact, according to them the whole of revelation gradually led up to the example and teaching of the nonviolent Jesus. While they admit that there are projections of human vindictiveness into the image of God in the Old Testament, according to these scholars the gradual unfolding of the Old Testament teaches that Yahweh does not need violence to establish his Kingdom. Development of that understanding culminates in the nonviolence of the Suffering Servant in Isaiah.

Häring's *The Healing Power of Peace and Nonviolence* makes it clear that the testimony of these scripture scholars is important to him. Even more important, however, for Häring's appreciation of Jesus' teaching on nonviolence is his appropriation of the teaching and example of Mohandas Gandhi. In fact, in all of Häring's writings he evidences not only a profound appreciation for but also a profound understanding of Gandhi. Gandhi's life and thought shed new light on Häring's understanding of the New Testament.

Häring turned to Gandhi for inspiration during periods of personal pain and suffering—such as what he endured from officials of the Holy Office who conducted an inquiry into his writings on sexuality and medical ethics, an enquiry that dragged on for years and hurt him deeply. Häring decided to go public with what was happening. He confronted the injustice done to him in the mode of satyagraha; he believed satyagraha was the way the whole church should approach its reform. He wrote:

> My intensive concern with the nonviolence of Gandhi...leads me to the conclusion that at this point we are in need of *satyagraha*, the powerful and liberating truth expressed with love. From long service as a medic I know that one must open wounds before healing can begin.

In the spirit of Gandhi's practiced transparency, and also his *Ahimsa*, his intimate sympathy, I wish in the following discussion to lay my hands on the wounds which need healing on the institutional level, knowing full well that all of us in the best of cases are no more than wounded healers.[84]

In *To Do Justice*, when he was attempting to communicate what the peace mission of a Christian is, he felt compelled to use the term "satyagraha" and invoke the example of Gandhi:

Mahatma Gandhi and Martin Luther King risked their lives, and ultimately sacrificed them, for *satyagraha*, a system of nonviolence which emphasizes the power of truth, love, justice, and solidarity in the service of the downtrodden. Gandhi, though not formally a Christian, was a fervent disciple of Christ; he was convinced that this method embodies the central message of the Sermon on the Mount and the life and death of Christ...

The only way we can break out of the vicious circle of the armaments race is for all of us to take on the attitude of and apply the skill of *satyagraha*...

In today's world, this method of nonviolence is perhaps the best way we can give witness to our faith in Christ, the Prince of Peace.[85]

Later in his life Häring helped a number of religious orders, both of men and of women, set up houses of prayer with the purpose of integrating faith, the struggle for justice, and the spiritual life. He admitted that Gandhi's example and Gandhi's ashrams served as the model and inspiration for his work, saying:

For me...there was always added the example of the *ashram* which Mahatma Gandhi set up in the perspective of a spirituality of non-violence and a non-violent liberation. I visited the first *ashram* founded by Gandhi in South Africa where I met a part of the Gandhi family. In the center of the "house of prayer," as I see it, is the Gospel of peace.[86]

With that as a background, the following recapitulation of Häring's teaching on the nonviolence of Jesus will show just how much Häring depends on Gandhi's witness to illuminate the teaching. Consistently, when he quotes a Christian scripture scholar, he follows up with a quote from Gandhi to buttress his interpretation.

First, according to Häring, the power of the nonviolence of Jesus rests on the fact that it is rooted in truth. Truth has a liberating and saving power as it unmasks the lies embedded in violence. The devil is the father of lies. Nonviolence requires an ongoing search for the truth and a constant process of realizing one's own entanglement in violence and need for grace. Häring invokes Gandhi to illuminate the point about truth:

> Gandhi concentrates on two key concepts of his message and his experience: satyagraha and ahimsa. Satyagraha means the strength of trust in the might of truth, done in love ... A Satyagrahi is a man or woman who is committed to the cause of truth and love, justice and peace, and determined to use only the means of nonviolent love and truthfulness in all situations.[87]

The second characteristic of the nonviolence of Jesus is that no individual is ever beyond the pale, lost, or a case to be written off. Referencing Heinrich Spaemann's comments on Romans 12:17–20 ("Never pay back evil for evil ... If your enemy is hungry, feed him; if he is thirsty, give him a drink; by doing this you will heap live coals on his head. Do not let evil conquer you, but use good to defeat evil") and 1 Peter 3:9 ("Do not repay wrong with wrong, or abuse with abuse; on the contrary retaliate with a blessing, for a blessing is the inheritance to which you yourselves have been called"), Häring writes:

> Nonviolence, which has its ground and roots in God, trusts that in the other too, there is the germ of life which responds to the living God, the Nonviolent, just as the germ grain reacts to the light of the sun.[88]

He then invokes the example and words of Gandhi to confirm the point:

> We hope one day the whole pastoral ministry, fully dedicated to the gospel of peace and nonviolence, will be marked by the faith and confidence of Gandhi: "It is an article of faith that no man has fallen so low that he cannot be redeemed by love."[89]

Third, for Häring, Christian nonviolence attempts to build the Kingdom of God on earth, not by ignoring or fleeing evil and oppression but by taking responsibility for the earth and wading into the struggle against violence. He calls on the witness not only of Gandhi but also of Martin Luther King to demonstrate what that entails:

> Gandhi and Martin Luther King and other pioneers of nonviolent liberation have understood well the Gospel's interpretation of love

of enemies (as well as friends) as the mightiest attack on oppression, lies and injustice. "Nonviolence means neither negligent tolerance nor intolerant enforcement." This offensive by peaceful healers uses all the "weapons" of peace offered by Jesus Christ, including the willingness to suffer rather than inflicting suffering on others.[90]

A fourth point that Häring makes about Jesus' nonviolence is that, far from being passive, it calls for bravery and creativity. Häring refers to Gandhi's recommendations on how to oppose Hitler's hangman and then goes on to say in the same spirit:

Had Christians been raised in a spirit of nonviolent resistance and creative liberty, less drastic means may have served to prevent the holocaust. For instance, on the day on which Hitler ordered Jews to wear on their clothes the distinctive sign of the "Star of David," all believers, all dedicated Christians should have worn the same sign.[91]

Finally, for Häring, Jesus' example and teaching on nonviolence are normative for Christians, not something to consider, not a counsel for those who are called to a life of perfection, but central to discipleship for all who call themselves Christians. "There is no ambiguity in Jesus' teaching. His disciples are those who love their enemies."[92]

Häring recognized, with Roland Bainton and others, that the early church was pacifist until the time of Constantine. For Häring, however, normativity is not to be understood as a burden or in a restrictive sense. Satyagraha is for those who are seized by the love, freedom, and power for action that the gospel brings to those who believe in Jesus' way. It is not a norm that hems us in but one that breaks us out of the vicious circle of violence. It is the way forward. Häring explains:

The seven-time repeated "But I say to you" of the Sermon on the Mount is an expression of the messianic ordering of peace. It expresses the messianic consummation of the "law" and in this sense it possesses a normative value ... The Christian who believes that the Kingdom of God is near proceeds in the direction of the sevenfold "But I say to you." The path is obligatory and clearly marked ... we are here concerned with a directive leading us to a goal, and not merely with a restriction.[93]

Häring understood how strong is the inclination to justify and believe in the efficacy of violence. Nonetheless, with Girard, he found it "mysterious" that "faced with the absolute clarity of the gospels, the 'things hidden since the foundation of the world' and revealed in Jesus Christ could remain still hidden and denied by much of Christianity up to our time."[94]

As Häring reflected on the signs of the times," particularly on the threat from nuclear war to humankind and the whole ecological system, the loss of a sense of civilian immunity from harm during war, and the lack of proportion in modern wars between violence done and outcome secured, he saw little room for the traditional teaching on the just war. He wrote:

> Everyone who has not lost his right mind should agree with Cardinal Roy that "war no longer seems only a crime but an absurdity as well." After all the experiences through which history teaches us, and in view of the deadly arsenal of weapons that can destroy humankind and the whole ecological system, it should be clear, that even on its own reasoning, the traditional "just war" theory can no longer be applied.[95]

Häring understood that the real value of the just war teaching had always been to limit wars; it had been of little use in keeping leaders from entering into wars. He was pleased, therefore, with the progress the official Catholic Church had made just in his lifetime to move toward an authentic vision of peacemaking. He recalled that only forty years ago the only discussion of peace in the handbooks of moral theology was a chapter with the title "Concerning the State's Right to War." The Vatican Council's declaration that "any act of war aimed at the indiscriminate destruction of population centers is a crime against God and humanity" heartened him; but he knew that logically that such a stance had to be broadened to include not just the act but the intention to use weapons of mass destruction and, by extension, the building and possession of them.

Häring knew that the threat of violence of one country against another remained real. That is why he advocated, in season and out of season, nonviolent civilian defense as an alternative to war. His reasoning for nonviolent civil defense is similar to what we saw Gandhi's to be. He recalled the example of the resistance of the people of Czechoslovakia against the Soviet invasion of 1968 as a testimony to the possibility of nonviolent resistance by an entire people or nation. He was encouraged by the fact that several influential bishops' conferences, and especially the U.S. bishops, had called for serious consideration of the alternative of civilian defense.

Häring outlined how nonviolent civilian defense would work:

> As a first step, war-minded superpowers might only be able to understand this model as a different mode of "deterrence" where-

by (1) in the case of taking advantage and trying to submit the "disarmed" nation, they have to fear that their own population, including many soldiers, will refuse to participate or co-operate in an invasion; (2) in any case, they would draw no advantage of invasion and occupation, since civilian resistance by non-cooperation would frustrate all their purposes; (3) their ideologies and political ambitions would be unmasked in the face of the whole world.[96]

Consistent with the entire corpus of his work as a moral theologian, Häring was more interested in pointing out the way to the fullness of life in Christ than in pointing to where the line between right and wrong lay. That is why he felt that the great task and challenge for the church was to return to the New Testament message of nonviolence and rally Christians to their positive task of confronting violence, domination, and oppression nonviolently in their roles as peacemakers. Häring was not about simply rejecting war; he was about waging peace. He recognized a great opportunity for the Catholic Church to be a credible, valuable resource to humanity—to embrace being a true peace church.

In a very interesting contretemps with Charles Curran, Häring's true hope for the church became clear. Curran had said in response to the U.S. Catholic Bishops' 1983 Pastoral Letter on Peace and War, that "the whole Church cannot be pacifist in our present circumstances," and that the bishops justify nonviolence as a choice only for some individuals. In response Häring wondered if Curran had missed the point entirely, that European peace researchers were giving much praise to the document because it appealed to all to give proper attention to nonviolent defense as a moral alternative to war. Häring wrote:

I would like to invite those who think like Curran to remember the history of slavery, when theologians and Churchmen held the opinion that "some individuals" might well set free their slaves but that the whole Church could not reject the institution of slavery.[97]

Häring counseled tolerance for those who consider nonviolent civilian defense a utopian "impossible possibility" and understanding for politicians who might not feel enough democratic support for such a stance, but he went on to state his real vision and hope for the church:

But my conviction is that "the whole Church" should firmly and intelligently promote the cause of nonviolence, including the option for nonviolent defense. For this we must make it clear that we do not speak about a passive pacifism but rather of a most committed option for peace and justice, with all their "spiritual armor." Such an option should not be compared with a special religious vocation for some individuals. At this crossroad of human history the whole of humankind should become "pacifist" and ban any option for war.[98]

We have seen that Häring enriched moral theology by infusing it with biblical scholarship and the insights of spiritual and systematic theology. The process goes the other way as well. As Häring charted out the centrality to the gospel of Jesus' nonviolence, it became clear to him that some long-held tenets of *systematic* theology had to change as well. In particular, he called for rethinking the way "salvation" had been taught and for reformulating the understanding of Jesus' death on the cross and the meaning of human suffering.

The teaching of the Sermon on the Mount, and Jesus' own example, according to Häring, make clear the priority of loving one's enemies and taking the initiative to reach an opponent through the power of love. The gospel does not give priority to righting wrongs by punishing the evildoers and goes way beyond the tit for tat of retributive justice. That is why Häring had no time for theories of redemptive sacrifice that ignored Jesus' nonviolence and instead based their concept of redemption on a theory of vindictive justice.

> Think for instance, of the theories on the redemptive sacrifice of Christ which pay no attention to Jesus' nonviolence in fulfillment of his redemptive mission and at the same time emphasize vindictive justice as foundation of theories on New Testament sacrifice. Especially in view of the signs of the times, this was and is a dangerous narrowing of the Testament.[99]

Häring says man-made religions project their own violence onto their image of God. That is not the picture in the New Testament. Jesus reveals, through his nonviolent love, the true image of God, not a God of vengeance but one who treats all with mercy, who sends the rain and the sun on the just and unjust alike. For Häring, atonement theories that portray Jesus' death as a vicarious punishment for sin miss the dynamic portrayed in the New Testament, the savior who withstands human violence without turning to the same methods as his persecutors:

> [Jesus] dies as revealer of the liberating and healing truth, and bears the full burden of humankind. By his very nonviolence he fully restores the honor of the Father, revealing the Father's true image. He dies for those who crucify him, for all of us sinners. And by his healing love he breaks up the circle of enmity, violence and

vindictiveness, and shows us the way to a healing peace in justice...It is not possible to speak of Christ's sacrifice while ignoring the role of nonviolence.[100]

Consistent with this approach to salvation, Häring also called for a revised understanding of why Jesus died. For Häring, Jesus did not die because the Father willed it. He died because human beings in their political blindness killed him. Jesus lived out his nonviolent outreach to the end, even to forgiveness from the cross:

> The Father's honor has surely not required his Son's cruel suffering, as such, to be offered for any reason of vindictive justice. He is in no way accountable for the wickedness suffered by his Son. Cruelty is not wanted by the Father or the Son. The responsibility is ours, each time we sin, especially if we sin by any kind of violence against any one of Christ's brothers and sisters.[101]

Finally, in this view of salvation, suffering is not a value in and of itself. Jesus suffered because he was being faithful to his vision of the Truth even as it collided with the powers of the time. For Häring, only suffering that comes with the effort to break through the cycles of violence and oppression is redemptive. As Häring wrote, "Suffering is not to be sought for itself but has to be taken up in the troublesome process of breaking the vicious circle of enmity and violence."[102]

Häring is saying, in effect, that the way people view violence seems to determine how they will construe the message and work of Christ. If violence is permissible, if war is permissible, and if retributive justice is the goal—then there arise theories of penal substitution and the nonviolent Jesus disappears. If, on the other hand the spirit of satyagraha is embraced, the gospel of Jesus transparently means the way of nonviolence. The moral decision determines the systematic theology and vice versa. Häring concludes that

> [o]nly a theology which justifies wars and is alienated from the Gospel of peace could misinterpret the redemption as a sacrificial work to assuage a God filled with revengeful righteousness.[103]

WALTER WINK: JESUS' THIRD WAY

Walter Wink (1935–) is a professor of biblical interpretation at Auburn Theological Seminary in New York City. Wink is especially well known and respected for his trilogy of books that explore the ways "power" is addressed and described in the New Testament and what Jesus taught concerning power in confrontation with domination and violence: *Naming the Powers, Unmasking the Powers,* and *Engaging the Powers.* The books bring back into the center of theological discussion the mysterious and all-pervasive language in the New Testament, ignored and overlooked for centuries, about the "principalities and powers." Wink has gradually, through his life experience and study of the New Testament, embraced nonviolence as central to Jesus' life and teaching.

Wink's life experience has taken him all around the world. A critical turning point in his life was in 1982, when he spent a sabbatical semester in Chile to learn what it was like to live under a military dictatorship. He and his wife spent weeks living in *favelas* and barrios, meeting with priests and nuns who were struggling for human rights and political freedom, meeting with people who had been tortured and those representing families who had "disappeared," appreciating with increasing clarity how, as in his words:

> unjust systems perpetuate themselves by means of institutionalized violence... Against such monolithic Powers it was and is tempting to use violence in response. But we have repeatedly seen how those who fight domination with violence become as evil as those whom they oppose. How then can we overcome evil without doing evil—and becoming evil ourselves? I found myself reluctantly pushed, simply by the logic of the inquiry, to a position of consistent nonviolence.[104]

The myth at the heart of the domination system can be so well promulgated, and the very people whose lives are oppressed by the system can be so thoroughly socialized to believe the myth, that they will be the very ones to sacrifice their lives in its defense. The only way for people to be freed from the domination system and the myth that animates it is to be caught up in a lived, countervailing, and transcending vision and practice. That, for Wink is precisely what the gospel and the "Kingdom of God" or "reign of God" are designed to be, a remedy for the evils of the domination system, the "most powerful antidote for domination the world has ever seen."[105] Wink writes:

> The gospel is not a message of personal salvation *from* the world, but a message of a world transfigured, right down to its basic structures. Redemption means actually being liberated from the oppression of the Powers, being forgiven for one's own sin and for complicity with the Powers, and being engaged in liberating the Powers themselves from their bondage to idolatry.[106]

Wink renames Jesus' "kingdom of heaven"; he calls it God's "domination-free order" to express how directly the gospel is designed to be an answer to the "powers that be."

The final prop of the domination system that Jesus' reign of God is designed to overcome is the threat and use of force to discourage any whiff of dissent and to keep the entire system in place. The spirituality of the domination system is the belief in the redemptive power of violence. It is the "religion" of the domination system, the fundamental belief. If God is what you turn to when you are really up against it and all else fails, then violence is God—that to which one turns for deliverance. When threatened, only might will really do. The domination-free order that Jesus preached and practiced did not ignore the reality of violence. Instead, Jesus proposed an entirely new way of dealing with violence. As we already have seen in the work of John Howard Yoder, Jesus was confronted historically with the basic options of fight or flight: withdrawal, in the mode of the Essenes and Pharisees, or armed resistance, in the mode of the Sicarii and Zealots. Instead, Jesus proposed what Wink calls the "Third Way."

Jesus' Third Way: Nonviolent Engagement

The classic text is Matthew 5:38–42:

> You have heard that it was said, "An eye for an eye and a tooth for a tooth." But I say to you, Do not resist an evildoer. But if anyone strikes you on the right cheek, turn the other also; and if anyone wants to sue you and take your coat, give your cloak as well; and if anyone forces you to go one mile, go also the second mile. Give to everyone who begs from you, and do not refuse anyone who wants to borrow from you.

As we saw in our discussion of John Howard Yoder, Christians through the centuries have found numerous ways to discount this text. It has been ignored; it has been dismissed as an impossible ideal, an interim ethic, or something to be practiced only by those who have professed vows and have no responsibilities for others;[107] and it has been interpreted as nonresistance.[108]

Wink builds on the work of other scholars[109] and offers the following exegesis. He first asks "why the *right* cheek"? His answer is that the blow is not from a right-hand fist; that would strike on the left cheek of the one struck. It is instead a backhanded slap with the right hand, a blow that is meant to be an insult, the usual way of admonishing inferiors. Masters backhanded slaves; husbands, wives; parents, children; Romans, Jews. The expected response was cowering submission. As Wink notes:

> To hit the right cheek with a fist would require using the left hand, but in that society the left hand was used only for unclean tasks. Even to gesture with the left hand at Qumran carried the penalty of ten days' penance. The only way one could naturally strike the right cheek with the right hand would be with the back of the hand. We are dealing here with insult, not a fistfight. The intention is clearly not to injure but to humiliate, to put someone in their place.[110]

The counsel of Jesus to the humiliated person in this situation is not to submit meekly to the insult; it is instead to turn the other cheek, to show that you are not humiliated. Take the initiative, in other words, and communicate the fact that you are not cowed. You are not retaliating either, but standing up as a free, worthwhile person who will not go along with the intended intimidation:

> The superior has been given notice that this underling is in fact a human being. In that world of honor and shaming, he has been rendered impotent to instill shame in a subordinate. He has been stripped of his power to dehumanize the other. As Gandhi taught, "The first principle of nonviolent action is that of noncooperation with everything humiliating."[111]

The second example in the series—"and if anyone wants to sue you and take your coat, give your cloak as well"—is set in a court of law. Jesus' stories are filled with examples of debts and debtors because they were so prevalent in first-century Palestine. Rome taxed heavily to fund its wars. Herod was pressing landowners for taxes for his lavish building projects. The landowners in turn pressured their tenants. Exorbitant interest rates drove landowners deeper into debt and to loss of their lands. Stripped of their land, their goods, and finally even their outer garments, what should they do? Give over their undergarments as well. March out of court stark naked. Wink points out that

> [n]akedness was taboo in Judaism, and shame fell less on the naked party than on the person viewing or causing the nakedness. By stripping the debtor has brought shame on the creditor...The entire system by which debtors are oppressed has been publicly unmasked. The creditor is revealed to be not a legitimate money-lender but a party to the reduction of an entire social class to land-

lessness and destitution. This unmasking is not simply punitive, since it offers the creditor a chance to see, perhaps for the first time in his life, what his practices cause, and to repent.[112]

This is another instance and example of how one who is oppressed can turn the tables on the oppressor without violence. Wink cites a modern example of the same kind of dynamic: a group of women in a squatters' camp in South Africa, whose shacks are about to be demolished by police bulldozers, sensing the puritanical streak in rural Afrikaners, stripped naked before the bulldozers, causing the police to flee. The context of the third example in the series[113]—"and if anyone forces you to go one mile, go also a second mile"—is the practice of impressed labor by the occupying Roman army and with the relatively enlightened practice of limiting the amount of forced labor to a single mile. The soldiers' packs weighed sixty to seventy pounds. Impressment caused much resentment in occupied territories, so to minimize the resentment Rome limited the distance; for a soldier to impress someone any more than a mile was an infraction of the military code and could incur punishment of the soldier by the centurion. This counsel is, therefore, another example of the way an oppressed person could regain the initiative and assert his human dignity. Wink writes:

> From a situation of servile impressments, the oppressed have once more seized the initiative... They have thrown the soldier off balance by depriving him of the predictability of his victim's response ... Imagine a Roman infantryman pleading with a Jew to give back his pack. The humor of this scene may have escaped us, but it could scarcely have been lost on Jesus' hearers... To those whose lifelong pattern has been to cringe before their masters, Jesus offers a way to liberate themselves from servile actions and a servile mentality...Jesus' teaching on nonviolence is thus integral to his proclamation of the dawning of the reign of God. Here was indeed a way to resist the Powers That Be without being made over into their likeness.[114]

The other key passage that Wink uses to make clear what this "Third Way" is all about is "loving your enemies." Why? Because God does so, and we are to be like him. God makes "the sun rise on the evil and the good, and sends rain on the righteous and on the unrighteous" (Matt 5:45). Jesus did not wait for people to repent. In him everything is reversed. As Wink notes:

> Jesus lived this new creation out in his table fellowship with those whom the religious establishment had branded outcasts, sinners,

renegades: the enemies of God. He did not wait for them to repent, become respectable, and do works of restitution . . . Instead he audaciously bursts upon these sinners with the declaration that their sins have been forgiven, prior to their repentance . . . You are forgiven; now you can repent.[115]

"Be perfect, therefore, as your heavenly Father is perfect" (Matt 5:48). For Wink, this does not mean some never-reachable ideal of perfectionism; it means "be all-inclusive in your love as the heavenly parent is all-inclusive." The enemy is a gift to us, forcing us to recognize the log in our own eyes. We see in ourselves the mix of just and unjust. Wink writes:

And if God is compassionate toward us, with all our unredeemed evil, then God must treat our enemies the same way. As we begin to acknowledge our own inner shadow, we become tolerant of the shadow in others. As we begin to love the enemy within, we develop the compassion to love the enemy without.[116]

Love of enemy is perhaps the most distinctive message Christianity offers to humankind, reversing centuries of tit-for-tat notions of retributive justice. Jesus' "forgive them for they know not what they do" invites human beings to a largeness of heart that never gives up on the possibilities of others and to a bold, creative style of outreach, of attempts at understanding and meeting. According to Wink:

Loving our enemies has become, in our time, the criterion of Christian faith. It may seem impossible; yet it can be done. At no point is inrush of divine grace so immediately and concretely perceptible as in those moments when we let go our hatred and relax into God's love. No miracle is so awesome, so necessary, and so frequent.[117]

As real-life examples—such as Gorbachev's inaugurating radical new directions in the Soviet Union or de Klerk's quietly directing the dismantling of apartheid—confirm, people can and do change. Nonviolent direct action, as exemplified in the life of Jesus, is the way to synchronize the divine source of renewal within us and in our "enemy." Wink begins his chapter on "love of enemies" with the following:

In the spiritual renaissance that I believe is coming to birth, it will not be the message of Paul that this time galvanizes heart, as in the Reformation and the Wesleyan revival, but the human figure of Jesus. And in the teaching of Jesus, the sayings on nonviolence and love of enemies will hold a central place...I submit that the ulti-mate religious question today should no longer be the Reformation's question, "How can I find a gracious God?" but rather, "How can we find God in our enemies?" What guilt was for Luther, the enemy has become for us: the goad that can drive us to God.[118]

Gandhi and Wink

In his work, Wink quotes Gandhi frequently. Wink came to his firm belief in nonviolence only gradually and somewhat reluctantly. It developed as described above, from a combination of life experience, particularly his experiences in South America and South Africa, and from his reading of the New Testament as it illuminated that experience. Gandhi was not, therefore, the sole or direct inspiration for Wink's understanding of Jesus' nonviolence. Gandhi's life and teaching, however, clarified for Wink some key aspects of nonviolence, demonstrating that the teaching of "love your enemies" and "turn the other cheek" are not impossible ideals but a feasi-ble, realistic way of confronting evil in this world. Moreover, Gandhi's life and teaching also clarified for Wink, as they did for Yoder, that the nonvi-olence of Jesus was not passive but creative, courageous, and assertive.

First, Gandhi demonstrated for Wink the obligation of opposing evil and the need to first name the powers:

Gandhi insisted that we must never accept evil, even if we cannot change it. Accepting evil, no matter how monolithic, inevitable, or entrenched, serves to deaden moral sensitivity...Calling evil by its name—naming as evil what others regard as custom (wife beating) or natural (homophobia) or even moral (executing political critics or religious heretics)—maintains the moral nerve even in circum-stances where change seems impossible.[119]

Gandhi helped Wink understand that nonviolence is the opposite of passivity in the face of evil, and that it takes more courage to be nonviolent than it takes to be violent. Nonviolence is fighting but with different meth-ods. As Wink notes:

Gandhi insisted that no one could join him who was not willing to take up arms for independence...One cannot pass directly from "Flight" to "Jesus' Third Way." One needs to pass through the "Fight" stage, if only to discover one's own inner strength and capacity for violence. One need not actually become violent, but one needs to own one's fury at injustice and care enough to be willing to fight and, if necessary, die for its eradication. Only then can such a person freely renounce violence and embrace active nonviolence.[120]

In fact, nonviolence is so assertive that not only will nonviolent persons fight when the fight comes to them, but they will often find themselves having to seek out the conflict. In Wink's words:

The "peace" that the Gospel brings is never the absence of conflict, but an ineffable reassurance at the heart of conflict, a peace that surpasses understanding. Christians have all too often called for "nonviolence" when they really meant tranquility. Nonviolence, in fact, seeks out conflict, elicits conflict, exacerbates conflict, in order to bring it out into the open and lance its poisonous sores.[121]

In conclusion, all four of these theologians reject a model of Christian salvation that leaves out the way Jesus lived and that makes his death not the doing of humans but the doing of a God of wrath and vengeance. In the next chapter we will review the multiple models developed through the centuries to express the meaning of what it means to be saved, giving special attention to the most commonly used model, Anselm's satisfaction theory.

CHAPTER FOUR

The Multiple Versions of Salvation Theologies

Throughout the history of Christianity the story of the first disciples' experience of Jesus' saving presence has been passed on in fresh, creative ways to new audiences with new questions and new life situations. The synoptic gospels themselves reflect distinct audiences with distinct concerns. The touchstone of the stories told and retold was, however, the historical Jesus.

In recent years many authors have been addressing the questions involved in "soteriology."[1] Soteriology is the technical theological term used for the "study of salvation." It derives from the Greek terms: *logos*, meaning study, knowledge or meaning and *soter*, which means savior. Soteriology attempts to understand the first disciples' experience of Jesus in a way that is relevant to our time and place and culture. It asks:

- What are we saved from?

- How are we saved?

- What does it mean that Jesus Christ has saved the world through the cross? Through his blood?

- For what are we saved?

Many of the ways those questions have been answered and expressed in the past have little meaning and resonance for people today. As Schillebeeckx put it, "Jesus is still regularly explained to us as salvation and grace in terms which are no longer valid for our world of experience."[2]

SALVATION, SOCIAL SIN, AND VIOLENCE

For the first time in history, humankind has the capability to destroy itself completely. Organized mass violence or war is still the assumed answer to conflicts between peoples, but it is organized savagery such as the world has never before seen. One nation after another is acquiring nuclear capability for its "defense." The danger increases that terrorists will use nuclear weapons against their enemies. The threat of total war continues to loom. Violence is our cultural heritage, supplies our icons, forms our mythology, and dictates the way we write history. Humankind might feel up to the task of feeding the hungry. There is after all enough food for all, and compassion still abides for the victim. Humankind might find ways to restore the health of the planet. But to confront, absorb, neutralize, and root out violence? That seems well beyond our reach.

In past centuries, the issue of violence was not front and center for theology. Salvation was typically discussed in terms of deliverance from personal sin, the personal evil within human beings. Augustine wrestled with his sinful self and struggled to withstand sexual temptation. Luther cried to God for deliverance from his wretched sense of personal guilt.

In our time the sense of social sin has become more acute. We recognize that it is not just personal sin but sinful structures that are the source of evil. Behind the "powers that be," legitimating them and protecting them, is the threat of violence against those who attempt to change them. It is not enough to change and redeem the social structures. Salvation has to reach, absorb, and redeem the violence that pervades those structures.

THE MULTIPLE MODELS OF SALVATION IN SACRED SCRIPTURE

The experience of salvation that Jesus' first disciples had was so rich and dynamic that they expressed it with multiple expressions, analogies, and symbols. Michael Slusser identifies five different primitive soteriological themes in the New Testament: victory over death, atonement, revelation, eschatological judgment, and exemplar.[3] Joseph Fitzmyer counts eight ways of expressing the meaning of Christ's saving event in Paul's writings alone: sanctification, justification, expiation, freedom, salvation, transformation, reconciliation, and new creation.[4] In his book, *Christ: The Experience of Jesus as Lord*, Schillebeeckx presents sixteen distinct expressions.

The distinct expressions come from just about every corner of human experience. In the words of Elizabeth Johnson:

> They spoke in financial categories of redemption or release from slavery through payment of a price; in legal categories of advocacy, justification, and satisfaction; in cultic categories of sacrifice, sin offering, and expiation; in political categories of liberation and victory over oppressive powers; in personal categories of reconciliation after dispute; in medical categories of being healed or made whole; in existential categories of freedom and new life; and in

familial categories of becoming God's children by birth (John) or adoption (Paul).[5]

Mark wrote his gospel at a time when the Jewish people were approaching a confrontation with Rome. The fledgling community of Christians was being challenged to declare one way or another: fight, flight, or accommodation. As a result, the Marcan gospel takes on a much more political tone, and salvation is described as discipleship following in the distinctive "way" that Jesus walked.

Matthew's gospel was written in the context of a Jewish community wrestling with the inherited weight of the law. Salvation is described as entering a new kingdom where the forces that are keeping human beings apart are overcome, where the poor and the sick and the outcast are welcomed, and where the law once again serves humanity and not the entrenched powers.

Luke's gospel was written as the church reached out to the gentiles. Salvation is described in terms that are congenial to a Hellenistic world: light and wisdom, service and freedom.

On through the rest of the New Testament, soteriology continued to adapt and morph depending on the life situations (*sitz im Leben*) of the distinctive audiences for whom each of the books was written. The witness to the saving presence of Jesus the Christ was understood to be a living witness and not bound to sacrosanct or rigid formulas. Such books as Colossians and Hebrews develop completely fresh articulations of the meaning of salvation. Colossians uses the language and philosophies current in Asia Minor at the time.[6] In the letter to the Hebrews, the author uses completely original *pesher* exegesis to communicate with his Jewish audience.[7] Through an extended exegesis of the passages involving Melchizedek and Abraham, the author shows that Melchizedek is a being higher than Abraham, without beginning and without end, and appears as both a king and a priest, a type for Jesus. Melchizedek is a priest of a transcendent order, much higher than the Jewish priesthood. Through Jesus, the Messiah, all humans have direct access to God at all times and not, as through the high priest, just once a year. As Jesus takes up God's cause in solidarity with humankind, so the apostolic experience of salvation from God in Jesus can be equally well expressed in *priestly* terms. According to Schillebeeckx:

> All this seems to be a fantastic exegesis of the Tanach, but this was not the case for the Jews of his time... Evidently he does not mean to say anything new. He seeks to articulate the apostolic faith in terms which for some reason are popular in the churches in which this homily will be delivered or read out.[8]

For Schillebeeckx, Hebrews is the most subtle book in the New Testament and is one of the best New Testament examples of presenting the one and same fundamental message about salvation in Jesus in totally new ways to meet the needs of a changing world.

> Hebrews is one of the best New Testament examples of the prob-
> lem presented by the relationship between experience and (theo-
> logical) interpretation...It leaves open the possibility that,
> inspired by what we have heard in the New Testament about inter-
> pretative experiences of Jesus Christ, we should again be able to
> experience the same Jesus differently within a new and different
> horizon of experience.[9]

The diversity of theologies of salvation and richness of metaphor in the New Testament era demonstrate the vitality of the early church's experience of God's saving action in Jesus. It also makes clear that no one metaphor or theology is absolute.

FOUR SOTERIOLOGIES AFTER THE NEW TESTAMENT

The work of interpreting anew the experience of salvation continued after the New Testament era. The early and later fathers of the church developed theologies of salvation to answer the concerns and needs of their own communities. The theologies of, for example, Irenaeus, Athanasius, Anselm, and Abelard, elaborated upon distinctive metaphors that continue to influence the present.

Irenaeus of Lyons (c. 135–c. 202) understood the whole of history to be a drama in three acts. Creation is the first act. The Word, through whom all was created, is knowable through creation, but humanity did not, for the most part, recognize the Word in creation. The second act is therefore the reign of sin and evil. In the third act, the Word becomes one with us as God always intended; we can now see and really know the Word. The incarnation is a "surge of new life and energy."[10] The preexistent Word becomes the second Adam and saves us first by assuming human reality, body and all, and thus, as Roger Haight writes:

> uniting this humanity to himself...[B]y living the whole course of
> human life from beginning to old age, he sanctifies every act of
> human existence...This sanctification is effected by complete
> obedience to the will of God.[11]

In this obedience, Jesus educates us and shows us how to live in a way that unites us now in a mystical union with God and prepares us for our deification, which will come about after death. The key word for this process, the new metaphor developed by Irenaeus, is *recapitulation*.

For we have shown that the Son of God did not begin to exist then since he always existed with the Father. But when he became incarnate and was made man, he recapitulated in himself the long line of the human race, procuring for us salvation summarily, so that what we had lost in Adam, that is, being in the image and likeness of God, we should regain in Jesus Christ.[12]

Irenaeus therefore stresses the goodness of creation and the human body in opposition to the Gnostic currents of his time and sees, in the process of sanctification, a continuous relationship between creation and grace—a vision that has been a lasting trait of the Eastern Church.[13] Like the other Greek fathers, he believed in the reality of the devil and maintained that he had to be conquered. Irenaeus speaks of a ransom paid to Satan, but it is not as central to his formulation as his understanding of Christ as the New Adam who recapitulates in himself all creation, renewing and bringing it to completion.

Athanasius (c. 295–373) continued in the Eastern tradition of Irenaeus, highlighting the action of the divine Word, but emphasized even more strongly that humans were *deified* as a result of the incarnation. As he wrote in *De Incarnatione* (54.3), "For he was made man that we might be made God."

In defending the faith against the Arians, he argued that the Logos must be God, since only God could re-create humanity. If the Logos is the Son by nature, humans can be sons and daughters by adoption. Humanity participates in the divine nature to such a degree that we are eventually freed from corruption and death. Denis Edwards notes that

[d]eification has remained an evocative way of understanding God's action in Jesus Christ among Orthodox Christians. It has also had a long history in the Catholic tradition, where it has been used by the great mystical writers to express the transforming action of God upon the human soul.[14]

These two representative Eastern thinkers' models of salvation, with their positive views in which humanity progresses from sanctification to divinization in the mutual embrace of the Word, contrast starkly with the Western models that emphasize, as in Augustine, humanity's sinfulness and the need for forgiveness.

Anselm of Canterbury (1033–1109) was among the most influential of those Western thinkers. He elaborated upon the biblical metaphor of "satisfaction" and made it the central leitmotiv of his theology of salvation. He developed his theory in *Cur Deus Homo*, "Why God Became Man" or more loosely but more completely translated, "Why God Had to Become Incarnate for Humanity to Be Saved."

For Anselm, the basic problem lies in the fact of original sin, which was an infinite offense against God. Humanity is in a deep pit and powerless to climb out of it.

> Thus man is inexcusable, for he voluntarily incurred that debt which he could not pay, and by his own fault lapsed into the inability, so that he could neither fulfill the obligation he had before— that is, to avoid sin—nor pay the debt he owes because he sinned. For his very inability is a fault he ought not have.[15]

That sin could be dealt with in only three ways: by forgiveness, by eternal punishment, or by satisfaction. Forgiveness is out of the question for Anselm, for two reasons. Such mercy would upset the order of the universe and it would be contrary to God's justice.

> And if he remits what he has to take away from man against his will, on account of man's inability to repay what he should voluntarily repay, then God is relaxing the penalty and making a man happy on account of his sin, because he would be possessing what he should not possess...But divine mercy of this sort is quite opposed to God's justice which allows for nothing but punishment to be the return for sin.[16]

The only alternative, therefore, to eternal punishment is satisfaction, which means not just making up for what is due but, over and above that, a "more" that repairs the injury, a work of "supererogation." But only God can offer an infinite satisfaction for an infinite offense.

> And if no one but God can make that satisfaction and no one but man is obliged to make it, then it is necessary that a God-man make it.[17]

> [I]t is necessary that one and the same person be perfect God and perfect man to make this satisfaction.[18]

This then is the answer to the question posed by the title of the book— why did God become human? To do what only a God-man could do: make satisfaction for humanity's sin. But why did he have to die? Because to give oneself up to death is the greatest possible gift a human can give, and it was necessary to give humanity the most powerful lesson possible.

> [M]an absolutely cannot give himself more fully to God than when he commits himself to death for God's honor.[19]...Do you not understand that when he bore with generous patience all inflicted

upon him...he gave us a far greater example to influence every person not to hesitate to give back to God.[20]

Later interpreters of Anselm simplified his soteriology so as to make it seem that the Father gave his Son up to die. Anselm's own words, however, reveal that he was more subtle than that.

> Anselm: God the Father did not treat that man in the way you seem to think, nor did he hand over the innocent to death in place of the guilty. For God did not compel him to die, or allow him to be slain, against his will; rather he himself, by his own free choice, underwent death to save men.[21]

When pressed further, Anselm does admit that in a way the Father willed the death of his Son:

> ...because he did not will the world to be saved except by a man performing some outstanding deed. Since no one else could perform such a deed, this was equivalent to the Father commanding the son to die, since the son willed the salvation of all men.[22]

The final step in Anselm's theological construct is in the transfer of the merit won by the Son to humanity. All human beings have to die because of sin. But if there were one sinless human, then he or she would not have to die, and if that person did die, that death would have the quality of being transferable. If, in addition, that person was infinite, his or her death could be a credit for many people or all of humanity.

> If the Son willed to give to another what is due Himself, could the Father legitimately prevent Him, or refuse it to the one to whom the Son transfers his right?[23]

That completes the idea: satisfaction is made by an innocent, infinite God-man, and the merit is transferred to humanity.

This carefully reasoned elaboration of a soteriology of satisfaction has been called the most successful work of theology in history. Elizabeth Johnson has written of it:

> I sometimes think that Anselm should be considered the most successful theologian of all time. Imagine having almost a thousand-year run for your theological construct! It was never declared a dogma but it might just as well have been, so dominant has been its influence in theology, preaching, devotion and the penitential system of the Church, up to our own day.[24]

A generation after Anselm, Abelard (1079–1142), a professor of theology at the University of Paris, rejected the idea that a debt had to be paid because of sin. He maintained that the central issue was estrangement of humans from God and proposed that it was Christ's example—of his life, death and resurrection—that achieved reconciliation. This approach has been traditionally called the moral influence theory. Abelard notes that humans can hardly be said to have been saved if their lives are not better and that change in individuals comes about as they witness Christ's example of love manifested in his life and his giving of his life for us. When a person reflects on Christ's life and death, according to Abelard,

> [e]veryone becomes more righteous—by which we mean a greater lover of God—after the Passion of Christ than before. [25]

Abelard criticized the satisfaction theory by pointing out that if Adam's lesser fault required such a satisfaction, how much greater ought to be the satisfaction due for what humans did to Christ.

His formulation, emphasizing as it does the power of love and example for humans, has had adherents through the centuries, but it has been consistently dismissed for making salvation dependent on human initiative, the human work of imitation.

THE REFORMERS

The Reformers stayed with the themes of substitution and vicarious punishment. Luther taught we are saved from the wrath of God due to sin. The believer clings to Christ, and through this relationship comes the "wonderful exchange" in which what is Christ's becomes ours. He is punished instead of us. Luther takes Anselm slightly further—into a doctrine of penal substitution—but the two central ideas, satisfaction and substitution, carry forward.

For Calvin too, Christ substituted for humanity:

> Christ was offered to the Father in death as an expiatory sacrifice that when he discharged all satisfaction through his sacrifice, we might cease to be afraid of God's wrath.[26]

Protestantism has generally embraced and taught the satisfaction position. As John Howard Yoder comments:

> Since the Middle Ages there have been no new systems. Protestantism has generally not only reaffirmed the satisfaction position,

but made it more dominant and more nearly a test of faith than had been the case in the Middle Ages.[27]

For Catholicism as well, the satisfaction paradigm has been the dominant one for some eight hundred years. It has been passed on to generations of Catholics through the neoscholastic manuals that were used to educate diocesan priests and through catechisms used to educate children. The catechisms were designed to pass on the formulas of faith in as short and pithy a manner as possible.

As Diane Steele puts it:

> The mystery of salvation was reduced to a set of propositions, and Anselm's tightly argued rationale for why God became human was reduced to little more than a paragraph.[28]

To demonstrate her contention, she presents a quote from a famous neoscholastic manual of theology by Adolf Tanquerey:

> According to the Council of Trent, Christ "by his most holy passion ...merited for us justification and made satisfaction for us to God the Father."
>
> The Council attributes meritorious and satisfying force and value to Christ's death alone because of the *divine ordinance* by which God wished Christ's death to be the price of human salvation...
>
> Therefore Christ redeemed us by *vicarious* satisfaction, through which He repaired the offense given to God, and by the *merit* through which He restored to us lost benefits.[29]

Steele then presents the corresponding passage from the famous and widely used Baltimore Catechism. In lesson 8, question 90, "What is meant by Redemption?" the children were taught:

> By the redemption is meant that Jesus Christ, as the Redeemer of the whole human race, offered his sufferings and death to God as a fitting sacrifice in satisfaction for the sins of men, and regained for them the right to be children of God and heirs of heaven...If he forgave us without any satisfaction, His justice would not have been satisfied and we would always feel guilty.[30]

The vivid, pulsing, flesh-and-blood life of Jesus of Nazareth, his thrilling words, his arresting personality, his terrible death—the whole of what he did—all turned into a cold, bloodless courtroom scene. And that is to be Good News? It is no wonder that this message of "salvation" has so little appeal or meaning to people today. It is a wonder that this version, this extended metaphor, has endured for so long. In the middle of the twentieth century, strong critiques began to appear.

A Critique of Anselm's Soteriology

A Misleading Image of God

Among the first in recent years to enter a critique of the satisfaction theory as it had devolved through history were Joseph Ratzinger[31] and Avery Dulles.[32] The critique concerned the image of God that the theory projected, an angry God who needs to be satisfied by the blood of his Son.

> Even in its classical form it is not devoid of one-sidedness, but when contemplated in the vulgarized form which has extensively moulded the general consciousness it looks cruelly mechanical and less and less feasible . . . Many devotional texts actually force one to think that Christian faith in the cross visualizes a God whose unrelenting righteousness demanded a human sacrifice, the sacrifice of his own Son, and one turns away in horror from a righteousness whose sinister wrath makes the message of love incredible.[33]

Anselm was locked into a view that God's mercy and justice were in conflict and that the conflict had to be decided in favor of justice. In *Cur Deus Homo*, at one point, the interlocutor, Boso, objects: "God commands us to forgive those who offend us,"[34] meaning, why does God not simply forgive us? Why does he not act as he would have us act? Anselm replies chillingly: "For it belongs to no one to carry out vengeance except to him who is Lord of all."[35]

Roger Haight points out that there were two interpretative schemes governing Anselm's view of the world, schemes that we no longer share. They were, first, feudalism's understanding of honor and, second, the monastic and contemplative view that God's justice is a dimension of the beauty, order, and harmony of the universe.

Anselm's era was the era of feudalism. Lords ruled. Serfs obeyed. Dishonoring the lord shook the whole system. The greater the personage whose honor was offended, the greater the punishment and credit needed to restore the balance. It was against this interpretative horizon that Anselm formulated his paradigm. God's honor is the main reason why Anselm could not see God simply forgiving sin.

Reinforcing this worldview was the conviction that the world was arranged in a harmonious, hierarchical order. Human happiness was to be found in contemplating and maintaining the world in harmony. Even God works within the rules of the orderly universe. Haight comments on this part of Anselm's worldview:

> God necessarily operates within a framework of what is fitting and just. This quality of justice in God cannot be reduced to legal justice. One should regard this notion within the framework of a monastic and contemplative theology. God's justice is a dimension of the beauty, order, and harmony of the universe. Anselm was an ascetic, and monastic life was governed by rules. But a larger framework is at work here.[36]

This understanding is the further reason why, according to Anselm, God could not just give sin a free pass and why justice had to trump mercy. God had to punish humanity for sin and demand satisfaction so that sin would not be free to infect the order of the universe. Anselm wrote: "It is, however, not seemly to let something inordinate pass into his kingdom."[37]

Understanding the interpretative lenses at work makes it more understandable that Anselm could read the New Testament and see the God depicted therein as a lord of the manor, infinitely above us, infinitely ready to take offense, caring only about the restoration of order. Nonetheless, in our day, it is a repulsive image of God.

A Theory That Is Not Biblical

Anselm's theory is unbiblical because it abandons the New Testament view that God is the initiator and agent of humanity's reconciliation in Christ. It makes God the object rather than the subject of the saving action.

> All this is from God, who reconciled us to himself through Christ and has given us the ministry of reconciliation; that is, in Christ God was reconciling the world to himself. (2 Cor 5:18–19)

The satisfaction theory makes God the object of the saving action, thereby reversing the meaning of the cross. The cross is made into a mechanism of injured right instead of the expression of radical love. In Joseph Ratzinger's words:

> [T]he scriptural theology of the cross represents a real revolution as compared with the notions of expiation and redemption entertained by non-Christian religions . . . In other world religions expiation usually means the restoration of the damaged relationship with God by means of expiatory actions on the part of men . . . In

the New Testament the situation is almost completely reversed. It is not man who goes to God with a compensatory gift, but God who comes to man, in order to give to him.[38]

The satisfaction schema presents us with a vision of God as a judge. On the other hand, Jesus, in the New Testament, proclaimed a reconciling and loving Father, with whom he knew such intimacy that he called him "Abba."

No Consideration of the Life of Christ

For Anselm, salvation is located in a mythical transaction associated with the heroic deed that provided the supererogation required by the offense. No attention is given to the life of Jesus, nor is any value placed on it. The only focus is on the death of Jesus. But that once again turns the New Testament on its head. Jesus proclaimed the coming of the Kingdom, and the presence of saving grace in and through his life-actions. Jesus approached sinners and the outcasts of society. He did not demand that they first reform their lives. He did not ask them to examine their consciences and repent before he would deign to be in their presence. He typically took the initiative and in so doing revealed the way of his Father. It was the way Jesus acted that revealed who God is for us.

There is an intrinsic relationship between the way that Jesus lived and his death on the cross. He died because of the way he lived, proclaiming equality for all, accepting the outcasts and marginal of society, critiquing and challenging those in power. He died because of the way he had lived and what he had proclaimed. Those in power, as a result of his message, killed him. The connection between his life and death is cut and rendered irrelevant by the satisfaction theory. As Jon Sobrino writes:

> In Anselm's theory Jesus' death is obviously framed in the context of a preexisting theological schema...One seeks to arrive at knowledge of the cross on the basis of some previously held conception of God, when in fact one should try to arrive at God on the basis of Jesus' cross.[39]

Removing the cross from history and the connection with the life of Jesus puts the locus of salvation outside this world, outside the world in which we live. Consequently salvation has nothing to do with the concrete political, social, and economic realities real people confront. The brutal death of Jesus becomes a cosmic drama rather than an event that releases liberating power for the struggles people face in this life. According to the satisfaction theory, salvation comes from a juridical reordering of the universe; there is no need for human beings to struggle with the vicissitudes of history. It has already all been done. To separate Jesus' death from his career, according to Schillebeeckx, is to "turn his death into a myth, sometimes even a sadistic, bloody myth."[40]

The satisfaction theory, by cutting the link between Jesus' death and his life, is, therefore, fundamentally ahistorical. What is really important happens outside history. The purpose of the saving act itself is to deliver us to the place outside history. As Anselm says in his rationale for submission at the beginning of *Cur Deus Homo*, "human nature was created for the very purpose that the whole person, body and soul, should enjoy peaceful immortality."[41] The purpose of salvation is to deliver us safely to the next life. Nothing is said about how to live in this one.

Human Suffering Ignored

The satisfaction model narrows the "from what are we saved" to forgiveness of sins. That is far from the sweeping gospel of the Kingdom of God that Jesus proclaimed. That gospel included liberation from oppression, healing of the sick, love between equals, hope for the future for those without hope, and a call to discipleship to bring the kingdom to others. According to Jon Sobrino:

> The danger of the explanatory models is that they tend to interiorize salvation... they tend to treat salvation in terms of inner life, explaining how the cross can bring forgiveness of sins, while neglecting to treat of salvation in relationship to the world outside and the problems of externalized injustice and sinfulness. The issue at stake is not just how God can *pardon* an "offense" against him insofar as it is an internal human act; it is how God can *take away* an external sin that leads to the cross of his Son and to all the crosses of history.[42]

The satisfaction theory does not suggest a way for individual Christians to appropriate salvation for themselves in their lives. Another way of saying this is: there is no call to discipleship. Christians are not called to struggle with evil, the social, political, and economic forces that oppress the poor, let alone with the central fact of violence in the world—even though all the texts of the New Testament concerning the followers of Jesus needing to take up their crosses or endure sufferings are all in the context of a call to action (Matt 10:38; Mark 8:34ff.; Luke 14:27; John 15:20; 2 Cor 1:5, 4:10; Phil 1:29, 2:5–8, 3:10; Col 1:24ff.; Heb 12:1–4; 1 Pet 2:21ff.; Rev 12:11). In these texts the concept of discipleship is most clearly taught. There is no room for these texts in the satisfaction theory—

as there is no need to enter the fray to confront human suffering. John Howard Yoder writes:

> Under the satisfaction theory these passages make no sense at all. The Christian's "cross" neither placates an offended holiness nor is the Christian's suffering a transaction with the Father. Unless the work of Christ has an ethical sense this whole strand of New Testament thought has no place to fit in. This explains why in preaching about Christian life many proponents of the Anselmic view abandon it in practice if not in theory.[43]

The satisfaction theory operates as if there is no ongoing problem of evil and suffering for human beings and certainly does not focus on the need to attack and eliminate the causes of that suffering. Much of Christian preaching and practice, as a result, has focused exclusively on the development of I-Thou personal relationships between believers and God.

The satisfaction theory skates along confident that human beings have been saved—even as human beings suffer what Schillebeeckx refers to as the "barbarous excess of suffering"[44]; the one reality has nothing to do with the other. As Francis Schüssler Fiorenza points out:

> Human existence faces . . . not only its limitations, especially the radical limit of death, but it also faces the constructive task of social and political life. Must not an understanding of redemption take this fundamental principle of human existence into consideration also?[45]

A Mystification of Suffering

The satisfaction theory presents the schema of a disobedient humanity being delivered from itself by a lamb who put his head down and obeyed. He obeyed even though it brought him great suffering. The implication for Christian spirituality is that we are most like Christ when we put our heads down and obey, even though our obedience may mean suffering. Such a schema can be destructive in three ways.

First, for many human beings the problem, on a personal level, is not that they are headstrong, imperious, and proud, but just the opposite. Many human beings are timid, fearful, and unsure of themselves. Many find it difficult to stand up for themselves, let alone others. Their problem is not disobedience but pusillanimity. As a result, they are all too willing to act as victims rather than as responsible adults. Cynthia Crysdale writes:

> [N]ote how destructive a lopsided teaching on healing and forgiveness could be (and has been). To assume that salvation is only about

forgiveness of sins—taking responsibility for one's failures and one's self-destruction—will overpower those who have a broken sense of agency in the first place. At the individual level, to counsel someone who is in desperate need of relief from victimization that they need to confess their sins and clean up their act is to further destroy what is already fragile. At the social level it is the script that has been written into the socialization of so many oppressed persons . . . This produces the double bind where those who don't wield power are held responsible for the behavior of those who oppress them.[46]

The spirituality of the satisfaction theory can work therefore to keep those who are weak in spirit from ever growing into their human potential and taking their rightful place in the sun as free, active sons and daughters of a saving God, whose Son died out of strength and not out of weakness.

Second, the satisfaction theory mystifies suffering by cutting the link between suffering and discipleship. Following Jesus does not mean simple passivity and resignation. His example was to stand against all human suffering: sickness, mental illness or possession, poverty, social isolation, inequality of the sexes, oppression by religious and secular rulers. The suffering that a Christian should expect to experience is the suffering that comes with following Jesus. Suffering is not a good in itself or even a means to an end. It is instead a by-product of discipleship. Jon Sobrino notes that

[s]pirituality based on the cross does not mean merely the acceptance of sadness, pain, and sorrow; it does not mean simply passivity and resignation . . . rather it is a spirituality focused on the following of Jesus. Not all suffering is specifically Christian; only that which flows from the following of Jesus is.[47]

Not all suffering is blessed. Suffering is not a good. In fact, the Christian, following Christ, attempts to stand against human suffering. Elizabeth Johnson writes:

. . . God intends to put an end to all the crosses of history. If so, soteriology shifts from the model of God as perpetrator of the disaster of the cross to the model of God as participant in the pain of the world. In Jesus the Holy One enters into solidarity with suffering people in order to release hope and bring new life.[48]

Third, satisfaction theory's emphasis on obedience and guilt, as it has been passed on through the generations, has served on a political level to freeze the status quo in place. The evils and sufferings of this world are to be endured as the will of God. This is a message that plays to the benefit of those who are in charge. As Schillebeeckx points out:

It can be claimed, for example, that for centuries churches and religions have directed their proclamation of guilt and sinfulness at the little people who cannot defend themselves, while the great and the mighty have gone free. Furthermore the oppressed in society have been kept down by playing on their sense of sinfulness and the torments of hell.[49]

People were instructed to "offer up" their sufferings without those who counseled such advice doing much to relieve the causes of that suffering. Unjust and oppressive social structures were allowed to stand as the faithful were taught to bear their burdens without complaint and to unite their sufferings with those of their Savior. The meaning of the "take up your cross and follow me" passages was nicely subverted to serve those in power. As Green and Baker write:

> When the Spanish arrived on Latin-American shores, two images of the adult Christ were introduced . . . [the] suffering Jesus was the image with which the native peoples were to identify, while the image of the conquering Christ was embodied by those conquistadores who brought Christian faith and Spanish rule to the Aztecs, Mayas and Incas.[50]

IMPLICATIONS FOR A THEOLOGY OF SALVATION

As we have seen, the life of Jesus is left entirely out of the picture in Anselm's theory of satisfaction. Salvation is an ahistorical transaction wholly within God's own self as he sends his Son as a sacrifice that satisfies his offended honor and justice. When we focus on the life of Jesus and look at the way he announced and practiced the reign of God, then the role of the powers that be come back into our understanding of salvation. Walter Wink writes:

> The earliest Epistles and all the Gospels had attested that Jesus was executed by the Powers. Jesus' own view of his inevitable death at the hands of the Powers seems to have been that God's nonviolent reign could only come in the teeth of desperate opposition and the violent recoil of the Domination System.[51]

In Anselm's theory and the subsequent penal substitution theory, the powers disappear from the picture. There is no real-life historical struggle with the powers in Jesus' life. There is no triumph over the powers through Jesus' nonviolent self-sacrifice. In the early church, on the contrary, as it lived in conflict with the Roman Empire, the theme of conflict was used consistently to explain the efficacy of the cross. Wink adds:

The *Christus Victor* or social theory of the atonement (more a set of images than a systematic doctrine) proclaimed release of the captives to those who had formerly been deluded and enslaved by the Domination System, and it set itself against that system with all its might... With the conversion of Constantine... preservation of the Empire became the decisive criterion for ethical behavior. The *Christus Victor* theology fell out of favor... because it was subversive to the church's role as state religion.[52]

As a result of this change, the demonic was perceived not in the empire but in the empire's enemies. Society was now regarded as Christian, and salvation became a highly individual transaction between the believer and God. The teaching on the reign of God, because it was no longer anchored in the life of Jesus, the way he lived it out, announced it, and taught it, was projected into an afterlife or the remote future. Salvation became a question of an individual's soul being saved for heaven, an afterlife. As Wink points out:

The *Christus Victor* or social theory of the atonement, by contrast, states that what Christ has overcome is precisely the Powers themselves. The forgiveness of which Col. 2:13–14 speaks is forgiveness for complicity in our own oppression and in that of others. Our alienation is not solely the result of our rebellion against God. It is also the result of our being socialized by alienating rules and requirements... Before we reach the age of choice, our choices have already been chosen for us by a system indifferent to our uniqueness.[53]

Focusing again on the *life* of Jesus, his nonviolent, preemptive forgiving way of living, and understanding his teaching of the reign of God entering history lead us back to understanding that salvation is not just saving the individual for an afterlife, it is overcoming the domination system at work in this life—overcoming domination hierarchies, economic injustice, patriarchy, racism, ranking, and violence. The God revealed by Jesus is a God of forgiveness and nonviolent love. In Wink's words:

The removal of nonviolence from the gospel blasted the keystone from the arch, and Christianity collapsed into a religion of personal salvation in an afterlife jealously guarded by a wrathful and terrifying God—the whole system carefully managed by an elite corps of priests with direct backing from the secular rulers now regarded as the elect agents of God's working in history.[54]

Focusing on the life of Jesus and rereading the Sermon on the Mount reveal how central to Christianity is nonviolence, not as a matter of legalism but of discipleship, the way God has chosen to overthrow the powers. Nonviolence is the praxis of God's system. Jesus distilled the long experience of his people in opposing evil in violent and nonviolent ways and opted for the way of opposing evil "without becoming evil in the process,"[55] namely nonviolence.

CRITERIA FOR A CONTEMPORARY SOTERIOLOGY

It follows from this historical review and critique of theologies of salvation that there is room for a soteriology that more adequately serves our time, while being faithful to the original experience of Jesus' saving presence and action. Such a soteriology would have the following hallmarks:

Historical Consciousness

Human beings today feel responsible for the future. More than ever we have a sense that we cannot blame anyone outside of human history for what happens to our world and to us. We are not able to blame God or say the devil made us do it; we are responsible. Such an understanding is a rather recent development. As Schillebeeckx notes:

> [W]e must remember here that an insight into historical conditions and the "pliability" of our world has entered deeply into the human consciousness only in modern times.[56]

In traditional cultures people believed that the future had to be like the past. The past was always the golden age. If no one thought the world could be changed, there were no conservatives or liberals in the modern sense of those terms.

A relevant soteriology will focus on human history as the locus of salvation, provide criteria for what is saving, and illuminate the relationship between what is possible in the present and the future. Along with historical consciousness comes the realization that all times are historically conditioned, the product of what humans do in human history. No one moment is normative for the rest.

A Way to Deal with Both Personal and Social Evil

Human suffering, we realize in our time, extends well beyond what happens due to forces of nature or individual acts of harm or injustice.

Barbarous human suffering comes about through the grinding effects of political, economic, and social structures. The way world markets are structured can have more to do with the suffering of an individual farmer in Nigeria or Cambodia than any individual action of a neighbor. The political situation in Uganda can have more to do with the suffering of starving children in that country than what any individual does or does not do. Gustavo Gutiérrez wrote:

> The approach we have been considering opens up for us—and this is of utmost importance—unforeseen vistas on the problem of sin. An unjust situation does not happen by chance; it is not something branded by a fatal destiny: there is human responsibility behind it... Sin is regarded as a social, historical fact... When it is considered in this way, the collective dimensions of sin are rediscovered. This is the Biblical notion that Jose Maria Gonzalez Ruiz calls the "harmartiosphere," the sphere of sin... that objectively conditions the progress of human history itself.[57]

A contemporary soteriology will have to point out how Jesus and the followers of Jesus are to confront social structures that cause human suffering.

A Link between the Life of Jesus and His Death and Resurrection

With the emphasis on history as the setting in which salvation occurs comes a renewed emphasis on Jesus' history, his life and deeds and the centrality of his message about the Kingdom of God. The Jesus that the first disciples experienced set the historical train moving when he chose them and commissioned them to preach and act the message he embodied. Unlike the models of salvation that focused only on the death of Jesus and lost the critical, liberating power of the example of his life and consequently the real impact of the cross, a soteriology that relates to our time will have to connect us to the Jesus of history, not just the Christ of faith.

A Model of Causality That Makes Sense

Once the models featuring cosmic transactions between God and Christ happening outside this world are rejected in favor of a radically historical approach to salvation, what is the nature of the causality at work?

The two main answers Christians give today are still either a substitution theory or an exemplary theory or some mixture of both. Abelard and Anselm live. Is there another plausible explication of causality—of *how* we are saved?

A Way to Exercise Power That Is of an Order Other Than Domination

That we live in a world of conflict is sharply experienced in our time. Especially if we embrace the challenge of Marx "that the challenge is not to understand the world but to change it," and if we accept the challenge to relieve people's suffering, we will find ourselves deeply in the middle of conflict. We will be putting our heads "where they do not belong." Where there is conflict, there is usually the threat of violence. Once the cycle of violence starts, no one can tell where it will end.

The radically different experience of our time, that there is the real possibility of ending human history through a violence-dealing apparatus such as the world has never seen, gives the idea of salvation a whole new depth. In the words of Rene Girard:

> [I]t has never been easier to change people's allegiance and alter their behavior, since the vanity and stupidity of violence have never been more obvious...[58]

> [T]he bomb does indeed seem like a prince of this world, enthroned above a host of priests and worshippers, who exist, it would seem, only to do it service...Humans have always found peace in the shadow of their idols...truly wonderful sense of the appropriate has guided the inventors of the most terrifying weapons to choose names that evoke ultimate violence in the most effective ways: names taken from the direst divinities in Greek mythology, like Titan, Poseidon and Saturn, the god who devoured his own children. We who sacrifice fabulous resources to fatten the most inhuman form of violence so that it will continue to protect us.[59]

Any discussion of "liberation" places one squarely into conflict with "the powers that be," and "the powers that be" have the power and might to keep things just the way they want them. If it is to be relevant in today's real world, soteriology will be about power. It will not take us out of the fray but lead us into its midst. It will summon us to deal with violence and the forces of power and might. It will reveal a source of power and a way to exercise power that is mightier than violence.

CHAPTER FIVE

Rethinking Christian Salvation in the Light of Gandhi's Satyagraha

The four theologians we have studied are all in substantive agree-ment on the key questions that need to be addressed in order to develop a statement on salvation that is coherent, faithful to the scriptures, and responsive to contemporary needs. Among those ques-tions are: Is salvation for this life or a life hereafter? Does salvation take place within and through the dynamics of human history or is it in some way outside of history? Why did Christ die? Are we saved through the death of Jesus or through his life and teachings? From what are we saved? How do people in our time experience a need for salvation? Are we saved through faith in a truth or through praxis? Does nonviolence have any-thing to do with Christian salvation? Did Jesus offer satisfaction to God for humankind's sins? Did Jesus experience punishment for sin on behalf of humankind?

Not only are the four theologians in substantial agreement on the answers to these questions, they are also in accord with Gandhi—or he with them. As we have seen, Gandhi was not averse to weighing in on questions of Christian theology. It would be overstating the case to say that Gandhi influenced their thinking on all these questions. On the pivotal issues, however, namely the centrality of nonviolence in Jesus' life and teaching and the political nature of the cross of Jesus, Gandhi did indeed, as we have seen, directly or indirectly influence these four thinkers. As a result of this stance they have rejected the satisfaction and penal substitu-tion theories of salvation—in fact any approach that attributes violence or retribution to God. Moreover, embracing an assertively nonviolent Jesus allows them to outline a fresh approach to Christian salvation.

This chapter will offer answers to the questions listed above by addressing the following topics—from the perspective of Gandhi and these theologians:

- Human responsibility for history

- The life, actions and teaching of Jesus as the ultimate criterion for evaluating approaches to salvation

- Why Christ died and the meaning of "carrying the cross"

- That from which we are saved

- The priority of praxis over theory

- The way of nonviolence: the calling of a disciple of Jesus

- The importance of the church for salvation and the mission of nonviolence

In a summary conclusion I will outline an approach to Christian salvation that is at once faithful to the scriptures and responsive to contemporary needs and sensibilities.

HUMAN RESPONSIBILITY FOR HISTORY

The four theologians understand history as open-ended, that human beings bear responsibility for the way things are but also have it in their power to resist evil and to build a better world. As John Howard Yoder writes:

> We are aware of history as a process. This awareness is characteristic of our age as it was not of earlier ages...History is the only reality we know; we do not think about essences any more, about substances and hypostases, about realities "out there" having being in themselves. We think of reality as happening in personal relationships, in institutional relationships, and in the passage of time...So we want a view of the atonement that is not tied to an archaic worldview...We want a view that is in history and not just in the mind of God or in some hypothetical heavenly courtroom.[1]

For Gandhi as well, history was in the hands of humans. He was constantly rallying his followers to stand up and make a difference for India and for humankind. He felt that, although one's previous karma limited the range and exercise of one's freedom, the doctrine of karma emphasized the human being as the architect of his or her own destiny. As he stated:

> Although I believe in the inexorable law of karma I am striving to do so many things; every moment of my life is a strenuous endeav-

or which is an attempt to build up more karma, to undo the past and add to the present.[2]

Gandhi insisted on human freedom and challenged himself and others to use that freedom in service of others. He called each person to resist and work to overcome the injustice and undeserved suffering that was the lot of so many. He wrote:

> I appreciate that freedom as I have imbibed through and through the central teaching of the Gita that man is the maker of his own destiny in the sense that he has freedom of choice as to the manner in which he uses that freedom.[3]

In this approach he seemed to belie the conventional wisdom about the attitudes of those who embraced "Eastern" modes of thought, in which typically one was cautioned not to fight evil but to transcend it. In the words of Paul Power:

> For all of his Hinduism Gandhi represented a departure from any tradition which accepts recurrent patterns of life and thought. He proclaimed a freedom and power of man to refashion destiny and to move, however painfully, out of fatalism and into a time of self-determination in individual and collective affairs.[4]

C. F. Andrews believed the same about the implications of the life and teaching of Jesus for Christians. He wrote:

> The merely negative process of refusal to participate in evil is not sufficient. It ought to lead on immediately to the positive endeavor to reconstruct a better order in which the old abuses shall no longer hold undivided sway.[5]

In our critique of Anselm's satisfaction theory we commented on its ahistorical nature, noting that it describes an interaction between God the Father and the Son that is outside of time. Salvation is accomplished once Jesus, the God-man, dies and makes satisfaction for our sins. The life and behavior of concrete human beings living in history are not really relevant in this view. As Jon Sobrino points out:

> Traditional Christology interpreted the cross as the transcendental reconciliation of God with human beings but outside the context of the historical conflict caused by historical human sins... and produced an image of Christ devoid of real conflict of history

and Jesus' stand on it, which has encouraged quietist or ultra-pacifist ideologies and support for anything going by the name of law and order.[6]

And, as Yoder writes:

> Some views of the atonement see God as annulling history. We were lost but God stepped in and wiped it off the record, blotted it out. Other views of the atonement that see God as suffering, accepting, enabling and healing history seem to be more biblical.[7]

For Gandhi and for our theologians, Christian salvation has meaning only if it leads to changed behavior in this world, only if it enlists the followers of Jesus in the fight against unjust suffering, only if it impels people to build a world that is more fully human. Christian salvation provides human beings with a new way of life that offers a way of fighting evil "without becoming evil in the process,"[8] namely nonviolence. As such, it is a profoundly this-worldly religion, not the "opiate of the people" that Marx accused it of being. As Walter Wink wrote:

> ...the removal of nonviolence from the gospel blasted the keystone from the arch, and Christianity collapsed into a religion of personal salvation in an afterlife jealously guarded by a wrathful and terrifying God.[9]

JESUS' LIFE, PRAXIS, AND TEACHING AS THE ULTIMATE CRITERION

For our four theologians the life, praxis, and teaching of Jesus are, taken together, the criterion against which any articulation of Christian salvation needs to be evaluated. Yoder, for example, anchors us in the world of Jesus—a Jew living in a country occupied by Rome, the great power of the time, and a country seething with political unrest. Yoder reviews the gospel of Luke in his classic work, *The Politics of Jesus*, to discover what Jesus *did* in relation to the "powers that be" of his time. We saw above that Wink takes the same approach as he sketches out the content and significance of the "domination-free order" that Jesus proclaimed and modeled. Andrews roots his theology in the historical Jesus—what he did and what he said. As M. M. Thomas wrote of Andrews: "His criterion is that the incarnation of God in Jesus Christ is historical and real, not mythical or docetic."[10] Bernard Häring broadened moral theology by asking how Jesus behaved and what he expected from his followers. All agree on the three ways that Jesus' praxis was distinctive, revolutionary, and normative for his followers.

First, Jesus behaved as if the Kingdom of God was already being revealed and made real by his actions and person. His actions showed that God was loving and faithful to his people even when they were in sin. Jesus, in the name of his Father, initiated the call. As a result of his presence, people changed. They felt the joyful nature of God's approach to them. Jesus did not ask for repentance first. He gave forgiveness and love first and as a result people felt forgiven, loved, and changed. In the words of Walter Wink:

> Jesus lived this new creation out in his table fellowship with those whom the religious establishment had branded outcasts, sinners, renegades: the enemies of God. He did not wait for them to repent, become respectable, and do works of restitution . . . Instead he audaciously bursts upon these sinners with the declaration that their sins have been forgiven, prior to their repentance . . . You are forgiven; now you can repent.[11]

Second, Jesus counseled "love your enemies" and then modeled that behavior for his followers. In so doing he revealed the nature of God. Jesus demonstrated that God shows unending, non-coercive patience with humanity. He makes the rain fall on the just and unjust alike. The fact that God acts toward humanity in this way and Christ expects us to forgive as God has forgiven us points to a nonviolent way of life as normative for Christ's followers.

Forgiveness is a creative act that restores people to positive relationships. One can forgive only if filled with a larger sense of what can and should happen between human beings and believe that people can change in response to initiatives of reconciliation. Forgiveness is a positive act, not a letting-off easy, because it has the potential to set relationships aright. In addition, it turns the victim of the offense from passivity to assertiveness. No longer a victim, the victim in forgiving becomes the carrier of the action, the protagonist.

As Häring expressed it:

> There is no ambiguity in Jesus' teaching. His disciples are those who love their enemies.[12]

Third, Jesus modeled a different way to exert power—power as service. His washing of the disciples' feet, one of the lowliest, most subservient acts possible in his culture, demonstrated what he taught in words. This way of exercising power contradicted the code of the Roman Empire that was built on the concept of patronage—a system of obligation of favor for favor and a strict hierarchy of power. In the words of Walter Wink:

According to the Fourth Gospel, Jesus washes his disciples feet, a duty considered so degrading that a master could not order a Jewish slave to perform it...The Church later developed this reversal of values in the magnificent infancy narratives...born in a stable...where shepherds, regarded as dishonest, unclean, no better than gentile slaves, and who were thus banned from being witnesses, are the sole witnesses of Jesus' birth.[13]

This new way of being powerful would be a way of justice and compassion instead of domination. Jesus showed himself to be in solidarity with the oppressed and outcast. As C. F. Andrews noted:

How could anyone who has the voice of Jesus saying, "I was sick, I was in prison," refuse to answer His call? For in their "afflictions, He was afflicted." In every one of those poor and distressed Indians, bound down to servile labor in the plantations...He the Son of Man, was suffering. It was all "done to him."[14]

The actions of Jesus spoke more loudly than his words and constituted the first level of revelation. His words were, however, also important because they clarified the meaning of his actions. Jesus' call to Zacchaeus, the most outcast of outcasts because he was the tax collector for the hated occupiers, to come down, that Jesus was going to visit him in his home, amplified and made even clearer the meaning of Jesus' actions. Words, such as the parable of the Prodigal Son, which could also be called the Profligately Loving Father parable, portrayed in a narrative story form what Jesus was teaching in his life actions.

By giving paramount importance to the praxis and teaching of Jesus, our theologians are able to resist interpreting the metaphors of Paul in the wrong way. They are able to understand them in their appropriate contexts—Paul attempting to convey the exciting news about Jesus and the benefits accruing to humankind from Jesus in ways his various audiences could appreciate and understand. They do not read the Pauline texts using the lenses of later models that attribute vengeance and retributive justice to God. Paul does in fact use the metaphors of sacrifice and expiation and ransom. They are useful metaphors if they are not twisted. Paul's fundamental picture of God is not that of an angry deity but of a God of boundless love who takes the initiative to save. That is consistent with and not contradictory to Jesus' life and message. For example, Paul writes in Romans 5:8: "While we were still sinners, Christ died for us." For Yoder the metaphor of sacrifice, when read as a metaphor and not an expanded full-scale theory, expresses well the nonviolent nature of Christ's death on the cross. Far from being a moment when the Father is carrying out a violent punishment of his Son in our stead as the later Calvinist model will have it, Christ responds nonviolently to the violence being done to him by human beings, thus absorbing the violence, ending violence's vicious cycle, and reaching out to those responsible with words of forgiveness even as he experiences the extremes of abandonment and pain. "Father forgive them, for they know not what they do."

Any new model of Christian salvation has to be faithful to scripture and do justice to the many metaphors used in the scriptures. Paul in particular makes use of multiple metaphors. In one passage, Romans 8:3, Paul uses three different metaphors, conflating three terms, condemnation (judicial), scapegoat, and sacrifice,[15] because it is rhetorically effective. Paul is trying to reach multiple audiences with different cultural backgrounds. He uses the dying hero image to appeal to the Romans and the metaphor of sacrifice for those whose lives have been filled with cultic devotions. As others point out, Paul has been so transformed by the message of the cross that no one or even a few metaphors can fully express his gratitude and awe. No single metaphor can capture the whole of what he is trying to express. But a metaphor (*meta*, meaning across and *pherein*, meaning to carry), referring to a word that carries meaning from one semantic field to another,[16] needs only one point of contact to be effective. There is blood in a sacrifice and in a political murder; this enables the murder of Jesus to be compared to a sacrifice.[17] The metaphor should not, however, be pushed beyond that one point of contact and made into a comprehensive model. To be faithful to the scriptures means first of all to appreciate the metaphors for what they are and, second, to convey in any new statement or metaphor the transforming message that flowed into Paul's metaphors and prompted it in the first place. The controlling criterion of evaluation is the life and teaching of the historical Jesus.

Jesus lived and taught nonviolence. Nonviolence can serve as a root metaphor for understanding salvation and allows us to understand sacrifice in a more adequate way. According to Yoder:

> The imagery of sacrifice is particularly relevant here. For the ultimate sacrifice, the sacrifice of self, is precisely giving oneself utterly to communion-obedience with God. This is what Jesus did in letting God express agape through his "obedience unto death, the death of the cross." Thus sacrifice, communion, and obedience are identical. Blood as the symbol of life given is the most striking way of saying this.[18]

In some ways it is hard to understand how models of Christian salvation that ascribe vengeance to the Father have continued to hold sway—given the clarity of the parable of the Prodigal Son and the consistent praxis of Jesus.

WHY CHRIST DIED AND THE MEANING OF "CARRYING THE CROSS"

Our four theologians answer the question in a consistently similar way. Christ died because of the way he lived—not because God the Father had him killed. Historically, Jesus' message and his actions upset the powers that be. As he inspired the crowds and recruited a band of followers, the Romans feared a violent uprising. The Jewish leaders feared that Jesus would continue to undercut their power, particularly in the way that he criticized the temple cult and his criticisms of the way the law was being interpreted and made a burden to the people. They also feared that, if Rome became concerned, he would upset the relationship that had been forged with their occupiers, a relationship that left them with some power and free to practice their religion. Jesus continued to practice and preach his alternative vision of the way human beings could live together even as it stirred up conflict with the leaders of society. He carried out his sense of mission to the fullest extent of his powers and to the end. As Borg and Crossan note:

> One may speak of Jesus sacrificing his life for his passion, namely for his advocacy of the kingdom of God...Did Good Friday have to happen? As divine necessity? No. As human inevitability? Virtually. Good Friday is the result of the collision between the passion of Jesus and the domination systems of his time.[19]

Through it all Jesus was faced with the same choices all others in his society faced—namely, go along with the way things were, secede from society as, for example, the Essenes did, or gear up to resist Rome violently. Jesus chose none of these but opted instead to respond nonviolently to the violence inflicted on him. In the words of Bernard Häring:

> He dies as a revealer of the liberating and healing truth, and bears the burden of mankind. By his very nonviolence he fully restores the honor of the Father, revealing the Father's true image. He dies for those who crucify him, for all of us sinners. And by his healing love he breaks up the circle of enmity, violence and vindictiveness, and shows us the way...It is not possible to speak of Christ's sacrifice while ignoring the role of nonviolence.[20]

Gandhi too interpreted the cross of Jesus in this way. Politically and historically it was the final step and consequence of a way of life, a life spent befriending those in need and resisting oppression and violence. As noted earlier, after seeing a simple crucifix at the Vatican Gandhi was very moved. He wrote:

It was not without a wrench that I could tear myself away from that scene of living tragedy. I saw there at once that nations like individuals, could only be made through the agony of the Cross and in no other way. Joy comes not out of infliction of pain on others, but out of pain voluntarily borne by oneself.[21]

Once these theologians understand the cross in terms of nonviolence, it is much clearer to them where the violence in the death of Jesus lay— not with God but with human beings. As Häring points out:

The father's honor has surely not required his Son's cruel suffering, as such to be offered for any reason of vindictive justice. He is in no way accountable for the wickedness suffered by His Son ... The responsibility is ours, each time we sin.[22]

As we have already seen, following Christ by taking up our cross does not refer to any and all suffering but to that suffering that results from acting as Jesus did, identifying with the poor and oppressed, laboring to relieve their suffering, and standing up to the powers that be. That is the kind of behavior that will bring a cross. Human suffering is not a good in itself. Human suffering is to be relieved, not praised—unless it is experienced as a consequence of the good cause that Jesus leads—nonviolent resistance to evil.

In his praxis of satyagraha Gandhi sheds light on how suffering endured as a consequence of involvement in nonviolent action can turn suffering into a positive force. In Yoder's words:

The cross of Christ was not an inexplicable or chance event which happened to strike him, like illness or accident... The cross of Calvary was not a difficult family situation, not a frustration of visions of self-fulfillment, a crushing debt or a nagging in-law; it was the political, legally to be expected result of a mortal clash with the powers ruling society.[23]

That from Which We Are Saved

The way Christian salvation is presented and explained has a lot to do with the way a particular era or culture experiences the need to be saved, or how the sense of being "lost" is felt. As John McIntyre writes:

... the appropriate soteriological model would "chime in" with equivalent spiritual distress of the hearer.[24]

Paul Fiddes reviews the historical record and finds, for example, that in the period of the New Testament church, sin was often seen as a kind of impurity or uncleanness that tainted life. People thus felt shut out of the sphere of the holy. Consequently, atonement was presented as sacrifice in which the blood of Christ was an agent of cleansing. Fiddes goes on to say that in the time of the early church fathers the human predicament was experienced as oppression by hostile heavenly powers. People felt out of control. Consequently salvation was presented as a victory of Christ over the powers and supernatural forces. In the period of the later church fathers, under the influence of Platonic philosophy, people felt the immortal soul, destined for eternal life, bound down in the life of the body. Salvation therefore was explained as raising humanity to share in the life of God or divinization. In the Middle Ages sin was understood to be the disruption of divinely ordered creation. Chaos resulted when loyalty and honor were not paid to the lord by his vassals. Salvation was consequently explained as satisfaction, paying the debts of honor. The period of the Reformation saw great political and social upheaval and the need to have the law enforced to guard the rights of those in power. Punishment of offenders was understood to be necessary for order to be restored. Consequently, salvation was articulated in terms of the demands of the law, with Jesus punished as a substitute for guilty humankind. The modern era has been characterized by a deep sense of alienation and anxiety. Salvation is consequently frequently articulated as healing of the sin-sick soul.[25]

Our four theologians, along with Gandhi, perceive "that from which we must be saved" in a way that is very similar to the way Paul sees it—when he talks about the "powers that be," the power of sin, the law, death and the evil powers. As Gustav Aulen observes:

> Paul's teaching is not a patchwork but... one central point concerning Redemption, that man is held in bondage under objective powers of evil... the purpose of Christ's coming is to deliver men from all these powers of evil—flesh, sin, law, death and demonic powers.[26]

The world is shot through with the power of evil. Evil is real. Evil corrupts, kills, and keeps millions in bondage. Evil cannot be explained; it can only be resisted.

The first thing our theologians realize is that evil is an active force over against us that is embedded not just in individuals but also in the structures of society. The power of social structures over human beings means there can be no individual salvation without at the same time challenging fallen institutions. Wink notes that

[t]he gospel then is not a message about the salvation of individuals from the world, but news about a world transfigured, right down to its basic structures.[27]

This theme is strongly echoed and reinforced in Gandhi's theory and practice. As far back as his publication of *Hind Swaraj* in 1909 he was critiquing the role that the social structures, both economic and political, were having on the daily life of Indians. His concept of liberation, or *swaraj*, therefore called for a radical change in the social, political and economic structures, not just a change of individual hearts. In the words of John Hick:

> According to Hindu (and Buddhist) tradition, the world of our ordinary, ego-centered perception, together with its pervasive values and concerns, is distorted, illusory, concealing reality from us. Gandhi's new insight was that the illusion of *maya*, which dominates ordinary human life, has a powerful socio-economic-political dimension. It includes the structure of false ideas, valuations and attitudes in virtue of which human beings despise, exploit and treat one another.[28]

If some would attribute the appreciation of the power of social structures to Marx, at least one author would attribute it to Gandhi. According to Dashrath Singh:

> In the history of human culture and civilization it was perhaps Mahatma Gandhi who for the first time could see the ocean of violence inherent in present social structures of different societies of the world and above all in Western civilization . . .[29]

Under Gandhi's influence, C. F. Andrews saw the social nature of sin and salvation in much the same way as Gandhi:

> But when we have to do with enormous social evils, which destroy millions of souls and make a wholesome life next to impossible for vast masses of the poor, are we then merely to fight a solitary battle in order to keep ourselves "unspotted from the world" while we drift along with the tide all the while and acquiesce in the evil system socially? Or is there a Way of Life, a Law of Love, whereby evil socially as well as individually may be overcome with good?[30]

Most of Walter Wink's lifetime of academic work has been devoted to understanding the language that Paul uses concerning the powers and principalities of evil. He makes it very clear that the salvation proclaimed in the New Testament is not a private affair between Jesus and individual souls. It entails a radical challenge to the social structures of evil. These institutions were originally good; they are fallen and they can be redeemed. They cannot be changed unless their inner spirits are reached. As Wink writes:

> By acknowledging that the Powers are good, bad and salvage-able—all at once—we are freed from the temptation to demonize those who do evil. We can love our enemies or nation or church or school, not blindly but critically, calling them back to their own highest self-professed ideals and identities. We can challenge institutions to live up to the vocation that is theirs from the moment they were created.[31]

The second realization that our four theologians share is that it is violence or the threat of violence that keeps the world as it is and from the path of salvation. This is the pressing and in some way new question—because the situation is new and the threat of all-consuming violence so overwhelming—that our post-modern era puts to the Christian tradition. This is the new "sign of the times." Does Jesus—does Christianity—have a way out of this hell? Humanity has continued to pursue the path of violence. As Christopher Hedges puts it: "[W]e too are strapping explosives around our waists with every new technological advance in destructive capabilities."[32] Humanity seems powerless to find a way out. In the words of the Second Vatican Council: human beings are "incapable of battling the assaults of evil successfully, so that everyone feels as though...bound by chains" (*Gaudium et spes*, 13).

Häring points to our mother-earth-ending, humanity-ending capabilities as one of the reasons why many feel a need to be saved. Humanity has a felt need to find a new way before it is too late. He notes that

> ...especially in view of the signs of the present time, when the alternative of non-violent conflict-solving becomes a question of "to be or not to be" for humankind...the fundamental option of faith in Jesus Christ requires faith in redemption from violence.[33]

Wink names violence as the spirituality of the "domination system," his term for the web of interlocking social structures that hold power over humanity. Violence is what the domination system turns to when really up against it, what it turns to for deliverance when threatened. Peter Ackerman and Jack DuVall point out that Mao embellished the myth even further when he said: "Power grows out of the barrel of the gun." That saying has inspired violent revolutionaries ever since and is also what has delayed China's liberation by more than fifty years.[34]

There is some recognition that with the tools of modernity such as communication and propaganda the violence is only getting worse.[35] Many thought we could never have another Auschwitz, but we have had a Rwanda and a Bosnia and a Darfur. Can we be saved from ourselves? Can we be saved from violence?

One other facet of the contemporary experience of "lostness," one other inheritance of a post-Auschwitz world deserves comment. In her book, *Evil in Modern Thought*, Susan Neiman reviews the history of the "problem of evil," the way philosophers have addressed it through the centuries, and points out that the concept of evil that has held sway since the Enlightenment, that human evil is what human beings will, that no one can be found guilty if they have not explicitly willed their wrongdoing—that concept no longer holds after Auschwitz. She refers to Hannah Arendt's work on the banality of evil that finds no correlation between the enormity of pure evil that was Auschwitz and the puny, barely-paying-attention human wills, like Adolf Eichmann's, that bore responsibility for it. Much greater evil can come from abdication of responsibility, from banal, irresponsible people doing nothing, than from acts of intentional wrong-doing.[36]

We need to be delivered from the social structures of evil, from violence and also from our inattention, our indifference, our fly-away, chaff-like selves.

As we review the contemporary experience of "lostness," it is clear that a metaphor/model of Christian salvation is needed that directly takes into account the no-exit of humanity's addiction to violence. Gandhi's theory and praxis of satyagraha has alerted us in a new way to a reading of Jesus' life and praxis that brings his nonviolence into full relief.

THE PRIORITY OF PRAXIS

A revived focus on the historical Jesus and a deeper reflection on hermeneutics have led to a renewed appreciation of the centrality of praxis for Christianity—both for discipleship and for theorizing. Praxis is prior in three ways: God reveals God's self in action not through theory; praxis is the way to grasping the truth; praxis is the one sure test of truth. The renewed appreciation for praxis has sparked a revised understanding of the meaning of the phrase "justification through faith alone."

First, God reveals God's self in action. Faith in Jesus began for those women and men who became his disciples with an encounter with him. As Elizabeth Johnson writes:

Their encounter with Jesus in his ministry, death and new resurrected life in the power of the Spirit unleashed positive religious experiences. They perceived that through Jesus the redeeming God of Israel, the God of boundless *hesed* and emeth, of loving kindness and fidelity, had drawn near to them in an intensely gracious way and moved their lives in a changed direction.[37]

The place of encounter with God has been desacralized. It is not to be found in a privileged locale but in service to others. In Jon Sobrino's words:

The privileged locus of access to God was not cultic worship, scholarly knowledge, or even prayer. It was service to the lowly and oppressed ... This ultimate solidarity with humanity reveals a God as a God of love in a real and credible way rather than an idealistic way.[38]

As N. T. Wright points out, even the meaning of "forgiveness of sins" was understood by Jesus' hearers as not a gift to individuals but an action of God for the sake of the whole people. Wright says that in Jesus' time the Jewish people were still yearning to be brought out of exile. Foreign powers still occupied their land. They believed the reason for their exile was their sins as a people. The declaration of forgiveness of sins by Jesus was equivalent to saying that in him God was present and had brought them home from exile. In him Yahweh was returning to Zion. It was not God declaring individuals to be not guilty but the return of the whole people into God's promised Kingdom.[39]

For Gandhi as well, God is revealed not in worship and not in meditative wisdom but in praxis. That is what he finds in the *Gita*, that neither *bhakti*, devotional acts, nor *jnana*, wisdom, but karma, the way of selfless action, is the way to knowing God and to *moksha*. God is essentially to be found in the truthful, moral act, performed in the here and now.

Second, Christian theology is returning to the realization that the truth is grasped fundamentally through praxis and only secondarily through thinking. First comes orthopraxis and then orthodoxy. The way Jesus acted contained the revelation. Sobrino writes:

For Jesus it was impossible to concretize his orthodoxy simply by pondering orthodoxy intellectually. It could only be concretized through a concrete praxis. Throughout his life Jesus would be involved in concretizing the meaning of such realities as "God," "hope," and "love" ... The contents of orthodoxy are limit-realities such as God, Christ, salvation and sin. They cannot be pondered or intuited in themselves. What we know or learn about them cannot be separated from the historical experiences that allow us to make general formulations that are reasonable.[40]

Gandhi also believed that the only way to truth was through a progressive process of testing relative truths in action, a corrective process of experimentation. As Rita Dadhich points out:

Gandhi does not remain merely satisfied by an advocacy of contemplation of Truth at the thought level. Rather his apotheosis of Truth stresses action instead of thought.[41]

Andrews expressed this same dynamic, that truth is caught, not taught, when he wrote: "No truth worth knowing can ever be taught; it can only be lived."[42] For Christianity the ultimate test of truth is praxis: "what you did to the least of my brothers and sisters." The life of a Christian lies first in action, only secondarily in a way of thinking. According to Sobrino:

Viewed theologically, the life of the Christian does not consist in knowing about that love but in receiving it and sharing it. Knowledge of it is subordinate to that process, though it is not to be disdained. To put it another way, it would be a complete contradiction to proclaim God's message solely so that it might be pondered and talked about; for that which is communicated is to be received as liberating love.[43]

So also for Gandhi, through a dialectic of conflict and nonviolent action the truth would be tested in terms of fulfillment of human needs. When Gandhi was asked how one knew one was in touch with the truth, he offered the following as a sure-fire test:

Whenever you are in doubt, or when the self becomes too much with you, apply the following test. Recall the fate of the poorest and weakest man whom you may have seen, and ask yourself if the step you contemplate is going to be of any use to him. Will that person gain by it? Will it restore that person to a control over his or her own life and destiny? In other words, will it lead to *swaraj* for the hungry and spiritually starving millions? Then you will find your doubts and your self melt away.[44]

This renewed appreciation of praxis as the source, norm, and way to truth allows for an enriched concept of faith, as in "justification by faith alone." There is no gap between the so-called subjective and objective accounts of faith when Christianity is understood first and foremost as praxis. Faith fully activated and alive has an element of trust and commitment to it. It is fully activated when it issues into discipleship and service. There is no gap between justification and sanctification. Yoder notes:

> We might try to affirm the unity of obedience, sanctification with justification, instead of distinguishing between being made righteous and being made good, the way traditional theology separates justification from sanctification as a separate process that comes later and makes us do good. The unity of these two in biblical thought links the unity of our obedience with God's work in Christ, his cross with ours, his death with our dying with him. This double unity is completely missing in Anselm but is present in the Bible.[45]

Not only does Christian faith issue into action and service, Christian faith springs from praxis as well—our encounter with others who believe, who, inspired by grace, witness the gospel through faithful performance. As Stanley Hauerwas expresses it:

> Christian faith is primarily an account of divine action and only secondarily an account of a believing subject. Our God is a performing God who has invited us to join in the performance that is God's life... Christian faith springs not from independently formulated criteria, but from compelling renditions, faithful performances.[46]

This highlights the importance of human action in cooperation with saving grace. As Elizabeth Johnson expresses it: "What is first of all God's gift is ultimately a human task."[47] Or as Glen Stassen, echoing Yoder, expresses it:

> Doing the deeds of Jesus is participation in delivering grace; the hypocrisy of not doing them while claiming goodness is participation in judgment... Gracious invitation must be joined with obedience.[48]

Our salvation is indeed *sola gratia*, by grace alone, and is due to God's initiative, not our own. This notion of faith in action is not "justification by works"; it is justification by faith informed by charity. It is to be faithful to the root meaning of the word "believe." As Marcus Borg writes:

> Believe did not originally mean believing a set of doctrines or teachings; in both Greek and Latin its roots mean "give one's heart to." The heart is the self at the deepest level. Believing, [be-*lieb*,

heart in German] therefore, does not consist of giving one's mental assent to something, but involves a much deeper level of one's self... It means to give one's heart, one's self at its deepest level to the post-Easter Jesus.[49]

Centuries of wrangling over this language seems to have been overcome when Catholics and Lutherans signed in 1999 the Joint Declaration on the Doctrine of Justification that rightly affirms both the priority of grace and the inseparability of faith and love.[50] As Gerhard Lohfink, reflecting on the synoptic tradition, wrote:

> For the people of God to exist as a community, its social order has to be put into practice... it would be a catastrophic mistake merely to listen to the word of Jesus. His word has to be *done*. It is astonishing how stubbornly the theme of doing Jesus' teaching can be found at all levels of the synoptic tradition.[51]

A renewed appreciation of praxis means therefore that a contemporary understanding of salvation will stress the "Way" of Jesus, a favorite expression of John's Gospel, and that "Way" is a way of acting in the world and in history. Gandhi always considered himself to be not a theoretician but a man of action. He admired Jesus and Mohammed for precisely that reason. They did not just talk, they did. So also the Christian.

THE WAY OF NONVIOLENCE

The question I have been pressing has been: Is there an answer in Jesus' life and the scriptures to our current experience of "lostness," our seeming inability to find a way out of the no-exit of violence and the oppressive structures of evil that hold the world in thrall? Partially (perhaps more than that) through the influence of Gandhi, we have begun to see the answer in the nonviolence of Jesus. As Martin Niemoeller, one of the first Christian leaders arrested by the Nazis, wrote:

> When the Christian church and Christian world did not do anything effective about peacemaking, God found a prophet of nonviolence in Mahatma Gandhi... In our days Gandhi has shown this [no hope in retaliation] to a great part of the world, and I wish that Christians would not be the last group of men and women to learn the lesson that God is teaching us through this prophet.[52]

In this section I will address three issues: whether nonviolence is indeed in the New Testament; the way nonviolence links the life, death and resurrection of Jesus; and the issue of the "wrath" of God and the harsh judgment sayings of Jesus.

Nonviolence in the New Testament

In our review of the four selected Christian theologians, we saw that many of the most eminent scripture scholars of the last few decades have concluded that Jesus did indeed embrace and teach nonviolence. When John Yoder, for example, revised his book, *The Politics of Jesus*, he had occasion to update the list of scholars who had provided support for his conclusions. There is no need to repeat that list here. We cited the many German scripture scholars who supported Bernard Häring's conclusions in his book, *The Healing Power of Peace and Nonviolence*. One of them, Norbert Lohfink, for example, wrote:

> In actuality everything the Gospels say depends on the fact that here a person appeared who himself was completely free and did not need to see anyone as his rival; a person who permitted every other person her or his own freedom and exercised no compulsion on them. Because he was nonviolent to the core, he could speak with absolute truth and no deception, of God as his father, and leave a transformed world along the way he trod. Only because people instinctively knew that no one had anything to fear from him could they abandon their own security and allow all those otherwise suppressed possibilities in their hearts to bloom.[53]

It is true that Christian theology through the centuries has developed many different ways to discount or put aside the nonviolence of Jesus and the clear teaching of the Sermon on the Mount. But in our time, because of the example of Gandhi and the many who have been inspired by him, such as Martin Luther King, Lech Walesa, and Nelson Mandela, nonviolence has been given new credibility. It is harder to accept a Niebuhr's wary "realism." In fact, Häring found it "mysterious" that the message has been put aside for so long, that,

> [f]aced with the absolute clarity of the gospels, the "things hidden since the foundation of the world" and revealed in Jesus Christ could remain still hidden and denied by much of Christianity.[54]

Walter Wink contributes to the new awareness of the power and potential of the Sermon on the Mount. His telling exegesis of the "turn the other cheek" passage (Matt 5:38–44) expresses well what other scholars who have pondered the type of language being used in the passage have come to understand—namely, that Jesus uses vivid, narrowly drawn examples to inspire creative, nonviolent behavior in situations of oppression. As Wink says, Jesus provides a spirituality for people at the bottom of society that can turn them from being passive victims into protagonists. That is similar, as we saw, to the way C. F. Andrews read the Sermon on the Mount sixty years before Wink and the way Gandhi himself read it, when the Sermon on the Mount "went straight to his heart."

In summary, there seems to be little scholarly doubt that the message of nonviolence really is central to Jesus' life and teaching and part and parcel of the belief of early Christianity. Robert Daly, SJ, in his article on nonviolence in the New Testament and the early church, cites Rene Coste's work:

> Rene Coste, for example, is summarizing a broad consensus of gospel criticism when he affirms: " It is an incontestable fact that Christ did preach nonviolence, both as a condition and a consequence of the universal love that he taught us. To pretend, as is sometimes is done, that his directives are only meant to be applied to individual or ecclesial relationships is a supposition that is nowhere justified in the writings of the New Testament."[55]

The Way Nonviolence Links Jesus' Life and Death

Earlier we saw that one of the limits of Anselm's theory of salvation is that it makes only the death of Jesus the cause of our salvation and pays no attention to the life and teaching of Jesus. Then we went on to note that a valid model of Christian salvation should show the relationship between the life and teaching of Jesus and his death.

As we have pointed out, the death of Jesus is really a consequence of the way he lived out the Sermon on the Mount. He did not just teach love of enemies; he lived it even to the end. The cross is not disjunctive with the way he lived but its consequence. The way he reacted to the actions of the "powers that be" was by rejecting the alternative of violence and practicing assertive nonviolence. As Anthony Bartlett writes:

> Jesus' personal final battle with evil was totally consistent with the Sermon on the Mount. As every other would-be messiah, he confronted the might of Rome, the pagan blasphemers in the land regarded by the Essenes as the sons of darkness, but he did so by a pathway that confronted the darkness itself.[56]

Jesus did not act the victim. His stance was not passive nonresistance. He continually tried to reach his opponents. He did not back away from conflict. In fact he seemed to seek it out at the end, forcing the action with his symbolic cleansing the temple. But when the powers gathered in retribution against him, he demonstrated even more clearly how God through him continued to love the enemy. The story of the cross is first of all a story of how God treats his enemies. As Raymund Schwager expresses it:

> [Jesus] did not fall back on the old mechanisms of retribution. Since his whole public ministry took place in the context of the dawning kingdom of God, after its rejection the question arose as to how God would react to those enemies who were not won over by the offer of unconditional forgiveness ... by his behavior he doubled his already gracious message of love of one's enemy.[57]

Jesus' proclamation of the love of the Father demonstrates complete respect for human freedom. It is a love that pursues, woos, and supports but does not coerce. Human beings are free to reject Jesus and his message. How then could the goodness of the Father reach human hearts that were closed to the message? The surprising answer of Jesus was allowing himself to be handed over to the dark powers and from within opening up a way out even for the hardened of heart. Again we turn to Schwager's words:

> He was the one taking action, and yet he became the victim of what he had released ... He allowed himself to be drawn into the process of self-judgment of his adversaries, in order, through participation in their lot, to open up for them from inside another way out of the diabolical circle and a new path to salvation ... he turned around the intensified evil and gave it back to them as love redoubled.[58]

There is no limit to Christ's and his Father's forgiveness. Christ's death can be understood and its saving significance can be fully grasped only in terms of its fulfillment of the arc of Jesus' life and mission. It is the "no limit" quality that provides a response to the "no exit" of violence. Bartlett writes:

> And the very quality of this "no limit" resists, subverts, overturns the hitherto irresistible damnation of death. Where before death inevitably ends in the rictus of the corpse, the sign of violence triumphs in the cross, the event of the crucified, it is changed endlessly into a glance of compassion and life begun over.[59]

The life, death, and resurrection are, therefore, one continuum. The resurrection happens because God's love has no limit. As Yoder notes:

Ontologically, it is a simple necessity. "Death could not hold him down" (see Acts 2:24). Psychologically, the resurrection is fundamental for discipleship, in that it vindicates the rightness, the possibility, and the effectiveness of the way of the cross . . . The resurrection proves that, even when humanity does its worst . . . so far as to kill God, we cannot destroy that love.[60]

The cross, understood as the final fate of a life lived according to the Sermon on the Mount, symbolizes assertive, courageous, nonviolent action in the face of violence. It is the symbol of Christ's new way to break out of the cycle and no exit of violence. The cross is not masochism. It stands for the belief that even "enemies" can be reached and changed. In Yoder's words, "the cross is not an instrument of propitiation, it is the political alternative to both insurrection and quietism."[61] Or as Ched Myers, making the link between Christ and Gandhi even clearer, writes:

> The cross is not only a reminder of the political cost of discipleship, but can also be seen as a symbol of what Gandhi called satyagraha.[62]

Raymund Schwager points out, in this context, that the Catholic Church holds that the Mass is a sacrifice—but not sacrifice in terms of destruction. Recent ecumenical agreement holds that the anamnesis or remembrance is a real making present again of the whole of Christ's work of salvation, the whole drama of Jesus' life: becoming man, humbling himself, his service, his teaching, his sacrifice, his suffering, resurrection, ascension and the sending of his spirit.[63]

The Wrath of God and Jesus' Judgment Sayings

It is relevant to comment on New Testament language that speaks of the wrath of God and to attempt to square the judgment sayings of Jesus with the message of love of enemies.

A number of scholars find the wrath of God statements in the New Testament to be quite consistent with the message of God's no limit, take-the-initiative love and respect for human freedom as depicted above. The wrath of God is simply letting human beings go their own way. It is God respecting human freedom and letting human beings create their own hells. Joel Green and Mark Baker express it this way:

> For Paul wrath in Romans 1 is the active presence of God's judgment toward all ungodliness and wickedness. The wrath of God is not vindictive indignation . . . not retributive justice . . . Paul is giving a diagnosis of the human condition . . . Sinful activity is the

result of God letting us go our own way... Our sinful acts do not
invite God's wrath but prove that God's wrath is already active.[64]

J. Denny Weaver says that statements about the retribution of God
were really a declaration of what those who reject the rule of God bring on
themselves... the offer of forgiveness always remains open.[65] Robert
Hamerton-Kelly writes that the revelation of wrath is the divine nonresistance to human evil, the way human beings turn on one another and
themselves in the absence of sacred order.[66] Bartlett says that when Luther
placed wrath and love in conflict within God, he created a theological
monstrosity.[67] Raymund Schwager writes:

> Paul does not even suggest that God himself intervenes violently
> ... According to Paul, God's anger consists only in the deliverance
> of humankind to themselves, their desires, passions and perverse
> thinking... God's wrath is identical with the granting of full
> respect for the human action that turns against God and leads to a
> complete perversion of personal relations.[68]

Häring points out that attributing violence to God has enabled theologians and others to sanction violence in the world. It seems to go the other
way as well: scholars who cannot imagine a world without violence assume
that God must be wrathful and violent. Hans Boersma, for example, cannot countenance any possibility that we could have a world without violence. He proceeds to build his model of salvation from that fundamental
stance and therefore endorses the sacrificial and punishment models. He
interprets the wrath of God in a similar vein:

> For God not to get angry when he is rejected... would demon-
> strate indifference not love.[69]

Jesus' rough statements of judgment, which can seem to be the opposite of nonviolent, are interpreted, on the other hand, not as a letting go of
his adversaries to their own self-made perdition but, quite the contrary, as
an example of Jesus trying to reach his adversaries and save themselves
from themselves. Leonardo Boff, for example, writes:

> He always leaves the other a space for freedom... Jesus never
> employs violence to make his ideas prevail. He appeals to, speaks
> to, consciences.[70]

Jesus argues and cajoles and in his controversies he is arguing for a radical message of the God of life to his opponents. Sobrino adds:

He appeals to their mercy and ultimate good sense even when their reaction is obstinate and hypocritical...(Mark 3:4; Luke 14:2). Sometimes he argues *ad hominem* (Luke 14:5; Matt. 12:11)...Sometimes he argues biblically, citing the Old Testament, as in the case of David and the bread of the Presence (see 1 Sam. 21:2–7; Mark 2:25–26).[71]

Jesus challenges his adversaries with hard sayings. He predicts that they will kill him as their ancestors killed the prophets before him but in response they refuse to admit any responsibility. That is what convinces Jesus that a dire fate awaits them. He can foresee the destruction of Jerusalem. According to Raymund Schwager:

They made the victims of violence into an object of veneration and thereby neutralized the question about their own behavior...It was their claim which rose from a totally false judgment about themselves...His pronouncements of woe are about something more fundamental, about instinctive self-deception.[72]

But after all his attempts at reaching them, Jesus realizes at the end that he has not succeeded. It fills him with sadness. He weeps over the city of Jerusalem and says that he would—if they would let him—gather them to him as a hen does her chicks. This interpretation of his hard sayings, as an attempt to break through to his adversaries, is fully in synch with the nonviolent practice of Gandhi centuries later.

THE IMPORTANCE OF THE CHURCH FOR SALVATION

As we have seen, Gandhi knew the importance of living in a supportive community. Wherever he moved, he initiated another ashram. This was not just for the sharing of goods in common or for social and moral support; it was, in his mind, a necessity for being able to live a life of nonviolence and service. Only through seeing others live that way of life could the individual continue to live it—for it called for continual unlearning of the usual ways of the world and continually modeling satyagraha for one another. As Yoder's disciple, Stanley Hauerwas, expresses it:

Discipleship is not a heroic endeavor of individuals, but rather a way of life of a community...The practice of peace among Christians requires constant care of our lives together, through which we discover the violence that grips our lives and compromises our witness to the world. [73]

As we have also seen, Yoder could embrace nonviolence only because he had seen others live it in his community. The narrative of Jesus' nonviolent way came alive in the praxis of believers. For Yoder, the way of nonviolence requires continual conversion, impossible without a living community of faith, a church. This was part of his critique of Niebuhr who believed that human beings gathered into groups were less likely to act selflessly. Yoder responded that Niebuhr had no living appreciation for what a vital church community can do for the individual. Nonviolence is not a rule, it is a call and that call can only be mediated through others. As Pheme Perkins expressed it: "The individual cannot be asked to 'love the enemy' independently of a community which supports him/her."[74]

In the words of Michael Gorman:

> To be in Christ is to live within a community that is shaped by his story, not merely to have a "personal relationship" with Christ ... Paul writes his letters to communities not individuals ... nearly all prescriptions for believers are couched in the plural "you" ... Paul did not set out merely to save or convert individuals to the gospel but to form communities shaped by the gospel into cruciform, and thereby alternative, theo-political entities.[75]

Häring and Wink also recognize the need for the church to be a "contrast society." They both long for the day when the church will take a clear-cut stance on nonviolence. We quoted Häring above concerning his disagreement with his friend Charles Curran concerning the church's stance on war. It is worth repeating part of that quote in this context:

> But my conviction is that "the whole church" should firmly and intelligently promote the cause of nonviolence, including the option for nonviolent civil defense. For this we must make it clear that we do not speak about a passive pacifism but rather of a most committed option for peace and justice.[76]

In a similar vein, Wink writes:

> I have slowly come to see that what the church needs most desperately is precisely such a clear-cut, unambiguous position. Governments will wrestle with the option of war, and ethicists can perhaps assist them with their decisions but the church's own witness should be understandable by the smallest child: we oppose violence in all its forms. No abuse or beatings. No rape. No more male supremacy or war. No more degradation of the environment.[77]

CONCLUSION

A nonviolent or, better in this context, a satyagraha,[78] reading of Jesus' life, teaching, death, and resurrection points us to a very different understanding of Christian salvation from that of the satisfaction and punishment models. Unlike the satisfaction and punishment models in which the transaction that saves humanity takes place outside of time, reading Jesus' life as a playing out of the Sermon on the Mount places Jesus squarely into the give and take and contingencies of history. He came with a new and exciting vision of the way human beings could live with one another and be in a love relationship with God. Because it was a world of iniquity and inequality, brimming with aspirations for privilege and wealth, and steaming with thoughts of retribution and violence, he needed people to help him build an alternative society. All he asked of people was that they trust him and his vision. Many did, and he would say—"your faith has saved you" to one after another. The synoptic gospels have him say that phrase six different times. These people were indeed saved. That was all it took, Jesus' vibrant presence that changed them, and their response, which included a commitment to help build the world he envisioned.

That message and its implications, however, disturbed the powers of the time. He persisted, gathered followers, appointed disciples; the resistance from the political powers built. They felt it was better that one man should die to protect the safety of what they had. His execution—as a shamed political prisoner, on a cross, in public—shocked, bewildered, and demoralized those who had put their trust in him. Cleopas and his companion on the road to Emmaus were emblematic. They reflected on their scriptures to find some way to reconcile the fact that a disgraced, executed convict could in some way be the one who had been promised. The Suffering Servant text of Isaiah helped. They realized that he died as he had lived. He had engaged his persecutors not with violence but with love. At one point he was silent before Pilate, giving Pilate a chance to have the truth of the situation dawn on him and find the courage to do what was right. Jesus refused to respond to their violence with violence. As Norbert Lohfink notes:

> And it is terrible to see how Jesus, with open eyes, let himself be impaled on the drawn knife—and yet could do no other without betraying the thing he had finally, finally brought into human history: the refusal to use violence.[79]

It was in the resurrection and the sending of the Spirit that the disciples realized the greatness of the way that Jesus had lived, that he had shown a new possibility for human history. Even more clearly did they see the cross as pivotal, that it revealed the way God dealt with enemies and how a real human being responds to violence and evil and exerts power. They saw the falseness of power as domination and the soundness of power as living the truth and being ready to suffer for it. They knew that they were to live that way as well. They were to take Jesus' mission forward into history. That mission is to resist evil in a way that does not cause more evil; to name, unmask and engage sinful social structures just as Jesus did; to practice concrete acts of charity for those in need, as Jesus did, and to build, as Jesus did, alternative communities of equality, nonviolence and charity. Living that way is to experience salvation, to be saved.

In this "satyagraha" or nonviolent reading of the New Testament, there is a real, objective change in the world as a result of Jesus' life and death. The "principalities and powers" have been defeated. Fiddes, following Wink, says that "the 'principalities and powers' refer to all the systems that lay claim to ultimate authority and demand absolute devotion from human beings."[80] These "powers that be" have been named; their illegitimacy has been revealed and they have lost their power to demand ultimate allegiance from humans. Sin—and sin is a word that covers all the ways that humans have been held captive and powerless—has been forgiven. In the words of Timothy Gorringe:

> Redemption was accomplished by the unmasking of the powers which destroy life and putting forgiveness in the place of revenge.[81]

Something genuinely new has happened in human history that opens up new possibilities of existence. As Fiddes observes, drawing on the thought of John Macquarrie:

> Here John Macquarrie helpfully points out two ways in which the victory of Christ actually creates victory in us. In the first place there is the power of revelation... Once a new possibility has been disclosed, other people can make it their own... what was once thought to be impossible... can be repeated and the new horizons of experience it opens up can be opened up for others... The author of Hebrews has this kind of picture in mind when he speaks of Jesus as the "pioneer" of our salvation.[82]

Nonetheless, before the eschaton, the coming of the fullness of the Kingdom inaugurated by Christ, evil still exists and humanity is still groaning for final salvation. Aulen calls Jesus' death the turning point in the struggle against evil.[83] It is a battle that has to continue. In the words of N. T. Wright describing the disciples' experience after the resurrection:

Jesus interpreted his coming death, and the vindication that he expected after that death, as the defeat of evil; but on the first Easter Monday evil still stalked the earth from Jerusalem to Gibraltar and beyond, and stalks it still... But they announced and celebrated the victory of Jesus over evil as something that had already happened, something that related pretty directly to the real world, their world. There was still a mopping up battle to be fought, but the real victory had been accomplished... This was the basis of their remarkable joy.[84]

A nonviolent or satyagraha reading of the New Testament and consideration of the meaning of salvation emphasizes this ongoing struggle against evil and the work that the followers of Jesus are commissioned to do. As Wright says:

Jesus... pointed to a further task awaiting his followers, that of implementing what he had achieved... envisaged followers becoming in their turn Isaianic heralds, lights to the world... But they would be people with a task not just an idea. [85]

Or, as Boff writes:

The reign of God will not come by magic. It will come as a result of the human effort that helps gestate the definitive future... suffering is the price we pay for the resistance the fatalizing systems put up to each and every quantum leap in history... social structure has a history that has been centuries in the weaving. It is the fruit of a historical project, and has deep mysterious ties to human freedom.[86]

It is precisely here that Gandhi helps us to broaden our understanding of what Jesus did in his life and on the cross and consequently what the ongoing task of a disciple of Christ is about. Jesus was not only nonresistant in the face of active aggression by refusing to resist an evil act with another evil act. During his life he was also actively nonviolently resistant to systemic evil. This is an important distinction. To be nonresistant, passively accepting a situation of systemic evil such as the way the law was interpreted and used in Jesus' time, or the way patriarchy was practiced, or the system that increasingly threw more and more peasants off the land, would be to acquiesce to the status quo. Jesus was more than nonresistant; he was actively, nonviolently resistant. For people in our time to be nonresistant to racism, family abuse or poverty, examples of systemic violence, would also be acquiescing to the status quo. Jesus practiced both nonresistance or non-cooperation when that was the appropriate stance and active, nonviolent resistance (satyagraha) when that was the appropriate stance. He did not acquiesce to the systemic violence of his time. Jesus spoke the truth to power. As we have seen, he upset the status quo and his teaching and praxis flew in the face of the systemic evils of his time. As Darby Kathleen Ray points out:

> Jesus' use of courage, creativity and the power of truth to uncover and disrupt the hegemony of power as control becomes a prototype for further strategies and action.[87]

Understanding this broader idea of nonviolence helps us understand what our task is as disciples of Jesus. To express this more active form of nonviolence, one could say—if it were not an expression out of its time—that Jesus was a *satyagrahi* and that the followers of Jesus are to be *satyagrahis*. J. Denny Weaver offers his own appreciation, in his own life, of this important distinction. He notes that

> ...the question of violence is not limited to the issue of pacifism and the refusal of military violence...slavery and racism and the enactment of white superiority are also forms of violence. So are poverty, sexism and patriarchy...recognizing that violence includes systemic forms of violence...makes painfully clear why the principle of nonresistance...is an inadequate peace stance...Nonresistance as a refusal to resist an evil act with another evil act has meaning when one faces active aggression. It means little, however, in the face of systemic violence such as racism or poverty. In fact, not resisting in that context can [be acquiescence] to...systemic violence... [A]ctive nonviolent resistance is to be embraced.[88]

It is in this faithful praxis of active, nonviolent resistance, in communion with Christ, that salvation is experienced. Salvation comes in the praxis of living this mission in history. In the words of Glen Stassen: "Doing the deeds of Jesus is participation in delivering grace."[89] Or, as Jon Sobrino writes:

> ...when we say that the cross brings salvation...we are saying that the culmination of our being loved by God is his work of preparing us to be introduced into his own historical process ...The cross does not offer an explanatory model that would make us understand what salvation is...Instead it invites us to participate in a process within which we can actually experience history as salvation.[90]

John Howard Yoder indicated that a revised understanding of salvation had to have at least three components. First it had to feature Christ's non-violence, "[t]he belief that nonresistance is part of the essential nature of 'agape,' of God's way of dealing with evil."[91] Second, it needed to feature the church as the community remembering and reenacting Christ's nonviolence in history. And third, it had to feature the notion of faith-union. Yoder thinks the notion of faith-union expressed by the Pauline term "in Christ" and the Johannine "abide in me" have been underappreciated. For Yoder, human beings fundamentally are made for communion with God. Faith is more than the acceptance of the proclamation that Jesus died. Yoder writes:

> Faith, likewise, must be understood biblically and de-Anselmized. It is not the mere acceptance of the proclamation that Jesus died because of our guilt. It is rather commitment to the faith-union of obedience made available to us through the perfect and triumphant obedience of Christ. In Pauline usage faith is identification with Christ's offering of himself in obedience to God.[92]

Being united with Christ in this way answers those who may think that salvation through nonviolent praxis is "Pelagian." It is not our actions that save us; it is our being united with Christ in his way of the cross that saves us. It is Christ acting in us and through us. This way of the cross continues across time through his Body, the church. Yoder's grasp of the biblical language provides us an opening to better understand the causality at work when we say someone is saved. Others have taken up this theme and explored the metaphors in Paul that express the sense that it is through an identification with Christ in his saving action that we are saved. Michael Gorman cites Albert Schweitzer's contention that "in-Christ" mysticism, not justification by faith, was the center of Paul's theology and experience. In 1977, E. P. Sanders also challenged the dominant interpretation of Paul suggesting that "participation in Christ," was the center of Paul's theology. In Gorman's words:

> The phrase "in Christ [Jesus]" occurs more than fifty times in the undisputed Pauline letters, while the phrases "in the Lord [Jesus/Jesus Christ]" and "in Christ Jesus our Lord" together appear a total of nearly forty times. Some of these texts refer to what God has done "in Christ," but the vast majority of these texts refer to existence in Christ. The language is not so much mystical as it is spatial: to live within a sphere of influence...but *to be "in Christ" principally means to be under the influence of Christ's power, especially the power to be conformed to him and his cross, by participation in the life of a community that acknowledges his lordship.*[93]

Paul mixes juridical and participationist metaphors, but according to Sanders "the real bite of his theology lies in the participatory categories."[94] Gorman goes on to point out that whenever Paul uses the phrase "in Christ," he is using plural pronouns in the Greek text. The experience of being one with Christ is not just for individuals but also for the community. Moreover, Gorman notes that the English expressions containing the word "with" simply do not do justice to much of Paul's language, experience, or thinking. He writes:

> The prefix "co-" does a better job; Paul says that we have been co-buried and co-crucified with Christ, that we have been co-formed with his death and will be co-formed with his resurrection in glory, that if we co-suffer with Christ we are coheirs with him and will be co-glorified with him...The focus of this participation is on suffering and death with Christ and on resurrection and glory in the future...that union with Christ's death is not a one-time past event but an ongoing reality.[95]

These categories help us get past the criticisms of Abelard's model of salvation, that being saved comes from "imitating" Christ. They also help us get past the criticism that it is "Pelagian" to conceive of salvation as nonviolent praxis. Salvation is continuing Jesus' work of nonviolent action through our nonviolent action. Being one with Christ through the remembering of him and the reenactment of his praxis in community today goes well beyond mere imitation. As Lohfink writes, echoing Yoder:

> The means by which the new society spread was not imitation, but discipleship: a non-envious identification with this person.[96]

Or, as Robert Barron put it:

> The Incarnation is not something to be admired from the outside, but rather an energy in which to participate...the Gospels want us not outside the energy of Christ, but in it, not wondering at it, but swimming in it...These beautiful organic images are meant to highlight our *participation* in the event of the Incarnation.[97]

The kind of causality at work here is one that we know in our everyday lives. We know that being in the presence of someone we love and admire changes us. The power of love has the power to create and generate love in response. I recently witnessed personally how this causality works. A few weeks after my wife and I saw the play, *Wicked,* and heard the song that culminates the play, "Because I knew you; because I knew you—I have been changed ... for good," we attended our grandson's graduation from high school. At the end of the graduation Mass, three graduates stood and ruefully sang the same words from *Wicked* to their classmates. The words of the song were no longer the words of one witch to another as in the play. In this setting the words conveyed the heartfelt gratitude these young people felt for one another and all that they had learned and received from one another, how, in their four years together, they had indeed changed. A few weeks later we attended a farewell party put on by a very vital parish community for their retiring, beloved pastor. After a raft of skits by various parishioners touching upon life and times with their pastor over the previous twelve years, the evening ended with the entire community standing and facing the priest and singing, some with tears in their eyes, all looking at him with gratitude and love, "Because I knew you, because I knew you—I have been changed ... for good." Never did a song seem so right. They clearly knew the causality of gracious love.

In the words of Jon Sobrino:

> When human beings have been in the presence of love they understand it as good news and deeply humanizing. And an invitation to be likewise ... This saving efficacy is shown more in the form of an exemplary cause than an efficient one ... It is not efficient causality but symbolic causality.[98]

Salvation then means to be given that intimate communion with God, not for the sake of a timeless I-Thou, but for the sake of the work that still needs to be done.

I indicated in chapter 4 that an adequate understanding of Christian salvation that is faithful to the scriptures and responsive to contemporary needs would have to satisfy the following criteria.

The soteriology has to

- have a thoroughgoing historical consciousness
- offer a way to deal with social as well as personal sin and evil
- link the life of Jesus with his death and resurrection
- present a model of causality that makes sense
- offer a way to exercise power that is of another order than domination

The restatement of Christian salvation influenced by Gandhi's concept of satyagraha satisfies all those criteria.

The "rethinking of Christian salvation in the light of Gandhi's satya-graha" is certainly not Anselmian. Gustav Aulen claims that the correct understanding of salvation, the one held widely by the early Church, is the *Christus Victor* model, Christ the Victor in the titanic battle with evil. Is then the understanding of Christian salvation inspired by nonviolence a *Christus Victor* or an Abelardian model? It is neither and it is both. It is rather a *Christus Viator* model—Christ the sojourner, Christ the pioneer, as in the letter to the Hebrews. This *Christus Viator* model insists that there is much more work to be done in history. Central to the model is the strug-gle against evil. In that it is similar to the *Christus Victor* model.

Satyagraha commits us to that struggle. Jesus' nonviolence shows us the way. The Way of the cross is the way for us who are wayfarers in his-tory to follow. The struggle can be carried out and accomplished, howev-er, only in community, through the loving inspiration of others who are learning the ways of nonviolence and unlearning the ways of domination. In that it is similar to the Abelardian model. Our salvation comes to us through and in the company of others who are faithfully performing the way of Christ in history, the community of believers, the church. Their witness and love transform us. But it is not mere mimesis or imitation, it is, in union with Christ, *discipleship*.

Epilogue

Embracing the New Testament teaching on nonviolent action changes us. It also influences the way we communicate with one another about our faith. In addition to the concept of salvation, which we have examined in this work, other fundamental tenets of our faith need to be recast as well. I have been asked, for example, if my understanding of the Eucharist has changed as I have come to understand the nonviolent Way of Jesus, and I realize that my understanding of the Eucharist has indeed evolved.

In my growing-up years I learned that the Eucharist was a sacrifice. We called it "the holy sacrifice of the Mass." In a mysterious but real way the sacrifice of Calvary is renewed at the Mass. The altar is the altar of sacrifice. I wasn't quite sure what "sacrifice" meant in that context. I did not make the associations one could make with ancient rituals that shed the blood of animals to appease a deity. I think I understood sacrifice mainly in its current colloquial sense—giving one's all for the sake of others or for a great cause. I understood that in the Mass Jesus was present again, giving his life for us. That is why in those years the words of consecration were the most important moment of the Mass. The "this" in the follow-on words, "Do this in memory of me," meant "Do this action, this sacrifice, in memory of me. When you do this action, you make me really present again under the species of bread and wine." That was the miracle referred to by the "this."

In subsequent years, the Second Vatican Council opened up for me a new understanding. The Mass is not just a sacrifice; it is also the celebration of a meal whose purpose, in the spirit of the Last Supper, is to form a community in Jesus' name. The council did not deny that the Mass is a sacrifice, but the new liturgy emphasized the Mass as a sacred meal. The altar was turned around and fashioned to look like a table for a meal. The language was not arcane Latin, understood only by the priest offering a sacrifice, but the vernacular through which all the participants could communicate with one another as in a family meal. We began to share the kiss of peace with the others present. The Mass was to prepare us to live our lives, supported by our family members, as Christians in the world. With this understanding of the Mass, the "this" in "Do this in memory of me" began to take on an additional meaning: "Do this community meal in such a way that you really do become a community that supports one another." The miracle referred to by "this" is that the community, the church, is formed and comes together.

Understanding Gandhian satyagraha has helped me understand and embrace Jesus' call to discipleship—following Jesus in his nonviolent Way of suffering, death, and resurrection. As a result, I understand what it means to be saved in a whole different way. It is to be united with him in the work of lifting up those whom society has left behind and in carrying on the work of building the Kingdom. This understanding has also given me a whole new understanding of the Mass. The Mass is not just an act of worship, an expression of a vertical relationship with God, nor is it only a meal that builds our horizontal relationships with our sisters and brothers. Even more important, in my life, the Mass is a summons to action, to live as Jesus did.

When I hear the words "Do this in memory of me," I am riveted. My back stiffens with resolve and my spirit and imagination are stirred. I think of the cloud of witnesses past and present who have modeled how to follow the nonviolent way, resisting oppression, caring for the poor and the sick, the outcast and the imprisoned, reaching out to "the enemy," confident in the love that possesses them. I think also of Gandhi's contention that it really is ahimsa that holds the world together, that violence is the rupture of the normal fabric of life—parents caring selflessly for their children, teachers engaging their students, people helping other people—that the daily round of human caring is what is real, not the *maya* of violence. Nonviolent action is the norm, not the exception.

I think also of how badly the world needs this message and this witness—how enmeshed our culture is in the belief in violence, how national security and the "nation" now command our deepest loyalty, how at risk we are because of our false idols.

The "this" in "Do this in memory of me" for me now means: "Do this way of acting that I have shown you. Do this way of resisting evil and returning good for evil that I lived and taught. Do it even if it is hard and stirs up resistance. Do it filled with love, because you know that you are loved." The Eucharist is now, for me, the call to follow Jesus' Way, united with him in his sacrifice and supported by a community of believers. It is the bread of life—sustenance for the journey, the Way that leads us outward and forward toward the suffering world.

Notes

Introduction

1. Andre Trocme, *Jesus and the Nonviolent Revolution* (Maryknoll, NY: Orbis Books, 2004),153, 156.

2. Norbert Lohfink, *Church Dreams* (N. Richland Hills, TX: Bibal Press, 2000),97.

3. Joel B. Green and Mark D. Baker, *Recovering the Scandal of the Cross* (Downers Grove, IL: InterVarsity Press, 2000), 24–25.

4. Christopher D. Marshall, *Beyond Retribution: A New Testament Vision for Justice, Crime and Punishment* (Grand Rapids, MI: William B. Eerdmans, 2001).

1: Mohandas Gandhi: A Hindu and More

1. *Young India*, August 6, 1925.

2. Ravindra Kumar, *Theory and Practice of Gandhian Non-violence* (New Delhi: Mittal Publications, 2002), 19.

3. C. F. Andrews, *Gandhi's Ideas* (London: George Allen and Unwin, 1929), 3.

4. Mohandas Gandhi, *An Autobiography or The Story of My Experiments with Truth* (Ahmedabad: Navajivan, 1927), 4.

5. Geoffrey Ashe, *Gandhi* (New York: Stein and Day, 1968), 6–7.

6. Gandhi, *Autobiography*, 32.

7. Ibid., 62.

8. Ibid., 63–64.

9. Raghavan Iyer, *The Moral and Political Writings of Mahatma Gandhi*, vol. 1 (London: Concord Grove Press, 1986), 145–46.

10. *Collected Works of Mahatma Gandhi* (hereafter cited as *CWMG*), 100 vols. (Delhi: Publications Division, Ministry of Information and Broadcasting, Government of India, 1958–94), 32:593.

11. B. R. Nanda, *In Search of Gandhi: Essays and Reflections* (New Delhi: Oxford University Press, 2002), 13.

12. *CWMG*, 4:408.

13. *Young India*, August 6, 1925.

14. Nanda, *In Search of Gandhi*, 31.

15. Quoted in Ashe, *Gandhi*, 125.

16. Nanda, *In Search of Gandhi*, 16.

17. Ibid., 327–28.

18. *CWMG*, 10:446.

19. Erik Erikson, *Gandhi's Truth* (New York: Norton, 1969), 36.

20. *CWMG*, 20:194.

21. *CWMG*, 4:409.

22. Judith Brown, *Gandhi: Prisoner of Hope* (New Haven: Yale University Press, 1989), 122. *Swaraj* is the Sanskrit word for freedom or liberation. It has many levels of potential meaning from political through religious.

23. *CWMG*, 23:271.

24. Madan Gopal Sinha, *The Political Ideas of Bipin Chandra Pal* (Delhi: Commonwealth Publishers, 1989), 35–36, quoted in Dennis Dalton, *Mahatma Gandhi: Nonviolent Power in Action* (New York: Columbia University Press, 1993), 4.

25. *CWMG*, 25:424.

26. *CWMG*, 37:250–51.

27. *Young India*, May 12, 1920.

28. Louis Fischer, *The Life of Mahatma Gandhi* (New York: Harper and Brothers, 1950), 430.

29. H. N. Brailsford, "Why India Follows Gandhi," *Forum*, 85 (May 1931): 287, quoted in Joan Bondurant, *Conquest of Violence* (Princeton: Princeton University Press, 1988), 122.

30. Vincent Sheehan, *Lead Kindly Light* (New York: Random House, 1949), 234.

31. Ibid., 22–23.

32. *CWMG*, 35:456.

33. *CWMG*, 23:242.

34. Raghavan Iyer, *The Moral and Political Thought of Mahatma Gandhi*, 2nd ed. (London: Concord Grove Press, 1983), 134.

35. Naryan Desai, "Gandhi's Method of Training for Nonviolence," in *Nonviolence, Peace, and Politics: Understanding Gandhi*, ed. Naresh Dadhich (Jaipur: Aavishkar Publishers, 2003), 59.

36. P. Spear, *India* (Ann Arbor: University of Michigan Press, 1961), 359, quoted in Iyer, *The Moral and Political Thought of Mahatma Gandhi*, 6.

37. The Khilafat movement was the push by Muslims throughout the world to have the Western powers, after World War I, restore the sultan of Turkey to power. Traditionally, the role of the caliph was not just political but also religious—he was the recognized leader of Muslims across many countries. The caliphate was especially important to the two Ali brothers who were members of Congress and received vigorous support from Indian Muslims. Gandhi went out on a political limb to support their cause. The Western powers, in particular the British, reneged on their war promises. The issue was rendered moot when the secular leader of Turkey, Ataturk, abolished both roles.

38. J. J. Doke, *M. K. Gandhi: An Indian Patriot* (Madras: Natesan, 1909), 142.

39. *CWMG*, 27:436.

40. *Harijan*, May 11, 1935.

41. *Harijan*, December 12, 1936.

42. *Harijan*, March 29, 1935.

43. Charles Freer Andrews was an Anglican priest and longtime friend of Gandhi and the Nobel Prize–winning poet, Rabinadrath Tagore, who lived his whole life on behalf of the Indian poor in many different parts of the world. We will discuss him in chapter 3.

44. Mohandas K. Gandhi, *The Message of Jesus Christ* (Bombay: Bharatiya Vidya Bhavan, 1986), 60.

45. Ibid., 3.

46. Ibid., 40.

47. *Harijan*, March 23, 1940.

48. *Young India*, October 27, 1927.

49. *Harijan*, March 6, 1937.

50. Gandhi, *The Message of Jesus Christ*, 18.

51. Ibid., 26.

52. *Young India*, March 31, 1927.

53. *Harijan*, June 18, 1938.

54. K. L. Seshagiri Rao, *Mahatma Gandhi and C. F. Andrews* (Patiala: Punjabi University Press, 1969), 31–32.

55. S. K. George, *Gandhi's Challenge to Christianity* (Ahmedabad: Navajivan, 1960), 74–75.

56. Mahadev Desai's *Diary*, as quoted in Margaret Chatterjee, *Gandhi's Religious Thought* (Notre Dame, IN: University of Notre Dame Press, 1983), 54.

57. Ibid., 242.

58. Gandhi, *The Message of Jesus Christ*, 14.

59. E. Stanley Jones, *Mahatma Gandhi: An Interpretation* (New York: Abingdon-Cokesbury Press, 1948), 105, 107.

60. *Young India*, December 31, 1931.

61. George, *Gandhi's Challenge to Christianity*, 23.

62. *Young India*, December 31, 1931.

63. Mohandas Gandhi, *Letter to Madame Privat*, November, 29, 1947, *CWMG*, 90:129.

64. *CWMG*, 37:261.

65. Leo Tolstoy, *The Kingdom of God Is within You*, trans. Constance Garnett (Lincoln: University of Nebraska Press, 1984; first published 1905), xv.

66. Gandhi, *Letter to Madame Privat*, *CWMG*, 90:129–30.

67. Iyer, *The Moral and Political Thought of Mahatma Gandhi*, 179.

68. *CWMG*, 9:243.

69. Chatterjee, *Gandhi's Religious Thought*, 89.

70. Tolstoy, *The Kingdom of God Is within You*, 380.

71. Leo Tolstoy, *The Gospel in Brief*, trans. Aylmer Maude (London: Noonday Press, 1958), 283.

72. J. T. F. Jordens, *Gandhi's Religion: A Homespun Shawl* (New York: Palgrave, 1998), 34.

73. William Robert Miller, "Gandhi and King: Pioneers of Modern Non-violence," *Gandhi Marg*, 13, no. 1 (1969): 21.

74. Iyer, *The Moral and Political Thought of Mahatma Gandhi*, 18.

75. *CWMG*, 63:339.

76. *CWMG*, 15:288.

77. *CWMG*, 20:369.

78. *CWMG*, 51:324–25.

79. Chatterjee, *Gandhi's Religious Thought*, 34.

80. *CWMG*, 14:146.

81. Rao, *Mahatma Gandhi and C. F. Andrews*, 35.

82. Unto Tahtinen, *Ahimsa: Non-violence in Indian Tradition* (Ahmedabad: Navajivan, 1976), 2.

83. S. B. Mookherji, "Ahimsa through the Ages: Gandhi's Contribution," *Gandhi Marg* 4 (July 1960): 221.

84. *Harijan*, July 6, 1940.

85. Iyer, *The Moral and Political Thought of Mahatma Gandhi*, 182.

86. Chatterjee, *Gandhi's Religious Thought*, 75.

87. Ibid., 77.

88. *Young India*, November 5, 1931.

2: Gandhian Satyagraha

1. *Collected Works of Mahatma Gandhi* (hereafter cited as *CWMG*), 100 vols. (Delhi: Publications Division, Ministry of Information and Broadcasting, Government of India, 1958–94), 29:94.

2. Raghavan Iyer, *The Moral and Political Thought of Mahatma Gandhi*, 2nd ed. (London: Concord Grove Press, 1983), 261.

3. *CWMG*, 29:93.

4. Ibid., 95.

5. Ibid., 95.

6. Ibid., 96.

7. Ibid., 92; see also *CWMG*, 7:455, 8:131–32.

8. *CWMG*, 29:92.

9. To avoid confusion it is helpful to define and distinguish the many terms that are used to convey the idea of nonviolence. Gene Sharp has developed a helpful taxonomy of the various terms in his article, "A Study of the Meaning of Nonviolence," *Gandhi Marg* 3 (1959): 265–73. In this schema he offers definitions, examples, and descriptions of advocate groups for nine distinct terms for nonviolence: nonresistance, active reconciliation, moral resistance, selective nonviolence, passive resistance, peaceful resistance, nonviolent direct action, satyagraha, and nonviolent revolution.

10. *CWMG*, 21:456.

11. *CWMG*, 22:382.

12. Ibid., 450.

13. *CWMG*, 42:426.

14. *From Yeravada Mandir*, chapter 1, as quoted in Mohandas Gandhi, *Satyagraha: Non-violent Resistance* (Ahmedabad: Navajivan, 1951), 38.

15. John Hick, introduction to part 2, *Gandhi's Significance for Today*, ed. John Hick and Lamont Hempel (London: Macmillan, 1989), 85–86.

16. Margaret Chatterjee, *Gandhi's Religious Thought* (Notre Dame, IN: University of Notre Dame Press, 1983), 61.

17. *Young India*, October 11, 1928, as quoted in Mohandas Gandhi, *Truth Is God*, ed. R. K. Prabhu (Ahmedabad: Navajivan, 1987), 7.

18. R. R. Diwakar, "Satyagraha: A New Way of Life and a New Technique for Social Change," *Gandhi Marg* 13, no. 4 (1969): 19.

19. E. Stanley Jones, *Mahatma Gandhi: An Interpretation* (New York: Abingdon-Cokesbury Press, 1948), 86.

20. M. K. Gandhi, *Young India* (1927–28).

21. Quoted in J. T. F. Jordens, *Gandhi's Religion: A Homespun Shawl* (New York: Palgrave, 1998), 114.

22. Iyer, *The Moral and Political Thought of Mahatma Gandhi*, 93.

23. Rex Ambler, "Gandhi's Concept of Truth," in Hick and Hempel, *Gandhi's Significance for Today*, 95.

24. As quoted in Nicholas Lobkowicz, *Theory and Practice* (Notre Dame, IN: University of Notre Dame Press, 1967), 411.

25. *CWMG*, 28:385, 30:66, 31:511, as quoted in Jordens, *Gandhi's Religion*, 242.

26. Lobkowicz, *Theory and Practice*, 74.

27. Ambler,"Gandhi's Concept of Truth," 93.

28. Ibid., 102.

29. Elton Hall, "Religious Universalism," in Hick and Hempel, *Gandhi's Significance for Today*, 168.

30. *Harijan*, June 18, 1938.

31. Mark Juergensmeyer, "Shoring Up the Saint: Some Suggestions for Improving Satyagraha," in Hick and Hempel, *Gandhi's Significance for Today*, 38.

32. *Harijan*, March 9, 1940.

33. *Young India*, June 24, 1925.

34. Joan Bondurant, *Conquest of Violence: The Gandhian Philosophy of Conflict*, new ed. (Princeton, NJ: Princeton University Press, 1988), 192, 196.

35. Juergensmeyer, "Shoring Up the Saint," 39.

36. *CWMG*, 29:92.

37. Bondurant, *Conquest of Violence*, 9.

38. Diwakar, "Satyagraha," 18.

39. *CWMG*, 40:58.

40. *CWMG*, 25:208.

41. *CWMG*, 68:389.

42. *CWMG*, 35:385.

43. *CWMG*, 47:276.

44. *CWMG*, 18:388.

45. *CWMG*, 39:459–50.

46. *CWMG*, 64:222.

47. *CWMG*, 69:122.

48. *CWMG*, 72:356.

49. *CWMG*, 83:204.

50. Chatterjee, *Gandhi's Religious Thought*, 76–77.

51. *CWMG*, 62:199.

52. Ibid., 200.

53. *CWMG*, 68:252.

54. *CWMG*, 72:226.

55. *CWMG*, 35:53.

56. *CWMG*, 19:233.

57. *CWMG*, 18:156.

58. *CWMG*, 72:307.

59. *CWMG*, 15:52.

60. *CWMG*, 34:3, 38:143.

61. *CWMG*, 68:13.

62. *CWMG*, 67:67.

63. *CWMG*, 68:14.

64. Ibid., 87.

65. Erik Erikson, *Gandhi's Truth* (New York: Norton, 1969), 373.

66. *CWMG*, 47:285.

67. *CWMG*, 39:220–21.

68. *CWMG*, 40:107.

69. *CWMG*, 69:163.

70. *CWMG*, 68:64.

71. *CWMG*, 37:135, 67:195, 14:356.

72. *CWMG*, 69:163.

73. *CWMG*, 28:305.

74. Juergensmeyer, "Shoring Up the Saint," 46.

75. *CWMG*, 69:122.

76. Ibid.

77. John Chattanatt, "Two Paradigms of Liberative Transformation: Approaches to Social Action in the Theological Ethics of Gandhi and Gutiérrez" (PhD diss., University of Chicago, 1991), 165.

78. B. R. Nanda, *In Search of Gandhi: Essays and Reflections* (New Delhi: Oxford University Press, 2002), 8.

79. Ibid., 77.

80. *CWMG*, 35:224.

81. Ibid., 225.

82. Richard B. Gregg, "Satyagraha as a Mirror," in *Gandhi: His Relevance for Our Times*, ed. G. Ramachandran and T. K. Mahadevan (Berkeley, CA: World Without War Council, 1967), 126.

83. Ibid., 127.

84. Rita Dadhich, *Modernity, Civilization and Conflict-Resolution* (Jaipur, India: Arihant Publishing House, 2001), 100.

85. Weyburn Woodrow Groff, "Nonviolence: A Comparative Study of Mohandas Gandhi and the Mennonite Church on the Subject of Nonviolence" (PhD diss., New York University, 1963), 112.

86. Gregg, "Satyagraha as a Mirror," 127.

87. Mark Juergensmeyer, *Gandhi's Way: A Handbook of Conflict Resolution* (Berkeley: University of California Press, 1984), 3.

88. Bondurant, *Conquest of Violence*, 195.

89. Richard B. Gregg, *The Power of Nonviolence* (New York: Schocken Books, 1966), 12.

90. *CWMG*, 48:402–3.

91. Sharp, "A Study of the Meaning of Nonviolence," 4.

92. *CWMG*, 40:365.

93. Rashmi-Sudha Puri, *Gandhi on War and Peace* (New York: Praeger, 1987), 213.

94. G. Ramachandran and T. K. Mahadevan, eds., *Quest for Gandhi* (New Delhi: Gandhi Peace Foundation, 1970), 133.

95. William James, *Memories and Studies* (London: Longmans, Green and Company, 1911), 276, 287–88.

96. Chris Hedges, *War Is a Force That Gives Us Meaning* (New York: Anchor, 2003).

97. Stanley Hauerwas, *Should War Be Eliminated? A Thought Experiment* (originally published as the 1984 Pere Marquette Theology Lecture [Milwaukee: Marquette University Press, 1984]), and "On Being a Church Capable of Addressing a World at War: A Pacifist Response to the United Methodist Bishops' Pastoral 'In Defense of Creation'" (originally published as the epilogue to *Speak Up for Just War or Pacifism: A Critique of the United Methodist Bishops' Pastoral Letter*, ed. Paul Ramsey [University Park, PA: Pennsylvania State University Press, 1988], 149–82).

98. *CWMG*, 48:420–21.

99. Ibid., 67:76.

100. *Harijan*, November 26, 1938.

101. *CWMG*, 67:405.

102. Ibid., 371.

103. Gene Sharp, "Gandhi's Political Significance for Today," in Ramachandran and Mahadevan, *Gandhi: His Relevance for Our Times*, 143.

104. *CWMG*, 60:50.

105. Naryan Desai, "Gandhi's Method of Training for Nonviolence," in *Nonviolence, Peace, and Politics: Understanding Gandhi*, ed. Naresh Dadhich (Jaipur, India: Aavishkar Publishers, 2003), 64.

106. Among them are Peter Ackerman and Jack DuVall, *A Force More Powerful: A Century of Nonviolent Change* (New York: Palgrave, 2000). They describe some twelve case studies. Michael Duffey, *Peacemaking Christians: The Future of Just Wars, Pacifism, and Nonviolent Resistance* (Kansas City, MO: Sheed and Ward, 1995), describes the Poland, Philippines, and East German campaigns because, consistent with his overall theme, in these campaigns the churches played a particularly important role. Gene Sharp, *Waging Nonviolent Struggle* (Boston: Extending Horizons Books, Porter Sargent Publishers, 2005), examines twenty-three nonviolent struggles of various kinds, from fending off a coup, to fighting for civil rights, to overthrowing an oppressive regime.

107. Walter Wink, *The Powers That Be: Theology for a New Millennium* (New York: Doubleday, 1998), 117.

108. Martin Luther King, *Stride toward Freedom* (New York: Harper and Brothers, 1958), 97–98.

109. Ackerman and DuVall, *A Force More Powerful*, 367.

110. Ibid., 368.

111. Duffey, *Peacemaking Christians*, 134.

112. Sharp, *Waging Nonviolent Struggle*, 227; the quote is from Bartolomiej Kaminski, *The Collapse of State Socialism: The Case of Poland* (Princeton: Princeton University Press, 1991), 215.

3: Selected Christian Theologians Who Have Embraced Nonviolence

1. K. L. Seshagiri Rao, *Mahatma Gandhi and C. F. Andrews* (Patiala: Punjabi University Press, 1969), 21.

2. Horace Alexander in the introduction to C.F. Andrews, *Gandhi's Ideas* (London: George Allen and Unwin, Ltd., 1929), 3.

3. *Collected Works of Mahatma Gandhi* (hereafter cited as *CWMG*), 100 vols. (Delhi: Publications Division, Ministry of Information and Broadcasting, Government of India, 1958–94), 16:315.

4. Ibid., 148.

5. C. F. Andrews, *Modern Review*, December 1907, as quoted in Daniel O'Connor, *The Testimony of C. F. Andrews* (Madras: Christian Literature Society, 1974).

6. C. F. Andrews, *What I Owe to Christ* (New York: Abingdon Press, 1932), 223.

7. C. F. Andrews, "Mahatma Gandhi's Greatest Weapon," *Modern Review*, November 1938, as quoted in P. C. Chaudbury, *C. F. Andrews: His Life and Times* (Bombay, Somaiya Publications, 1971), 75.

8. Andrews, *What I Owe to Christ*, 216.

9. Ibid., 215.

10. Benarsidas Chaturvedi and Marjorie Sykes, *C. F. Andrews: A Biography* (New York: Harper Brothers, 1950), 315.

11. C. F. Andrews, *The Sermon on the Mount* (London: G. Allen and Unwin, 1942), 85. This beautiful book was discovered in his drawer after his death.

12. Ibid., 118.

13. Ibid., 119.

14. Ibid., 122.

15. Ibid., 123.

16. Ibid., 124.

17. Ibid., 123.

18. C. F. Andrews, *Addresses and Other Records* (London: Tambaram Series, 1939), 7:92–99, as quoted in O'Connor, *The Testimony of C. F. Andrews*, 275.

19. Andrews, *What I Owe to Christ*, 206–7.

20. C. F. Andrews, *Christ in the Silence* (New York: Abingdon Press, 1933), 262.

21. Ibid., 131.

22. Andrews, *The Sermon on the Mount*, 96–97.

23. Ibid., 94–95.

24. John Hoyland, *C. F. Andrews: Minister of Reconciliation* (London: Allenson, 1940), 7.

25. Andrews, *Gandhi's Ideas*, 312–13.

26. Ibid., 347.

27. Ibid., 348.

28. Andrews, *The Sermon on the Mount*, 159.

29. See Kenneth Hallahan, "The Social Ethics of Nonresistance: The Writings of Mennonite Theologian John Howard Yoder Analyzed from a Roman Catholic Perspective" (PhD diss., The Catholic University of America, 1997). Hallahan concludes that Yoder's method does contrast sharply with the use of scripture as "proof texts" in the encyclicals—if quoted or mentioned at all.

30. John Howard Yoder, *The Politics of Jesus*, 2nd ed. (Grand Rapids, MI: William B. Eerdmans, 1994), 31.

31. Ibid., back cover.

32. Introduction to Stanley Hauerwas, Chris K. Heubner, Harry J. Heubner, and Mark Thiessen Nation, eds., *The Wisdom of the Cross: Essays in Honor of John Howard Yoder* (Grand Rapids, MI: William B. Eerdmans, 1999), x–xi.

33. John Howard Yoder, *The Original Revolution* (Scottdale, PA: Herald Press, 1977), 128.

34. Earl Zimmerman, "A Praxis of Peace: The 'Politics of Jesus' According to John Howard Yoder (PhD diss., The Catholic University of America, 2004), 60.

35. Mark Thiessen Nation, "John H. Yoder, Ecumenical Neo-Anabaptist: A Biographical Sketch," in Hauerwas et al., *The Wisdom of the Cross*, 5.

36. Yoder, *The Politics of Jesus*, 5.

37. Paul Ramsey, *Basic Christian Ethics* (New York: Scribner, 1950), 167ff., quoted in Yoder, *The Politics of Jesus*, 6.

38. Yoder, *The Original Revolution*, 19.

39. Ibid., 22–23.

40. Yoder, *The Politics of Jesus*, 32.

41. Ibid., 50.

42. John Howard Yoder, *He Came Preaching Peace* (Scottdale, PA: Herald Press, 1985), 20.

43. J. Denny Weaver, "Theology in the Mirror of the Martyred and Oppressed," in Hauerwas et al., *The Wisdom of the Cross*, 413.

44. Yoder, *The Original Revolution*, 29.

45. Yoder, *The Politics of Jesus*, 36.

46. Yoder, *The Original Revolution*, 56–57.

47. Yoder, *The Politics of Jesus*, 129.

48 Ibid., 131.

49. Ibid., 64, 68, 71.

50. John Howard Yoder, *Christian Attitudes towards War, Peace, and Revolution* (Durham, NC: Duke University Divinity School, 1983), 115.

51. Ibid., 98.

52. Yoder, *He Came Preaching Peace*, 21.

53. Yoder, *Christian Attitudes towards War, Peace and Revolution*, 356.

54. Craig Carter, *The Politics of the Cross: The Theology and Social Ethics of John Howard Yoder* (Grand Rapids, MI: Brazos Press, 2001), 45.

55. Yoder, *Christian Attitudes towards War, Peace, and Revolution*, 344–45.

56. Ibid., 505.

57. Ibid., 405.

58. Ibid., 333.

59. Guy F. Hershberger, *War, Peace, and Nonresistance* (Scottdale, PA: Herald Press, 1944), 1, as quoted in Zimmerman, "A Praxis of Peace," 39.

60. John Howard Yoder, *Nevertheless: The Varieties of Religious Pacifism* (Scottdale, PA: Herald Press, 1971), 38.

61. Yoder, *Christian Attitudes towards War, Peace, and Revolution*, 366.

62. Yoder, *Nevertheless*, 47–48.

63. Ibid., 119, 139.

64. Ibid., 141.

65. Yoder, *He Came Preaching Peace*, 40.

66. John Howard Yoder, *The Priestly Kingdom* (Notre Dame, IN: University of Notre Dame Press, 1984), 99.

67. Yoder, *The Original Revolution*, 39.

68. Yoder, *Christian Attitudes towards War, Peace, and Revolution*, 454.

69. Ibid., 437.

70. Ibid., 491, 546.

71. Joel Zimbelman, "The Contribution of John Howard Yoder to Recent Discussions in Christian Social Ethics," *Scottish Journal of Theology* 45 (September 1992): 388.

72. Glen Stassen, "The Politics of Jesus in the Sermon on the Plain," in Hauerwas et al., *The Wisdom of the Cross*, 160.

73. John Howard Yoder, *For the Nations: Essays Public and Evangelical* (Grand Rapids, MI: William B. Eerdmans, 1997), 35.

74. Bernard Häring, *My Witness for the Church* (New York/Mahwah, NJ: Paulist Press, 1992), 15.

75. Bernard Häring, *I Have Seen Your Tears* (Liguori, MO: Liguori Publications, 1995), 13.

76. Häring, *My Witness for the Church*, 24.

77. Ibid., 19.

78. Charles Curran, *Catholic Moral Theology in Dialogue* (Notre Dame, IN: Fides Publishers, 1972), 27.

79. Ibid., 64.

80. Kathleen Cahalan, "The Sacramental-Moral Theology of Bernard Häring: A Study of the Virtue of Religion" (Ph.D. diss., University of Chicago, 1998), 13.

81. Bernard Häring, *Free and Faithful in Christ* (New York: Crossroad, 1981), 359.

82. Bernard Häring, *The Healing Power of Peace and Nonviolence* (New York/Mahwah, NJ: Paulist Press, 1986), 89.

83. Rene Girard, *Violence and the Sacred* (Baltimore: Johns Hopkins University Press, 1977), 106.

84. Häring, *My Witness for the Church*, 90–91.

85. Bernard Häring, *To Do Justice: A Christian Social Conscience* (Liguori, MO: Liguori Publications, 1999), 77–79.

86. Häring, *My Witness for the Church*, 211.

87. Häring, *The Healing Power of Peace and Nonviolence*, 49.

88. Ibid., 58.

89. Ibid., 59.

90. Ibid., 55.

91. Ibid., 56.

92. Häring, *Free and Faithful in Christ*, 398.

93. Bernard Häring, *A Theology of Protest* (New York: Farrar, Straus and Giroux, 1970), 11–12.

94. Häring, *The Healing Power of Peace and Nonviolence*, 22.

95. Häring, *Free and Faithful in Christ*, 407.

96. Häring, *The Healing Power of Peace and Nonviolence*, 100.

97. Ibid., 65.

98. Ibid.

99. Ibid., 88.

100. Ibid., 88–89.

101. Ibid., 88.

102. Ibid., 57.

103. Häring, *My Witness for the Church*, 198.

104. Walter Wink, *The Powers That Be* (New York: Doubleday, 1998), 7–8.

105. Ibid., 48.

106. Ibid., 83.

107. Warren S. Kissinger, *The Sermon on the Mount: A History of Interpretation and Bibliography* (Metuchen, NJ: Scarecrow Press, 1975), 5–15, shows how all the ante-Nicene fathers of the church as well as Augustine understood the Sermon on the Mount to be the way of life applicable to all Christians, not just a select few.

108. So much depends on how interpreters understand the key word, *anthistemi*. Many continue, with Reinhold Niebuhr, to translate it as *nonresistance*, staying passive in the face of evil, and then write the passage off as irrelevant for the real world except as an impossible ideal. See, for example, John Stott, *The Message of the Sermon on the Mount* (Leicester, England: InterVarsity Press, 1978), 105. Robert Guelich, *The Sermon on the Mount: A Foundation for Understanding* (Waco, TX: Word Books, 1982), 219, 251, comes closer to the mark in translating *anthistemi* as "not seeking legal vindication." Wink rejects a translation that equates to "be complicit with your own repression and submit to evil." He points out that the term is used in the Septuagint primarily (forty-four out of seventy-one times) for armed resistance in military encounters. It means to resist violently, to revolt, to engage in an insurrection. Walter Wink, *Engaging the Powers: Discernment and Resistance in a World of Domination* (Minneapolis: Fortress Press, 1992), 185.

109. Wink is not alone in his interpretation of Matthew 5:38–42, rejecting the passivity interpretation of Niebuhr and so many others. He cites Pinchas Lapide, Gerhard Lohfink, Jean Lambrecht, SJ, and Jurgen Sauer as scholars who also understand the creative, active nature of these responses to oppression and violence. Moreover, many modern commentators appreciate the fact that this section of the Sermon on the Mount is not a new set of laws or rules, nor is it "works." The passage assumes that people first have heard the gospel and because they have been transformed by the message and example of Jesus, they can then live differently. It is first grace and then works. Joachim Jeremias articulates this point of view:

The sayings of Jesus which have been collected in the Sermon on the Mount are not intended to lay a legal yoke upon Jesus' disciples; neither in the sense that they say: "You ought actually to have done all of this, see what poor creatures you are" (theory of the impossible ideal); nor in the sense : "Now pull yourself together; the final victory is at hand" (interim ethic). Rather these sayings of Jesus delineate the lived faith. They say: You are forgiven; you are the child of God; you belong to the kingdom. The sun of righteousness has risen over your life. You no longer belong to yourself; rather, you belong to the city of God, the light of which shines in the darkness. Now you may also experience it: out of the thankfulness of a redeemed child of God a new life is growing. This is the meaning of the Sermon on the Mount. (Joachim Jeremias, *The Sermon on the Mount* [Philadelphia: Fortress Press, 1963], 34.)

110. Wink, *Engaging the Powers*, 175–76. It is perhaps no surprise that Wink's exegesis of these "commands" of Jesus is so similar to that in C. F. Andrews's *The Sermon on the Mount*, written some forty years earlier. Andrews witnessed Gandhi's life firsthand. Wink witnessed the multiple, historical examples of successful nonviolent action subsequent to, and inspired by, Gandhi.

111. Ibid., 176–77.

112. Wink, *The Powers That Be*, 104–5.

113. An important and influential article by Robert Tannehill, "The 'Focal Instance' as a Form of New Testament Speech: A Study of Matthew 5:39b–42," *Journal of Religion* 50 (1970): 372–85, illuminates and confirms Wink's exegesis from a slightly different direction. He too appreciates the fact that these examples are part of an open-ended series. Tannehill concentrates on the type of language at work here, a literary criticism approach, and calls the four specific and extreme commands—turn the other cheek, let the person have your cloak, go two miles, give to the one who begs from you—"focal instances." He writes, "We take them as examples which are relevant to many situations which have nothing to do with cheeks and forced service." Ibid., 377–78. The presence of a series of commands ensures that each command is not restricted to its specific scenario. The language is specific but open-ended. The extreme language shocks and provokes. As Tannehill writes, "It arouses the moral imagination, enabling the hearers to see their situation in a new way and to contemplate new possibilities of action . . . The focal instance serves as an illuminator of the hearer's situation. The hearer is invited to lay the saying alongside the hearer's own situation and, through the imaginative shock produced to see that situation in a new way." Ibid., 382–83.

114. Wink, *The Powers That Be*, 108–9.

115. Wink, *Engaging the Powers*, 266.

116. Ibid., 267.

117. Ibid., 275.

118. Ibid., 263.

119. Ibid., 307–8.

120. Ibid., 187.

121. Ibid., 193.

4. The Multiple Versions of Salvation Theologies

1. Monika Hellwig, "Changing Soteriology in an Ecumenical Context: A Catholic Reflection," *Proceedings of the Catholic Theological Society* 38 (1983): 14–21; Monika Hellwig, "Emerging Issues in Soteriology," *Theology Digest* 3/4 (1984): 129–32; William Loewe, "Toward a Responsible Contemporary Soteriology," in *Creativity and Method: Essays in Honor of Bernard Lonergan S.J.*, ed. Matthew Lamb (Milwaukee: Marquette University Press, 1985), 213–27; Jon Nilson, "Salvation," in *The HarperCollins Encyclopedia of Catholicism*, ed. Richard McBrien (San Francisco: HarperCollins, 1995), 1158; Francis Schüssler Fiorenza, "Critical Social Theory and Christology: Toward an Understanding of Atonement and Redemption as Emancipatory Solidarity," *Proceedings of the Catholic Theological Society* 30 (1975): 63–110; Francis Schüssler Fiorenza, "Redemption," in *New Dictionary of Theology*, ed. Joseph Komonchak, Mary Collins, and Dermot Lane (Wilmington, DE: Michael Glazier, 1987).

2. Edward Schillebeeckx, *Christ: The Experience of Jesus as Lord* (New York, Crossroad, 1980), 63.

3. Michael Slusser, "Primitive Christian Soteriological Themes," *Theological Studies* 44 (1983): 555–69.

4. Joseph Fitzmyer, "Reconciliation in Paul," in *No Famine in the Land: Studies in Honor of John L. McKenzie*, ed. James Flanagan and Anita Weisbord Robinson (Missoula, MT: Scholars Press, 1975), 156.

5. Elizabeth Johnson, "Jesus and Salvation," *Proceedings of the Catholic Theological Society of America* 49 (1994): 4.

6. For this section I draw on Edward Schillebeeckx, *Christ: The Experience of Jesus as Lord*, which devotes some 350 pages to reviewing the distinctive theologies of salvation in the various books of the New Testament

7. "*Pesher*" exegesis is found especially in the Dead Sea Scrolls. It often consists of taking a scriptural book and identifying its characters with individuals and situations of the writer's own day or of the expected near future. For example, a prophet's description of an Assyrian attack would be taken to refer to the recent Roman attack, and a prophecy of victory over the Assyrians would be taken as indicating a victory over the Romans.

8. Schillebeeckx, *Christ*, 252.

9. Ibid., 292–93.

10. Irenaeus, "Against the Heresies," in *The Ante-Nicene Fathers*, vol. 1, ed. Alexander Roberts and James Donaldson (Grand Rapids, MI: William B. Eerdmans, 1979), bk. 4, 20.7.

11. Roger Haight, *Jesus Symbol of God* (Maryknoll, NY: Orbis Books, 1999), 216.

12. Irenaeus, "Against the Heresies," bk. 3, 18.1, as quoted in Denis Edwards, *What Are They Saying about Salvation?* (New York/Mahwah, NJ: Paulist Press, 1986), 14.

13. J. Patout Burns, "The Economy of Salvation: Two Patristic Traditions," *Theological Studies* 37 (1976): 601, 608

14. Edwards, *What Are They Saying about Salvation?* 15.

15. Anselm of Canterbury, *Cur Deus Homo*, trans. Joseph Colleran (Albany, NY: Magi Books, 1969), bk. 1, 24, p. 113.

16. Ibid., bk. 1, 24, p. 114.

17. Ibid., bk. 2, 6, p. 124.

18. Ibid., bk. 2, 7, p. 126.

19. Ibid., bk. 2, 11, p. 136.

20. Ibid., bk. 2, 18, p. 156.

21. Ibid., bk. 1, 8, pp. 74–75.

22. Ibid., bk. 1, 9, pp. 79–80.

23. Ibid., bk. 2, 19, p. 160.

24. Johnson, "Jesus and Salvation," 5.

25. Abelard, *A Scholastic Miscellany*, ed. E. R. Fairweather (London: SCM, 1956), 284.

26. John Calvin, *Institutes of Christian Religion*, ed. John T. McNeill (Philadelphia: Westminster Press, 1960), bk. 2, chap. 16.5, p. 510.

27. John Howard Yoder, *Preface to Theology* (Grand Rapids, MI: Brazos Press, 2002), 298.

28. Diane Marie Steele, "Creation and Cross in the Later Soteriology of Edward Schillebeeckx" (PhD diss., University of Notre Dame, 2000), 34.

29. Adolf Tanquerey, *A Manual of Dogmatic Theology*, vol. 1, trans. Rt. Rev. Msgr. John J. Byrne (New York: Desclee, 1959), 74–75 (emphasis in the original).

30. *St. Joseph's Baltimore Catechism* (New York: Catholic Book, 1962–69), 53–54.

31. Joseph Ratzinger, *Introduction to Christianity* (New York: Herder and Herder, 1970).

32. Avery Dulles, *Survival of Dogma* (Garden City, NY: Doubleday, 1971).

33. Ratzinger, *Introduction to Christianity*, 172, 214.

34. Anselm, *Cur Deus Homo*, bk. 1, 12, p. 86.

35. Ibid.

36. Haight, *Jesus*, 228–29.

37. Anselm, *Cur Deus Homo*, bk. 1, 22, p. 86.

38. Ratzinger, *Introduction to Christianity*, 214.

39. Jon Sobrino, *Christology at the Crossroads* (Eugene, OR: Wipf and Stock, 2002), 193.

40. Edward Schillebeeckx, *Church: The Human Story of God* (New York: Crossroad, 1994), 120.

41. Anselm, *Cur Deus Homo*, preface, p. 61.

42. Sobrino, *Christology at the Crossroads*, 190.

43. Yoder, *Preface to Theology*, 303.

44. Schillebeeckx, *Christ*, 725.

45. Fiorenza, "Critical Social Theory and Christology," 75.

46. Cynthia Crysdale, *Embracing Travail: Retrieving the Cross Today* (New York: Continuum, 1999), 25.

47. Sobrino, *Christology at the Crossroads*, 215.

48. Johnson, "Jesus and Salvation," 15.

49. Schillebeeckx, *Christ*, 832.

50. Joel B. Green and Mark D. Baker, *Recovering the Scandal of the Cross* (Downers Grove, IL: InterVarsity Press, 2000), 24.

51. Walter Wink, *Engaging the Powers: Discernment and Resistance in a World of Domination* (Minneapolis: Fortress Press, 1992), 148.

52. Ibid., 150.

53. Ibid., 150.

54. Ibid., 217.

55. Walter Wink, *When the Powers Fall: Reconciliation in the Healing of Nations* (Minneapolis: Fortress Press, 1998), 10.

56. Schillebeeckx, *Christ*, 718.

57. Gustavo Gutiérrez, *A Theology of Liberation* (Maryknoll, NY: Orbis Books, 1973), 102.

58. Rene Girard, *Things Hidden since the Foundation of the World* (Stanford, CA: Stanford University Press, 1987), 201.

59. Ibid., 255–56.

5. Rethinking Christian Salvation in the Light of Gandhi's Satyagraha

1. John Howard Yoder, *Preface to Theology* (Grand Rapids, MI: Brazos Press, 2002), 306.

2. *Collected Works of Mahatma Gandhi* (hereafter cited as *CWMG*), 100 vols. (Delhi: Publications Division, Ministry of Information and Broadcasting, Government of India, 1958–94), 70:28.

3. *Harijan*, March 23, 1940.

4. Paul F. Power, "A Gandhian Model for World Politics," in *Gandhi: His Relevance for Our Times*, ed. G. Ramachandran and T. K. Mahadevan (Berkeley, CA: World Without War Council, 1967), 291.

5. C. F. Andrews, "Resistance to Evil," *Modern Review*, November 1923, as quoted in P. C. Chaudhury, *C. F. Andrews: His Life and Times* (Bombay, Somaiya Publications, 1971), 77.

6. Jon Sobrino, *Jesus the Liberator* (Maryknoll, NY: Orbis Books, 1993), 16.

7. Yoder, *Preface to Theology*, 320.

8. Walter Wink, *When the Powers Fall: Reconciliation in the Healing of Nations* (Minneapolis: Fortress Press, 1998), 10.

9. Walter Wink, *Engaging the Powers: Discernment and Resistance in a World of Domination* (Minneapolis: Fortress Press, 1992), 217.

10. M. M. Thomas, *The Acknowledged Christ of the Indian Renaissance* (Madras: Christian Institute for the Study of Religion in Society, 1970), 276.

11. Wink, *Engaging the Powers*, 266.

12. Bernard Häring, *Free and Faithful in Christ* (New York: Crossroad, 1981), 398.

13. Wink, *Engaging the Powers*, 112–13.

14. C. F. Andrews, *Sandyha Meditations* (Madras: G. A. Natesan, 1940), 126–27.

15. Stephen Finlan, *Problems with Atonement* (Collegeville, MN: Liturgical Press, 2005), 10.

16. Hans Boersma, *Violence, Hospitality, and the Cross* (Grand Rapids, MI: Baker Academic, 2004), 100.

17. Finlan, *Problems with Atonement*, 39.

18. Yoder, *Preface to Theology*, 311.

19. Marcus J. Borg and John Dominic Crossan, *The Last Week* (San Francisco: HarperSanFrancisco, 2007), 162.

20. Bernard Häring, *The Healing Power of Peace and Nonviolence* (New York/Mahwah, NJ: Paulist Press, 1986), 88.

21. *Young India*, December 31, 1931.

22. Häring, *The Healing Power of Peace and Nonviolence*, 88.

23. John Howard Yoder, *The Politics of Jesus*, 2nd ed. (Grand Rapids, MI: William B. Eerdmans, 1994), 132.

24. John McIntyre, *The Shape of Soteriology* (Edinburgh: T & T Clark, 1992), 190.

25. Paul Fiddes, *Past Event and Present Salvation* (Louisville: Westminster/John Knox Press, 1989), 7–12.

26. Gustav Aulen, *Christus Victor* (Eugene, OR: Wipf and Stock, 1931), 65.

27. Walter Wink, *The Powers That Be: Theology for a New Millennium* (New York: Doubleday, 1998), 36.

28. John Hick, "Introduction to Part Two," *Gandhi's Significance for Today*, edited by John Hick and Lamont C. Hempel (London: Macmillan, 1989).

29. Dashrath Singh, "Gandhi and the Concept of Structural Violence," *Gandhi Marg* 20 (July–September 1998): 197–210.

30. C. F. Andrews, *The Sermon on the Mount* (London: G. Allen and Unwin, 1942), 147.

31. Wink, *The Powers That Be*, 34.

32. Christopher Hedges, *War Is a Force That Gives Us Meaning* (New York: Anchor Books, 2003), 13.

33. Häring, *The Healing Power of Peace and Nonviolence*, 89.

34. Peter Ackerman and Jack DuVall, *A Force More Powerful: A Century of Nonviolent Conflict* (New York: Palgrave, 2000), 458.

35. Anthony W. Bartlett, *Cross Purposes: The Violent Grammar of Christian Atonement* (Harrisburg, PA: Trinity Press International, 2001), 21–22.

36. Susan Neiman, *Evil in Modern Thought* (Princeton, NJ: Princeton University Press, 2002).

37. Elizabeth Johnson, "Jesus and Salvation," *Proceedings of the Catholic Society of America* 49 (1994): 3.

38. Jon Sobrino, *Christology at the Crossroads* (Eugene, OR: Wipf and Stock, 1978), 368.

39. N. T. Wright, *Jesus and the Victory of God* (Minneapolis, MN: Fortress Press, 1996), 268–74.

40. Sobrino, *Christology at the Crossroads*, 390.

41. Rita Dadhich, *Modernity, Civilization and Conflict-Resolution* (Jaipur, India: Arihant Publishing, 2001), 18.

42. C. F. Andrews, a letter to *The British Weekly*, August 18, 1932 as quoted in Benarsidas Chaturvedi and Marjorie Sykes, *C. F. Andrews: A Biography* (New York: Harper Brothers, 1950), 234.

43. Sobrino, *Christology at the Crossroads*, 391.

44. *CWMG*, 89:125.

45. Yoder, *Preface to Theology*, 307.

46. Stanley Hauerwas, *Performing the Faith* (Grand Rapids, MI: Brazos Press, 2004), 76–78.

47. Johnson, "Jesus and Salvation," 13.

48. Glen Stassen, "The Politics of the Sermon on the Mount," in the *Wisdom of the Cross: Essays in Honor of John Howard Yoder*, ed. Stanley Hauerwas, Chris K. Heubner, Harry J. Heubner, and Mark Thiessen Nation (Grand Rapids, MI: William B. Eerdmans, 1999), 155.

49. Marcus Borg, *Meeting Jesus Again for the First Time* (San Francisco: HarperSanFrancisco, 1995), 137.

50. Michael J. Gorman, *Cruciformity: Paul's Narrative Spirituality of the Cross* (Grand Rapids, MI: William B. Eerdmans, 2001), 388.

51. Gerhard Lohfink, *Jesus and Community* (Philadelphia: Fortress Press, 1984), 58.

52. Martin Niemoeller, "The Way of Peace," in *Peace Is the Way*, ed. Walter Wink (Maryknoll, NY: Orbis Books, 2000), 62–63.

53. Norbert Lohfink, *Church Dreams* (N. Richland Hills, TX: Bibal Press, 2000), 97.

54. Häring, *The Healing Power of Peace and Nonviolence*, 22.

55. Robert Daly, SJ, "The New Testament and the Early Church," in *Nonviolence: Central to Christian Spirituality*, ed. Joseph T. Culliton (New York: Edwin Mellen Press, 1982), 41.

56. Bartlett, *Cross Purposes*, 219.

57. Raymund Schwager, *Jesus in the Drama of Salvation: Toward a Biblical Doctrine of Redemption* (New York: Crossroad, 1999), 94.

58. Ibid., 116.

59. Bartlett, *Cross Purposes*, 154.

60. Yoder, *Preface to Theology*, 311–12.

61. Yoder, *The Politics of Jesus*, 43, 47.

62. Ched Myers, *Binding the Strong Man* (Maryknoll, NY: Orbis Books, 1988), 438.

63. Schwager, *Jesus in the Drama of Salvation*, 225.

64. Joel B. Green and Mark D. Baker, *Recovering the Scandal of the Cross* (Downers Grove, IL: InterVarsity Press, 2000), 54–55.

65. J. Denny Weaver, *The Nonviolent Atonement* (Grand Rapids, MI: William B. Eerdmans, 2001), 41.

66. Robert G. Hamerton-Kelly, *Sacred Violence: Paul's Hermeneutic of the Cross* (Minneapolis: Fortress Press, 1992), 103.

67. Bartlett, *Cross Purposes*, 206.

68. Raymund Schwager, *Must There Be Scapegoats? Violence and Redemption in the Bible* (New York: Crossroad, 2000), 214.

69. Boersma, *Violence, Hospitality, and the Cross*, 49.

70. Leonardo Boff, *Passion of Christ, Passion of the World* (Maryknoll, NY: Orbis Books, 1987), 18.

71. Sobrino, *Jesus the Liberator*, 164.

72. Schwager, *Jesus in the Drama of Salvation*, 62.

73. Hauerwas, *Performing the Faith*, 172, 176.

74. Pheme Perkins, *Love Commands in the New Testament* (New York/Mahwah, NJ: Paulist Press, 1982), 125.

75. Gorman, *Cruciformity*, 350.

76. Häring, *The Healing Power of Peace and Nonviolence*, 65.

77. Wink, *The Powers That Be*, 144.

78. Note: The term "nonviolence," unfortunately, still has the ring of passive acceptance, simply not being violent; the Sermon on the Mount and Jesus' praxis is so much more proactive, risky and bold. The limits of the terms such as "nonviolence," "passive resistance," and so on are the very reason why Gandhi coined the term "satyagraha." Unfortunately, it is a term from another culture and language system. Nonetheless, given our exploration in chapter 3, it is appropriate to use it here to express the positive, building, confronting nature of Jesus' life and actions. Glen Stassen has coined the term "transforming initiatives," which, even though it is a mouthful, expresses well the Sermon on the Mount/satyagraha spirit and is more useful than other terms in English. Glen Stassen, *Just Peacemaking: Transforming Initiatives for Justice and Peace* (Louisville, KY: Westminster/John Knox Press, 1992).

79. N. Lohfink, *Church Dreams*, 101.

80. Fiddes, *Past Event and Present Salvation*, 122.

81. Timothy Gorringe, *God's Just Vengeance* (Cambridge: Cambridge University Press, 1996), 27.

82. Fiddes, *Past Event and Present Salvation*, 136.

83. Gustav Aulen, *The Faith of the Christian Church* (London: SCM, 1961), 226, as quoted in Fiddes, *Past Event and Present Salvation*, 111.

84. Wright, *Jesus and the Victory of God*, 659.

85. Ibid., 660.

86. Boff, *Passion of Christ, Passion of the World*, 125–26.

87. Darby Kathleen Ray, *Deceiving the Devil: Atonement, Abuse, and Ransom* (Cleveland: Pilgrim Press, 1998), 141.

88. J. Denny Weaver, "Theology in the Mirror of the Martyred and Oppressed," in Hauerwas et al., *The Wisdom of the Cross*, 424.

89. Glen Stassen, "The Politics of Jesus in the Sermon on the Plain," in Hauerwas et al., *The Wisdom of the Cross*, 155.

90. Sobrino, *Christology at the Crossroads*, 227.

91. Yoder, *Preface to Theology*, 308.

92. Ibid., 312.

93. Gorman, *Cruciformity*, 36.

94. E. P. Sanders, *Paul and Palestinian Judaism* (Philadelphia: Fortress Press, 1977), 43, as quoted in Gorman, *Cruciformity*, 36.

95. Gorman, *Cruciformity*, 46.

96. N. Lohfink, *Church Dreams*, 97.

97. Robert Barron, *And Now I See: A Theology of Transformation* (New York: Crossroad, 1998), 3.

98. Sobrino, *Jesus the Liberator*, 230.

Glossary

Agraha: Firmly hold; firmness, insistence, adherence

Ahimsa: Doing no harm

Atman: The innermost essence of each individual

Brahman: Ultimate reality

Bhakti: Devotion to God

Darshan: A blessing conferred by seeing or touching a holy person

Dharma: The law built into the universe that makes all cohere

Himsa: Harm or violence

Khadi movement: Reintroducing into India the production of homespun cloth, a capability that had been lost when the British had undercut the industry

Lathi: A long, steel-shod, bamboo rod

Mahatma: "Great Soul"

Maya: Illusion

Moksha: Liberation

"*Sanatani* Hindu": In our terms, an orthodox Hindu

Satya: The truth, that which is; the source of the moral law running through the universe

Satyagraha: Firmness in the truth; applying the principles of nonviolence and self-suffering to the struggle of masses against the forces of oppression and violence

Satyagrahi: A practitioner of satyagraha

Shastris: The scholars of the ancient texts

Swaraj: Self-governance; self-determination

Tapasya: Self-suffering; renunciation of self

Varna: The view that each individual's occupation fits into an order that extends before and around and after that individual's lifetime

Vedanta: The system of Hindu philosophy based on the Vedas

Bibliography

Abelard. *A Scholastic Miscellany*. Edited by E. R. Fairweather. London: SCM, 1956.

Ackerman, Peter, and Jack DuVall. *A Force More Powerful: A Century of Nonviolent Conflict*. New York: Palgrave, 2000.

Allison, Dale. *The Sermon on the Mount*. New York: Crossroad, 1999.

Appleby, R. Scott. *The Ambivalence of the Sacred*. Lanham, MD: Rowan and Littlefield, 2000.

Andrews, C. F. *Christ in the Silence*. New York: Abingdon Press, 1933.

———. *Gandhi's Ideas*. London: George Allen and Unwin, 1929.

———. "Resistance to Evil." *Modern Review*. November 1923.

———. *Sandhya Meditations*. Madras: G. A. Natesan, 1940.

———. *The Sermon on the Mount*. London: G. Allen and Unwin, 1942.

———. *The True India*. New Delhi: Inter-India Publications, 1985.

———. *What I Owe to Christ*. New York: Abingdon Press, 1932.

Anselm of Canterbury. *Cur Deus Homo*. Translated by Joseph Colleran. Albany, NY: Magi Books, 1969.

Arendt, Hannah. *Between Past and Future*. New York: Penguin Books, 1977.

———. *Eichmann in Jerusalem*. New York: Penguin Books, 1977.

———. *The Human Condition*. Chicago: University of Chicago Press, 1958.

———. *On Violence*. San Diego, CA: Harcourt Brace, 1970.

———. *The Origins of Totalitarianism*. San Diego, CA: Harcourt Brace, 1968.

Ashe, Geoffrey. *Gandhi*. New York: Stein and Day, 1968.

Athanasius. *On the Incarnation*. Crestwood, NY: St. Vladimir's Seminary Press, 1996.

Aulen, Gustav. *Christus Victor*. Eugene, OR: Wipf and Stock, 1931.

Avalos, Hector. *Fighting Words*. Amherst, NY: Prometheus Books, 2005.

Bailie, Gil. *Violence Unveiled*. New York: Crossroad, 1996.

Bainton, Roland H. *Christian Attitudes toward War and Peace*. Nashville: Abingdon Press, 1960.

Baker, Mark, ed. *Proclaiming the Scandal of the Cross*. Grand Rapids, MI: Baker Academic, 2006.

Barron, Robert. *And Now I See: A Theology of Transformation*. New York: Crossroad, 1998.

Bartlett, Anthony W. *Cross Purposes: The Violent Grammar of Christian Atonement*. Harrisburg, PA: Trinity Press International, 2001.

Beilby, James, and Paul R. Eddy, eds. *The Nature of the Atonement*. Downers Grove, IL: InterVarsity Press, 2006.

Berkhof, H. *Christ and the Powers*. Scottdale, PA: Herald Press, 1962.

Berry, Brian David. "Fundamental Liberation Ethics: The Contribution of the Later Theology of Edward Schillebeeckx." PhD diss., Boston College, 1995.

Betz, Hans Dieter. *Nachfolge und Nachahmung Jesu Christi im Neuen Testament.* Tubingen: Mohr, 1967.

———. *The Sermon on the Mount.* Minneapolis: Fortress Press, 1995.

Boersma, Hans. *Violence, Hospitality, and the Cross.* Grand Rapids, MI: Baker Academic, 2004.

Boff, Leonardo. *Liberating Grace.* Maryknoll, NY: Orbis Books, 1979.

———. *Passion of Christ, Passion of the World.* Maryknoll, NY: Orbis Books, 1987.

Boff, Leonardo, and Clodovis Boff. *Salvation and Liberation.* Maryknoll, NY: Orbis Books, 1984.

Bondurant, Joan. *Conquest of Violence: The Gandhian Philosophy of Conflict.* New ed. Princeton, NJ: Princeton University Press, 1988.

Bonhoeffer, Dietrich. *The Cost of Discipleship.* New York: Touchstone, 1995.

———. *Letters and Papers from Prison.* New York: Touchstone, 1997.

Borg, Marcus J. *Conflict, Holiness, and Politics in the Teachings of Jesus.* Harrisburg, PA: Trinity Press International, 1998.

———. *Meeting Jesus Again for the First Time.* San Francisco: HarperSanFrancisco, 1995.

Borg, Marcus J., and John Dominic Crossan. *The Last Week.* San Francisco: HarperSanFrancisco, 2007.

Bredin, Mark. *Jesus, Revolutionary of Peace.* Waynesboro, GA: Paternoster, 2003.

Brimlow, Robert W. *What about Hitler?* Grand Rapids, MI: Brazos Press, 2006.

Britton, Burnett. *Gandhi Arrives in South Africa.* Canton, ME: Greenleaf Books, 1999.

Brock, Rita Nakashima, and Rebecca Ann Parker. *Proverbs of Ashes.* Boston: Beacon Press, 2001.

Brown, Judith. *Gandhi: Prisoner of Hope.* New Haven, CT: Yale University Press, 1989.

Brueggemann, Walter. *Revelation and Violence: A Study in Contextualization.* Milwaukee: Marquette University Press, 1986.

Burghardt, Walter J. *Justice: A Global Adventure.* Maryknoll, NY: Orbis Books, 2004.

Burns, J. Patout. "The Economy of Salvation: Two Patristic Traditions." *Theological Studies* 37 (1976): 598–619.

Cahalan, Kathleen. "The Sacramental-Moral Theology of Bernard Haring: A Study of the Virtue of Religion." PhD diss., University of Chicago, 1998.

Cahill, Lisa Sowle. *Love Your Enemies.* Minneapolis: Fortress Press, 1994.

Calvin, John. *Institutes of the Christian Religion.* Edited by John T. McNeill. Philadelphia: Westminster Press, 1960.

Campbell, J. McLeod. *The Nature of the Atonement.* Eugene, OR: Wipf and Stock, 1999.

Carroll, James. *House of War.* Boston: Houghton Mifflin Company, 2006.

Carroll, John T., and Joel B. Green. *The Death of Jesus in Early Christianity.* Peabody, MA: Hendrickson, 1995.

Carson, D. A. *Jesus' Sermon on the Mount.* Grand Rapids, MI: Baker Books, 1978.

Carter, Craig. "The Pacifism of the Messianic Community: The Christological Social Ethics of John Howard Yoder." PhD diss., University of St. Michael's, 1999.

————. *The Politics of the Cross: The Theology and Social Ethics of John Howard Yoder.* Grand Rapids, MI: Brazos Press, 2001.

Carter, Warren. *What Are They Saying about Matthew's Sermon on the Mount?* New York: Paulist Press, 1994.

Casanova, Jose. *Public Religions in the Modern World.* Chicago: University of Chicago Press, 1994.

Cassidy, Richard J. *Christians and Roman Rule in the New Testament.* New York: Crossroad, 2001.

Chattanatt, John. "Two Paradigms of Liberative Transformation: Approaches to Social Action in the Theological Ethics of Gandhi and Gutiérrez." PhD diss., University of Chicago, 1991.

Chatterjee, Margaret. *Gandhi's Religious Thought.* Notre Dame, IN: University of Notre Dame Press, 1983.

Chase, Kenneth R., and Alan Jacobs, *Must Christianity Be Violent?* Grand Rapids, MI: Brazos Press.

Chaturvedi, Benarsidas, and Marjorie Sykes. *C. F. Andrews: A Biography.* New York: Harper Brothers, 1950.

Chaudbury, P. C. *C. F. Andrews: His Life and Times.* Bombay, Somaiya Publications, 1971.

Chopra, Deepak *Peace Is the Way.* New York: Harmony Books, 2005.

Clark, Robert Michael. "Towards a Theology of Peace: Contributions from the Thought of Bernard Lonergan." PhD diss., Boston College, 1994.

Cortright, David. *Gandhi and Beyond.* Boulder, CO: Paradigm Publishers, 2006.

Crossan, John Dominic. *The Birth of Christianity.* San Francisco: HarperSanFrancisco, 1998.

————. *In Search of Paul.* New York: HarperSanFrancisco, 2004.

Crysdale, Cynthia. *Embracing Travail: Retrieving the Cross Today.* New York: Continuum, 1999.

Culliton, Joseph T., ed. *Non-violence: Central to Christian Spirituality.* New York: Edwin Mellen Press, 1982.

Curran, Charles. *Catholic Moral Theology in Dialogue.* Notre Dame, IN: Fides, 1972.

Dadhich, Naresh, ed. *Nonviolence, Peace, and Politics: Understanding Gandhi.* Jaipur, India: Aavishkar Publishers, 2003.

Dadhich, Rita. *Modernity, Civilization and Conflict-Resolution.* Jaipur, India: Arihant Publishing House, 2001.

Dalton, Dennis. *Mahatma Gandhi: Nonviolent Power in Action.* New York: Columbia University Press, 1993.

Davies, W. D. *The Sermon on the Mount.* Cambridge: Cambridge University Press, 1966.

Dear, John. *Disarming the Heart.* Scottdale, PA: Herald Press, 1993.

————. *Jesus the Rebel.* Franklin, WI: Sheed and Ward, 2000.

————. *Living Peace.* New York: Doubleday, 2001.

Desai, Naryan. "Gandhi's Method of Training for Nonviolence." In *Nonviolence, Peace, and Politics: Understanding Gandhi*, edited by Naresh Dadhich, 40–65. Jaipur, India: Aavishkar Publishers, 2003.

Desjardins, Michael. *Peace, Violence, and the New Testament.* Sheffield, England: Sheffield Academic Press, 1997.

Diwakar, R. R. "Satyagraha: A New Way of Life and a New Technique for Social Change." *Gandhi Marg* 13, no. 4 (1969): 16–24.

Doke, J. J. *M. K. Gandhi: An Indian Patriot.* Madras: Natesan, 1909.

Douglass, James, *The Non-violent Cross.* London: Macmillan, 1968.

———. *The Nonviolent Coming of God.* Eugene, OR: Wipf and Stock Publishers, 2006.

Duffey, Michael. *Peacemaking Christians: The Future of Just Wars, Pacifism, and Nonviolent Resistance.* Kansas City, MO: Sheed & Ward, 1995.

———. *Sowing Justice, Reaping Peace.* Franklin, WI: Sheed & Ward, 2001.

Dulles, Avery. *Survival of Dogma.* Garden City, NY: Doubleday, 1971.

Dupuis, Jacques. *Who Do You Say I Am?* Maryknoll, NY: Orbis Books, 1994.

Easwaran, Eknath. *Gandhi the Man.* Tomales, CA: Nilgiri Press, 1997.

Edwards, Denis. *What Are They Saying about Salvation?* New York/Mahwah, NJ: Paulist Press, 1986.

Edwards, George. *Jesus and the Politics of Violence.* New York: Harper and Row, 1972.

Egan, Eileen. *Peace Be With You.* Maryknoll, NY: Orbis Books, 1999.

Erikson, Erik. *Gandhi's Truth.* New York: Norton, 1969.

Fiddes, Paul. *Past Event and Present Salvation.* Louisville: Westminster/ John Knox Press, 1989.

Fiorenza, Francis Schüssler. "Critical Social Theory and Christology: Toward an Understanding of Atonement and Redemption as Emancipating Solidarity." *Proceedings of the Catholic Theological Society* 30 (1975): 63–110.

———. "Redemption." In *New Dictionary of Theology.* Edited by Joseph Komonchak, Mary Collins, and Dermot Lane. Wilmington, DE: Michael Glazier, 1987.

Finlan, Stephen. *Problems with Atonement.* Collegeville, MN: Liturgical Press, 2005.

Fischer, Louis. *The Life of Mahatma Gandhi.* New York: Harper and Brothers, 1950.

Fitzmyer, Joseph. "Reconciliation in Paul." In *No Famine in the Land: Studies in Honor of John L. McKenzie,* edited by James Flanagan and Anita Weisbord Robinson, 155–78. Missoula, MT: Scholars Press, 1975.

Furnish, Victor Paul. *The Love Commandment in the New Testament.* Nashville: Abingdon Press, 1972.

Gandhi, Mohandas K. *All Men Are Brothers.* New York: Continuum, 1958.

———. *An Autobiography or The Story of My Experiments with Truth.* Ahmedabad: Navajivan, 1927.

———. *Christian Missions: Their Place in India.* Ahmedabad: Navajivan, 1941.

———. *The Collected Works of Mahatma Gandhi.* 100 vols. Delhi: Publications Division, Ministry of Information and Broadcasting, Government of India, 1958–1994.

———. *Discourses on the Gita.* Ahmedabad: Navajivan, 1960.

———. *The Essence of Hinduism.* Ahmedabad: Navajivan, 1987.

———. *Gandhi on Christianity.* Edited by Robert Ellsberg. Maryknoll, NY: Orbis Books, 1991.

———. *Gandhi on Nonviolence*. Edited by Thomas Merton. New York: New Directions, 1964.

———. *The Gospel of Selfless Action: The Gita According to Gandhi*. Translated by Mahadev Desai. Ahmedabad: Navajivan, 1946.

———. *Hind Swaraj or Indian Home Rule*. Ahmedabad: Navajivan, 1938.

———. *The Message of Jesus Christ*. Bombay: Bharatiya Vidya Bhavan, 1986.

———. *Mohandas Gandhi: Essential Writings*. Edited by John Dear. Maryknoll, NY: Orbis Books, 2002.

———. *My God*. Ahmedabad: Navajivan, 1955.

———. *My Religion*. Ahmedabad: Navajivan, 1955.

———. *Nonviolent Resistance (Satyagraha)*. New York: Schocken Books, 1961.

———. *Ruskin, Unto This Last: A Paraphrase*. Ahmedabad: Navajivan, 1956

———. *Satyagraha in South Africa*. Ahmedabad: Navajivan, 1928.

———. *Satyagraha: Non-violent Resistance*. Ahmedabad: Navajivan, 1951

———. *Truth Called Them Differently*. Ahmedabad: Navajivan, 1961.

———. *Truth Is God*. Edited by R. K. Prabhu. Ahmedabad: Navajivan, 1987.

George, Davis. *Dynamics of Power: The Gandhian Perspective*. New Delhi: Frank Brothers, 2000.

George, S. K. *Gandhi's Challenge to Christianity*. Ahmedabad: Navajivan, 1960.

Gioseffi, Daniela, ed. *Women on War*. New York: Feminist Press at the City University of New York, 2003.

Girard, Rene. *I See Satan Fall Like Lightning*. Maryknoll, NY: Orbis Books, 2001.

———. *Things Hidden since the Foundation of the World*. Stanford, CA: Stanford University Press, 1987.

———. *Violence and the Sacred*. Baltimore: Johns Hopkins University Press, 1977.

Gorman, Michael J. *Cruciformity: Paul's Narrative Spirituality of the Cross*. Grand Rapids, MI: William B. Eerdmans, 2001

Gorringe, Timothy. *God's Just Vengeance*. Cambridge: Cambridge University Press, 1996.

Gracie, David McI., ed. *Gandhi and Charlie, The Story of a Friendship: As Told through the Letters and Writings of Mohandas K. Gandhi and the Rev'd Charles Freer Andrews*. Cambridge, MA: Cowley Publications, 1989.

Grassi, Joseph A. *Informing the Future: Social Justice in the New Testament*. New York/Mahwah, NJ: Paulist Press, 2003.

Green, Joel B., and Mark D. Baker. *Recovering the Scandal of the Cross*. Downers Grove, IL: InterVarsity Press, 2000.

Green, Martin. *The Origins of Nonviolence*. New Delhi: HarperCollins, 1986.

Gregg, Richard B. *The Power of Nonviolence*. New York: Schocken Books, 1966.

Groff, Weyburn Woodrow. "Nonviolence: A Comparative Study of Mohandas Gandhi and the Mennonite Church on the Subject of Nonviolence." PhD diss., New York University, 1963.

Guelich, Robert A. *The Sermon on the Mount: A Foundation for Understanding*. Waco, TX: Word Books, 1982.

Guinan, Edward, ed. *Peace and Nonviolence*. New York/Mahwah, NJ: Paulist Press, 1973.

Gunton, Colin E. *The Actuality of Atonement*. London: T & T Clark, 1998.

Gutiérrez, Gustavo. *A Theology of Liberation*. Maryknoll, NY: Orbis Books, 1973.

Haight, Roger. "Jesus and Salvation: An Essay in Interpretation." *Theological Studies* 55 (1994): 225–51.

———. *Jesus Symbol of God*. Maryknoll, NY: Orbis Books, 1999.

Hallahan, Kenneth. "The Social Ethics of Nonresistance: The Writings of Mennonite Theologian John Howard Yoder Analyzed from a Roman Catholic Perspective." PhD diss., The Catholic University of America, 1997.

Hamerton-Kelly, Robert G. *Sacred Violence: Paul's Hermeneutic of the Cross*. Minneapolis: Fortress Press, 1992.

Hamilton, Neill. "Temple Cleansing and the Temple Bank." *Journal of Biblical Literature* 83 (December 1964): 365–72.

Häring, Bernard. *Free and Faithful in Christ*. New York: Crossroad, 1981.

———. *The Healing Power of Peace and Nonviolence*. New York/Mahwah, NJ: Paulist Press, 1986.

———. *I Have Seen Your Tears*. Liguori, MO: Liguori Publications, 1995.

———. *My Witness for the Church*. New York/Mahwah, NJ: Paulist Press, 1992.

———. *A Theology of Protest*. New York: Farrar, Straus and Giroux, 1970.

———. *To Do Justice: A Christian Social Conscience*. Liguori, MO: Liguori Publications, 1999.

———. *Toward a Christian Moral Theology*. Notre Dame, IN: University of Notre Dame Press, 1966.

Hauerwas, Stanley. *After Christendom?* Nashville: Abingdon Press, 1991.

———. *A Better Hope*. Grand Rapids, MI: Brazos Press, 2001

———. *Cross-Shattered Christ*. Grand Rapids, MI: Brazos Press, 2004.

———. "On Being a Church Capable of Addressing a World at War: A Pacifist Response to the United Methodist Bishops' Pastoral 'In Defense of Creation.'" In *Speak Up for Just War or Pacifism: A Critique of the United Methodist Bishops' Pastoral Letter*, ed. Paul Ramsey. University Park, PA: Pennsylvania State University Press, 1988.

———. *The Peaceable Kingdom*. Notre Dame, IN: University of Notre Dame Press, 1983.

———. *Performing the Faith*. Grand Rapids, MI: Brazos Press, 2004.

———. *Resident Aliens*. Nashville: Abingdon Press, 1989.

———. *Should War Be Eliminated? A Thought Experiment*. Milwaukee: Marquette University Press, 1984.

Hauerwas, Stanley, Chris K. Heubner, Harry J. Heubner, and Mark Thiessen Nation, eds. *The Wisdom of the Cross: Essays in Honor of John Howard Yoder*. Grand Rapids, MI: William B. Eerdmans, 1999.

Hauerwas, Stanley, and Frank Lentricchia, eds. *Dissent from the Homeland*. Durham, NC: Duke University Press, 2003.

Hedges, Christopher. *War Is a Force That Gives Us Meaning*. New York: Anchor, 2003.

Heim, S. Mark. *Saved From Sacrifice*. Grand Rapids, MI: William B. Eerdmans, 2006.

Hellwig, Monika. "Changing Soteriology in Ecumenical Context: A Catholic Reflection." *Proceedings of the Catholic Theological Society* 38 (1983): 14–21.

———. "Emerging Issues in Soteriology." *Theology Digest* 3/4 (1984): 129–32.

————. "Seminar on Christology: Exclusivist Claims and the Conflicts of Faiths." *Proceedings of the Catholic Theological Society* 31 (1976): 129–32.

Hengel, Martin. *Victory over Violence*. Philadelphia: Fortress Press, 1973.

Henry, Sarojini. "The Social Ethic of Gandhi, Including Some Comparisons with Reinhold Niebuhr's Political and Social Thought." PhD diss., Union Theological Seminary, 1987.

Hick, John, and Lamont Hempel, eds. *Gandhi's Significance for Today*. London: Macmillan, 1989.

Holmes, Robert L., and Barry L. Gan. *Nonviolence in Theory and Practice*. Long Grove, IL: Waveland Press, 2005.

Horsley, Richard. *Bandits, Prophets, and Messiahs*. Harrisburg, PA: Trinity Press International, 1999.

————. *Jesus and the Spiral of Violence*. Minneapolis: Fortress Press 1993.

Hoyland, John. *C. F. Andrews: Minister of Reconciliation*. London: Allenson, 1940.

Hubert, H., and M. Maus. "Essai sur la nature et function du sacrifice." *L'anee sociologique* 3 (1898–99): 29–138.

Irenaeus. "Against the Heresies." In *The Ante-Nicene Fathers*, vol. 1, ed. Alexander Roberts and James Donaldson. Grand Rapids, MI: William B. Eerdmans, 1979.

Iyer, Raghavan. *The Moral and Political Thought of Mahatma Gandhi*. 2nd ed. London: Concord Grove Press, 1983.

————. *The Moral and Political Writings of Mahatma Gandhi*. Vol. 1. London: Concord Grove Press, 1986.

James, William. *Memories and Studies*. London: Longmans, Green and Company, 1911.

Jeremias, Joachim. *The Sermon on the Mount*. Philadelphia: Fortress Press, 1963.

Jesudasan, Ignatius. *A Gandhian Theology of Liberation*. Maryknoll, NY: Orbis Books, 1984.

————. *Roots of Religious Violence*. Delhi: Media House, 2007.

Johnson, Elizabeth A. "Jesus and Salvation." *Proceedings of the Catholic Theological Society of America* 49 (1994): 1–18.

Jones, E. Stanley. *Mahatma Gandhi: An Interpretation*. New York: Abingdon-Cokesbury Press, 1948.

Jordens, J. T. F. *Gandhi's Religion: A Homespun Shawl*. New York: Palgrave, 1998.

Juergensmeyer, Mark. *Gandhi's Way: A Handbook of Conflict Resolution*. Berkeley, CA: University of California Press, 1984.

Kasemann, Ernst. *Jesus Means Freedom*. Philadelphia: Fortress Press, 1968.

Kelly, H. A. "The Devil in the Desert." *Catholic Biblical Quarterly* 26 (1964): 213–20.

King, Martin Luther. *Stride toward Freedom*. New York: Harper and Brothers, 1958.

Kirk-Duggan, Cheryl. *Misbegotten Anguish*. St. Louis, MO: Chalice Press, 2001.

Kissinger, Warren S. *The Sermon on the Mount: A History of Interpretation and Bibliography*. Metuchen, NJ: Scarecrow Press, 1975.

Korejo, M. S. *The Frontier Gandhi: Abdul Ghaffar Khan*. Karachi: Oxford University Press, 1993.

Kumar, Ravindra. *Theory and Practice of Gandhian Non-violence.* New Delhi: Mittal Publications, 2002.

Lamarche, P. "Le 'blaspheme' de Jesus devant le Sanhedrin." *Recherches Science Religieuse* 50 (1962): 74–85.

Lamb, Matthew L. *Solidarity with Victims.* New York: Crossroad, 1982.

Lederach, John Paul. *Journey Toward Reconciliation.* Scottdale, PA: Herald Press, 1999.

Lefebure, Leo. *Revelation, the Religions, and Violence.* Maryknoll, NY: Orbis Books, 2000.

Leidert, John, Paula Minaert, and Mark Mossa. *Just War, Lasting Peace.* Maryknoll, NY: Orbis Books, 2006.

Levering, Matthew. *Christ's Fulfillment of Torah and Temple.* Notre Dame, IN: University of Notre Dame Press, 2002.

———. *Studies in the Sermon on the Mount.* Grand Rapids, MI: William B. Eerdmans, 1959–60.

Lloyd-Jones, D. Martyn. *The Cross.* Westchester, IL: Crossway Books, 1986.

Lobkowicz, Nicholas. *Theory and Practice.* Notre Dame, IN: University of Notre Dame Press, 1967.

Loeb, Paul Rogat. *The Impossible Will Take a Little While.* New York: Basic Books, 2004.

Loewe, William. "Christus Victor Revisited: Irenaeus' Soteriology." *Anglican Theological Review* 47 (1985): 1–15.

———. "Toward a Responsible Contemporary Soteriology." In *Creativity and Method: Essays in Honor of Bernard Lonergan S.J.*, ed. Matthew Lamb, 213–27. Milwaukee: Marquette University Press, 1985.

Lohfink, Gerhard. *Jesus and Community.* Philadelphia: Fortress Press, 1984.

Lohfink, Norbert. *Church Dreams.* N. Richland Hills, TX: Bibal Press, 2000.

———, ed. *Gewalt und Gewaltlosigkeit im Alten Testament.* Freiburg in Breisgau: Herder, 1983.

———. *In the Shadow of Your Wings.* Collegeville, MN: Liturgical Press, 2003.

———. *Option for the Poor.* N. Richland Hills, TX: Bibal Press, 1987.

Lohfink, Norbert, and Rudolf Pesch. *Weltgestaltung und Gewaltlosigkeit: ethische Aspekte des Alten und Neuen Testaments in ihrer Einheit und ihrem Gegensatz.* Dusseldorf: Patmos-Verlag, 1978.

MacGregor, G. H. C. *The New Testament Basis of Pacifism.* New York: Fellowship of Reconciliation, 1936.

Maguire, Daniel. *A Moral Creed for All Christians.* Minneapolis: Fortress Press, 2005.

———. *The Horrors We Bless.* Minneapolis: Fortress Press, 2007.

Malotky, Daniel. "Faith and Force: Groundwork for Social Responsibility in the Thought of Reinhold Niebuhr and Stanley Hauerwas." PhD diss., University of Chicago, 1999.

Marshall, Christopher D. *Beyond Retribution: A New Testament Vision for Justice, Crime, and Punishment.* Grand Rapids, MI: William B. Eerdmans, 2001.

Massaro, Thomas J., and Thomas Shannon. *Catholic Perspectives on Peace and War.* Lanham, MD: Sheed and Ward, 2003.

Mauser, Ulrich. *The Gospel of Peace.* Louisville: Westminster/John Knox Press, 1992.

May, Rollo. *Power and Innocence.* New York: W. W. Norton & Company, 1972.

McDaniel, Jay. *Gandhi's Hope.* Maryknoll, NY: Orbis Books, 2005.

McDonald, H. D., *The Atonement of the Death of Christ* Grand Rapids, MI: Baker Book House, 1985.

McGrath, Alister E. *Justitia Dei.* Cambridge: Cambridge University Press, 1986.

McIntyre, John. *The Shape of Soteriology.* Edinburgh: T & T Clark, 1992.

McSorley, Richard. *It's a Sin to Build a Nuclear Weapon.* Baltimore, MD: Fortkamp Publishing, 1991.

———. *New Testament Basis of Pacifism.* Scottdale, PA: Herald Press, 1979.

Meier, John P. *A Marginal Jew: Rethinking the Historical Jesus.* 3 vols. 1991–1994; reprint, New York: Anchor, 2001.

Merton, Thomas. *Conjectures of a Guilty Bystander.* Garden City, NY: Image Books, 1968.

———. *Faith and Violence.* Notre Dame, IN: University of Notre Dame Press, 1968.

———. *Thomas Merton on Peace.* New York: McCall Publishing, 1969.

Metz, Johannes B. "The Church's Social Function in the Light of a 'Political Theology.'" In *Faith and the World of Politics,* edited by J. B. Metz, 2–18. New York: Paulist Press, 1968.

———. "The Future in the Memory of Suffering." *Concilium* 76 (1972): 9–25.

Miller, William Robert. "Gandhi and King: Pioneers of Modern Nonviolence." *Gandhi Marg* 13, no. 1 (1969): 21–28.

———. *Nonviolence: A Christian Interpretation.* New York: Schocken Books, 1966.

Mookherji, S. B. "Ahimsa through the Ages: Gandhi's Contribution." *Gandhi Marg* 4 (July 1960): 220–28.

Morris, Leon. *The Atonement: Its Meaning and Significance.* Downers Grove, IL: InterVarsity Press, 1983.

Mukherjee, Subrata, and Sushila Ramaswamy, eds. *Non-violence and Satyagraha.* New Delhi: Deep & Deep Publications, 1998.

Musto, Ronald G. *The Catholic Peace Tradition.* New York: Peace Books, 2002.

Myers, Ched. *Binding the Strong Man.* Maryknoll, NY: Orbis Books, 1988.

———. *Who Will Roll Away the Stone?* Maryknoll, NY: Orbis Books, 1994.

Nagler, Michael N. *Is There No Other Way?* Maui, HI: Inner Ocean Publishing, 2001.

Nanda, B. R. *In Search of Gandhi: Essays and Reflections.* New Delhi: Oxford University Press, 2002.

Neiman, Susan. *Evil in Modern Thought.* Princeton, NJ: Princeton University Press, 2002.

Niditch, Susan. *War in the Hebrew Bible.* Oxford: Oxford University Press, 1993.

Niebuhr, H. Richard. *Christ and Culture.* New York: Harper, 1951.

Niebuhr, Reinhold. *Interpretation of Christian Ethics.* New York: Harper, 1936.

———. *Moral Man and Immoral Society.* Louisville: Westminster/John Knox Press, 2001.

Nilson, Jon. "Salvation." In *The HarperCollins Encyclopedia of Catholicism,* ed. Richard McBrien, 1158. San Francisco: HarperCollins, 1995.

Nojeim, Michael J. *Gandhi and King: The Power of Nonviolent Resistance*. Westport, CT: Praeger, 2004.

North, Robert. *Sociology of the Biblical Jubilee*. Rome: Pontifical Biblical Institute, 1954.

———. "Violence and the Bible: The Girard Connection." *Catholic Biblical Quarterly* 47 (1985): 1–27.

O'Connor, Daniel. *Gospel, Raj, and Swaraj*. New York: P. Lang, 1990.

———. *The Testimony of C. F. Andrews*. Madras: Christian Literature Society, 1974.

O'Keefe, Mark. *What Are They Saying about Social Sin?* New York/Mahwah, NJ: Paulist Press, 1999.

Organ, Troy Wilson. *Hinduism: Its Historical Development*. Woodbury, NY: Barron's Educational Series, 1974.

Pawlikowski, John T., and Donald Senior, eds. *Biblical and Theological Reflections on The Challenge of Peace*. Wilmington, DE: Michael Glazier, 1984.

Perkins, Pheme. *Love Commands in the New Testament*. New York/Mahwah, NJ: Paulist Press, 1982.

Puri, Rashmi-Sudha. *Gandhi on War and Peace*. New York: Praeger, 1987.

Rahner, Karl. "Christianity and the Non-Christian Religions." In *Theological Investigations*, vol. 5, trans. David Morland, 115–34. Baltimore: Helicon Press, 1966.

———. "Current Problems in Christology." In *Theological Investigations*, vol. 1, trans. Cornelius Ernst, 149–200. Baltimore: Helicon Press, 1964.

———. "The One Christ and Universality of Salvation." In *Theological Investigations*, vol. 16, trans. David Morland, 199–226. New York: Seabury, 1979.

Ramachandran, G., and T. K. Mahadevan, eds. *Gandhi: His Relevance for Our Times*. Berkeley, CA: World Without War Council, 1967.

———. *Quest for Gandhi*. New Delhi: Gandhi Peace Foundation, 1970.

Ramsey, Paul. *Basic Christian Ethics*. New York: Scribner, 1950.

Rao, K. L. Seshagiri. *Mahatma Gandhi and C. F. Andrews*. Patiala, India: Punjabi University Press, 1969.

Ratzinger, Joseph. *Introduction to Christianity*. New York: Herder and Herder, 1970.

Ray, Darby Kathleen. *Deceiving the Devil: Atonement, Abuse, and Ransom*. Cleveland, OH: Pilgrim Press, 1998.

Reid, Barabara E. "Violent Endings in Matthew's Parables and Christian Nonviolence." *Catholic Biblical Quarterly* 66, no. 2 (April 2004): 237–55.

Richard, Lucien. *What Are They Saying about the Theology of Suffering?* New York/Mahwah, NJ: Paulist Press, 1992.

Ringe, Sharon. *Jesus, Liberation, and Biblical Jubilee*. Philadelphia: Fortress Press, 1985.

Ruether, Rosemary Radford. *Introducing Redemption in Christian Feminism*. Sheffield, England: Sheffield Academic Press, 1998.

Sanders, John, ed. *Atonement and Violence*, Nashville: Abingdon Press, 2006.

Schillebeeckx, Edward. *Christ: The Experience of Jesus as Lord*. New York: Crossroad, 1980.

———. *Church: The Human Story of God*. New York: Crossroad, 1994.

———. *Jesus: An Experiment in Christology*. New York: Vintage Books, 1981.

Schmidt, David. "Theological Ethics and Public Policy: An Analysis of Argument in Public Policy Testimonies by Paul Ramsey and Stanley Hauerwas." PhD diss., University of Chicago, 1987.

Schmiechen, Peter. *Saving Power: Theories of Atonement and Forms of the Church*. Grand Rapids, MI: William B. Eerdmans, 2005.

Schottroff, Luise, Reginald Fuller, Christoph Burchard, and M. Jack Suggs. *Essays on the Love Commandment*. Philadelphia: Fortress Press, 1978.

Schwager, Raymund. *Jesus in the Drama of Salvation: Toward a Biblical Doctrine of Redemption*. New York: Crossroad, 1999.

———. *Jesus of Nazareth*. New York: Crossroad, 1998.

———. *Must There Be Scapegoats? Violence and Redemption in the Bible*. New York: Crossroad, 2000.

———. *Der wunderbare Tausch: zur Geschichte und Deutung der Erlösungslehre*. Munich: Kosel, 1986.

Sharp, Gene. *Gandhi as a Political Strategist*. Boston: PorterSargent, 1979.

———. *The Methods of Nonviolent Action*. Boston: PorterSargent, 1973.

———. *The Politics of Nonviolent Action*. Boston: PorterSargent, 1973.

———. "A Study of the Meaning of Nonviolence." *Gandhi Marg* 3 (1959): 265–73.

———. *Waging Nonviolent Struggle*. Boston: Extending Horizons Books, Porter Sargent Publishers, 2005.

Sheehan, Vincent. *Lead Kindly Light*. New York: Random House, 1949.

Sherman, Robert. *King, Priest, and Prophet*. New York: T & T Clark International, 2004.

Shirer, William L. *Gandhi: A Memoir*. New York: Simon & Schuster, 1979.

Shridharani, Krishnalal. *War Without Violence*. New York: Harcourt, Brace, 1939.

Singh, Dashrath. "Gandhi and the Concept of Structural Violence." *Gandhi Marg* 20 (July–September, 1998): 197–210.

Slusser, Michael. "Primitive Christian Soteriological Themes." *Theological Studies* 44 (1983): 555–69.

Smock, David R. *Interfaith Dialogue and Peacebuilding*. Washington, DC: United States Institute of Peace Press, 2002.

Sobrino, Jon. *Christology at the Crossroads*. Eugene, OR: Wipf and Stock, 2002.

———. *Christ the Liberator*. Maryknoll, NY: Orbis Books, 2001.

———. *Jesus the Liberator*. Maryknoll, NY: Orbis Books, 1993.

Sobrino, Jon, and Ignacio Ellacuria, eds. *Systematic Theology: Perspectives from Liberation Theology*. Maryknoll, NY: Orbis Books, 1993.

Southern, R. W. *St. Anselm: A Portrait in a Landscape*. Cambridge: Cambridge University Press, 1990.

St. Joseph's Baltimore Catechism. New York: Catholic Book Publishing Co., 1962–69.

Stassen, Glen H., ed. *Just Peacemaking: Ten Practices for Abolishing War*. Cleveland: Pilgrim Press, 1998.

———. *Just Peacemaking: Transforming Initiatives for Justice and Peace*. Louisville: Westminster/John Knox Press, 1992.

Steele, Diane Marie. "Creation and Cross in the Later Soteriology of Edward Schillebeeckx." PhD diss., University of Notre Dame, 2000.

Stott, John. *The Message of the Sermon on the Mount*. Leicester, England: InterVarsity Press, 1978.

Stringfellow, William. "Jesus the Criminal." *Christianity in Crisis* 30, no. 8 (June 8, 1970): 119–25.

Stump, Eleonore. ed. *Reasoned Faith*. Ithaca, NY: Cornell University Press, 1993.

Swartley, William. *Covenant of Peace*. Grand Rapids, MI: William B. Eerdmans, 2006.

———. *The Love of Enemy and Nonretaliation in the New Testament*. Louisville: Westminster/John Knox Press, 1992.

Tahtinen, Unto. *Ahimsa: Non-violence in Indian Tradition*. Ahmedabad: Navajivan, 1976.

Tannehill, Robert. "The 'Focal Instance' as a Form of New Testament Speech: A Study of Matthew's 5:39b–42." *Journal of Religion* 50 (1970): 372–85.

Tanquerey, Adolf. *A Manual of Dogmatic Theology*. Vol. 1. Translated by Rt. Rev. Msgr. John J. Byrne. New York: Desclee, 1959.

Thomas, M. M. *The Acknowledged Christ of the Indian Renaissance*. Madras: Christian Institute for the Study of Religion in Society, 1970.

Tinker, Hugh. *The Ordeal of Love*. Delhi: Oxford University Press, 1979.

Tolstoy, Leo. *The Gospel in Brief*. Translated by Aylmer Maude. London: Noonday Press, 1958.

———. *The Kingdom of God Is within You*. Translated by Constance Garnett. Lincoln: University of Nebraska Press, 1984.

Trocme, Andre. *Jesus and the Nonviolent Revolution*. Maryknoll, NY: Orbis Books, 2004.

Vanderhaar, Gerard. *Christians and Nonviolence in the Nuclear Age*. Mystic, CT: Twenty-Third Publications, 1982.

Von Balthazar, Hans Urs. *Dare We Hope That All Men Be Saved?* San Francisco: Ignatius Press, 1988.

Weaver, J. Denny. *The Nonviolent Atonement*. Grand Rapids, MI: William B. Eerdmans, 2001.

Williams, James G. *The Bible, Violence, and the Sacred*. Valley Forge, PA: Trinity Press International, 1991.

Wink, Walter. *Engaging the Powers: Discernment and Resistance in a World of Domination*. Minneapolis: Fortress Press, 1992.

———. *The Human Being*. Minneapolis: Fortress Press, 2002.

———. *Jesus and Nonviolence: A Third Way*. Minneapolis: Fortress Press, 2003.

———. *Naming the Powers: The Language of Power in the New Testament*. Philadelphia: Fortress Press, 1984.

———, ed. *Peace Is the Way*. Maryknoll, NY: Orbis Books, 2000.

———. *The Powers That Be: Theology for a New Millennium*. New York: Doubleday, 1998.

———. *Unmasking the Powers: The Invisible Forces That Determine Human Existence*. Philadelphia: Fortress Press, 1986.

———. *When the Powers Fall: Reconciliation in the Healing of Nations*. Minneapolis: Fortress Press, 1998.

———. "Write What You See: An Odyssey." *Fourth R* 7 (May–June 1994).

Winter, Paul. "Magnificat and Benedictus: Maccabean Psalms?" *Bulletin of the John Rylands Library* 37 (1954–55): 328–40.

Witherington, Ben, III. *The Jesus Quest: The Third Search for the Jew of Nazareth.* Downers Grove, IL: InterVarsity Press, 1995.

Woito, Robert. *To End War: A New Approach to International Conflict.* New York: Pilgrim Press, 1982.

Wolpert, Stanley. *India.* Berkeley: University of California Press, 1991.

Wright, N. T. *Evil and the Justice of God.* Downers Grove, IL: InterVarsity Press, 2006.

———. *Jesus and the Victory of God.* Minneapolis: Fortress Press, 1996.

———. *Paul in Fresh Perspective.* Minneapolis: Fortress Press, 2005.

Yoder, John Howard. *Body Politics.* Scottdale, PA: Herald Press, 2001.

———. *Christian Attitudes towards War, Peace, and Revolution.* Durham, NC: Duke University Divinity School, 1983.

———. *The Christian Witness to the State.* Scottdale, PA: Herald Press, 2002.

———. "The Disavowal of Constantine." In *The Royal Priesthood: Essays Ecclesiological and Ecumenical,* ed. Michael Cartwright, 242–61. Grand Rapids, MI: William B. Eerdmans, 1994.

———. *Discipleship as Political Responsibility.* Scottdale, PA: Herald Press, 2003.

———. *For the Nations.* Grand Rapids, MI: William B. Eerdmans, 1997.

———. *He Came Preaching Peace.* Scottdale, PA: Herald Press, 1985.

———. *Karl Barth and the Problem of War.* Nashville: Abingdon Press, 1970.

———. *Nevertheless: The Varieties of Religious Pacifism.* Scottdale, PA: Herald Press, 1971.

———. *The Original Revolution.* Scottdale, PA: Herald Press 1977.

———. *The Politics of Jesus.* 2nd ed. Grand Rapids, MI: William B. Eerdmans, 1994.

———. *Preface to Theology.* Grand Rapids, MI: Brazos Press, 2002.

———. *The Priestly Kingdom.* Notre Dame, IN: University of Notre Dame Press, 1984.

———. *What Would You Do?* Scottdale, PA: Herald Press, 1983.

———. *When War Is Unjust.* Eugene, OR: Wipf and Stock, 1996.

Zimbelman, Joel. "The Contribution of John Howard Yoder to Recent Discussions in Christian Social Ethics." *Scottish Journal of Theology* 45 (September 1992): 367–99.

Zimmerman, Earl. "A Praxis of Peace: The 'Politics of Jesus' According to John Howard Yoder." PhD diss., The Catholic University of America, 2004.

Zinn, Howard, ed. *The Power of Nonviolence: Writings by Advocates of Peace.* Boston: Beacon Press, 2002.

Index

Abelard, 140
Ackerman, Peter, 82, 164
action, importance of, 10–11
Adam, Karl, 116
Advaita Vedanta, 10
Against the Nations (Hauerwas), 114
agitation, 74
agraha, 52–53
ahimsa, 7, 19, 51; as active force pitted against violence, 58–61; five facets of, 53–64; Gandhi recasting fundamental concept of, 34–35; Hinduism's largest contribution to Indian culture, 53–54; as normal law of human nature, 61–62; as the way of the strong and the brave, 62–64
Alexander, Horace, 85
Ambler, Rex, 46, 48–49
Andrews, C. F., 6, 84, 156; answering questions about Jesus' teaching on nonviolence, 91–94; as friend of Gandhi's, 85; on the future of nonviolence, 94–96; on Gandhi's significance, 86–87; on implications of Jesus' life for Christians, 155; on Jesus' solidarity with oppressed and outcast, 158; making Christianity live, for Gandhi, 96; new understanding for, of the New Testament, 87–91; on social nature of sin and salvation, 163; on truth being caught, 167
anekantavanda, 73
Anselm of Canterbury, 137–40, 142–45
Arendt, Hannah, 165

Arnold, Edwin, 8
asceticism, 92–93
Ashe, Geoffrey, 7
Athanasius, 137
atman, 10, 13
Augustine, 134
Aulen, Gustav, 162, 178, 184

Bainton, Roland, 121
Baker, Mark D., 3, 148, 173–74
Baltimore Catechism, 141
Banerjee, Kali Charan, 11
Barron, Robert, 182
Barth, Karl, 96
Bartlett, Anthony, 171
belief, original meaning of, 168–69
Bhagavad Gita, 8, 32, 113
Bhatt, Shamal, 7, 9
Bhave, Vinoba, 70
Bible, Gandhi's early reading of, 8–9
blame, assigning, 3
Boersma, Hans, 174
Boer War, 12
Boff, Leonardo, 174, 179
Bondurant, Joan, 51, 52, 73–74
Borg, Marcus, 160, 168–69
boycott, 74
Brahman, 11
Brailsford, H. N., 18
bread labor, 31
British, non-cooperation campaign against, 68–70
Brown, Judith, 15–16

Cahalan, Kathleen, 117
Calvin, John, 140